Introduction

Abacus Evolve fully covers the curriculun ;, which have been planned to match the blocked structure recommenc Each block is planned to provide sound progression through mathematics

The blocks in *Abacus Evolve* match those recommen Framework:

- Block A: Counting, partitioning and calculating
- Block B: Securing number facts, understanding shapes
- Block C: Processing, presenting and interpreting data and measures
- Block D: Calculating, measuring and understanding shapes
- Block E: Securing number facts, relationships and calculating.

To help further with progression, the blocks in *Abacus Evolve* have been broken down into four smaller units: a, b, c and d. So, for example, *Abacus Evolve* Blocks A1.a, A1.b, A1.c and A1.d all match the PNS block A1, but are presented in smaller, more manageable chunks.

A 30-week programme allows space for 'spreading out' the maths teaching where needed, for example to consolidate or return to concepts, to plan in problem-solving weeks, or to accommodate other school activities such as school trips.

The plans and activities in this book are based on Years 1 and 2 of *Abacus Evolve*. If you wish to use the other products that are referred to in this book (workbooks, textbooks, photocopy masters and Talk Maths pupil software), you can buy them as part of the *Abacus Evolve* scheme.

Objectives

The objectives in *Abacus Evolve* are based on the objectives outlined by the Primary National Strategy in the Renewed Framework and are broken down in smaller, more focused objectives in order to make the progression of learning clear and to help you find resources that are exactly matched to your pupils' level of understanding.

Mental oral starters

Abacus Evolve provides a systematic structure of mental oral maths activities to ensure that pupils rehearse key skills on a regular basis, and that they make real progression in mental maths. There is a rich variety of teaching styles and activities, and maximum pupil participation is encouraged.

Main teaching

For most weekly plans, the main teaching will be split fairly evenly between the whole class together (indicated by the heading 'All') and the two year groups.

Often the teacher starts with the whole class and then sends one year group, for example Y1, to work on differentiated activities and independent tasks, preferably with the TA. Meanwhile, the teacher retains the other year group, for example Y2, on the carpet for further teaching. The following day, the teaching starts with the whole class, and then Y2 go off to do activities, whilst Y1 are taught on the carpet. This structure applies throughout the mixed-age planning.

In most cases, the whole class will work on the same objectives, but occasionally one year group will be doing a separate topic, for example Y2 may need to do multiplication when Y1 do not. The plans allow for this, whilst also enabling differentiation through the range of activities. The use of investigative and problem-solving activities enables the TA to be exploring one topic in more depth with one whole year group whilst the teacher teaches the other year group.

'Complex' weeks

In teaching mixed-age classes, there is always a difficulty in covering the larger curriculum for the higher year group. The fact that these older children have to do more (and not just harder) maths means that, inevitably, there are a very small number of weeks in which the teacher has to cover two quite different maths topics. In some of these weeks, it may be advisable to omit some of the mental oral starters. The days for which you may choose to do this are those in which the first part of the main teaching is best regarded as revision for one of the year groups, and so this section effectively takes the place of a mental oral starter. You may wish to omit the starter altogether, or move it to a different time in the day.

In weeks 26 and 28 of Year 1–2 we have suggested swapping parts of two complex weeks around to create one week which covers time (C3.c/d), and one week which covers adding and subtracting (D3.c/d). This results in two weeks which look a little different from the others because activities are taken from another week, but we recommend that this will be the most practical way to teach these two weeks.

Differentiated activities

For each day's teaching, four practical activities suitable for pairs, groups or the whole class are planned in. These activities give all pupils progression in their learning and a balance between reinforcement and challenge.

The *Abacus Evolve* weekly plans divide a Y1/Y2 mixed-age class into four groups:

Group 1: mainly Y1 •/••

Group 2: mainly Y1 ••/•••

Group 3: mainly Y2 •/••

Group 4: mainly Y2 ••/•••

These groupings are given as a guide only. We recommend that your groups be based on attainment level, rather than purely on chronological age.

The T and TA icons indicate which activities we recommend that the teacher and the teaching assistant (if one is available) supervise. We recommend that if you have focused on a particular year group during the main teaching, then the TA, if there is one, should focus on the other. As mentioned earlier, the use of problem solving, investigational and exploratory activities enables the TA to provide further teaching of a topic in a practical context. This is particularly useful when the teacher is working with the other year group.

Alternative activities that cover the same objectives are also suggested on the Activities pages, to provide more flexibility and choice.

Plenaries

Plenary sessions allow you to draw together the learning for the whole class, and they often involve a game or fun way of ending the lesson.

Outcomes

The weekly plans give outcomes for each day, which describe what the children in each group should achieve by participation in the main teaching and the suggested activities. These outcomes enable you to review each child's achievements and adapt future plans to suit children's needs.

Icon key

- Lower-ability activity
- Middle-ability activity
- Higher-ability activity
- Textbook
- Textbook (use top half)
- Textbook (use bottom half)
- Photocopy Master (PCM)
- Paired activity
- Paired activity: teacher required
- Group activity
- Group activity: teacher required
- Whole-class activity
- Talk Maths software activity
- Teacher required
- Teaching assistant recommended
- Resources

Contents

Week	Block		Strands	Objectives
1	Block A1.a: Count on or back in 1s or 10s; read and write numbers in words and figures	Y1	Knowing and using number facts Counting and understanding number	• Count on in 1s to 20 and on to 100 • Read numbers up to 20 in words and figures • Estimate a number of objects up to 30 • Count on and back in 10s from a multiple of 10
		Y2	Counting and understanding number	• Count on and back in 1s or 10s from a 2-digit number • Read and write numbers up to 100 in figures
	Block A1.b: Estimate a number of objects and count by grouping in 5s or 10s	Y1	Counting and understanding number	• Estimate a number of objects up to 30 • Estimate a number of objects and count by grouping in 10s
		Y2	Counting and understanding number	• Estimate a number of objects up to 50 • Begin to count up to 100 objects by grouping in 5s or 10s
2	Block A1.c: Partition numbers into T and U and recognise the value of each digit	Y1	Counting and understanding number	• Recognise the value of each digit in a 'teens' number
		Y2	Counting and understanding number	• Know what each digit in a 2-digit number represents, including 0 as a place holder • Partition 2-digit numbers into T and U
	Block A1.d: Compare and order numbers	Y1	Counting and understanding number	• Say which is more or less of two numbers
		Y2	Counting and understanding number	• Order numbers up to at least 100 and position them on a 100-square
3	Block B1.a: Y1 Say the number 1 more; Y2 Add by counting on in 1s	Y1	Counting and understanding number Knowing and using number facts	• Say the number that is 1 more than a given number • Count on 1 from a given number
		Y2	Calculating	• Recognise addition as counting on • Add by counting on in 1s from the larger number, crossing a multiple of 10
	Block B1.b: Y1 Say the number 1, 2, 3 or 4 more; Y2 Add three numbers by counting on	Y1	Knowing and using number facts Calculating	• Count on 1, 2, 3 or 4 from a given number • Begin to use the + and = signs to record addition sentences • Relate counting on to addition and to addition sentences
		Y2	Calculating	• Add three numbers by putting the largest number first • Recognise that addition can be done in any order • Use the + and = signs to record addition sentences

Week	Block		Strands	Objectives
4	Block B1.c: Know addition and subtraction facts for numbers that total up to 6 or 9	Y1	Counting and understanding number Knowing and using number facts	• Recognise a number of objects up to 6 without counting • Know by heart addition facts for pairs of numbers that total up to 6
		Y2	Knowing and using number facts Counting and understanding number	• Rehearse addition and subtraction facts for pairs of numbers that total up to 9 • Use the +, – and = signs to record addition and subtraction sentences
	Block B1.d: Rehearse addition and subtraction facts and record number sentences	Y1	Knowing and using number facts Counting and understanding number	• Begin to know by heart addition facts for pairs of numbers that total up to 7 • Relate addition facts for pairs of numbers to an understanding of addition, including use of + and = signs
		Y2	Calculating Knowing and using number facts	• Recognise the use of a symbol to stand for an unknown number • Rehearse addition and subtraction facts for pairs of numbers that total 10 • Relate addition and subtraction facts to missing number sentences
5	Block C1.a: Compare lengths and heights, and estimate and measure in centimetres	Y1	Measuring	• Compare two or more lengths or heights by direct comparison
		Y2	Measuring	• Estimate, measure and compare lengths using standard units: centimetres • Use a ruler to draw and measure lines to the nearest centimetre
	Block C1.b: Estimate and measure lengths in non-standard units or metres	Y1	Measuring	• Estimate then measure lengths, recording estimates • Measure lengths using uniform non-standard units (whole, half and quarter)
		Y2	Measuring	• Estimate, measure and compare lengths using standard units: metres • Recognise relationship between metres and centimetres

Week	Block		Strands	Objectives
6	Block C1.c: Know days of the week and hours in a day, and order events in time	Y1	Measuring	• Order familiar events in time • Know the days of the week
		Y2	Measuring	• Use units of time and know the relationship between them: hours in a day, days in a week
	Block C1.d: Know the months and seasons of the year	Y1	Measuring	• Begin to know and order the months of the year • Know the seasons of the year
		Y2	Measuring	• Use units of time and know the relationship between them: months in a year, seasons in a year • Order the months of the year
7	Block D1.a: Use names of common 2D shapes and describe their features	Y1	Understanding shape	• Begin to use the names of common 2D shapes; circle, square, rectangle, triangle • Describe features of familiar 2D shapes: number of sides and corners, types of sides
		Y2	Understanding shape	• Use the names of common 2D shapes, including: pentagon, hexagon, octagon • Sort 2D shapes and describe their features: number of sides and corners
	Block D1.b: Rehearse features of 2D shapes and begin to recognise line symmetry	Y1	Understanding shape	• Begin to use the names of common 2D shapes; circle, square, rectangle, triangle • Describe features of familiar 2D shapes: number of sides and corners, types of sides
		Y2	Understanding shape	• Begin to recognise line symmetry • Make symmetrical patterns by folding and cutting • Begin to sketch the reflection of a simple shape in a mirror line
8	Block D1.c: Say the number 1 less, and count back in 1s	Y1	Counting and understanding number Knowing and using number facts	• Say the number that is 1 less than a given number • Count back 1 from a given number
		Y2	Calculating	• Count back in 1s, not crossing a multiple of 10 • Extend understanding of subtraction as taking away
	Block D1.d: Subtract a 1-digit number by counting back	Y1	Calculating	• Subtract a 1-digit number from a 'teens' number by counting back, not crossing 10 • Subtract one 1-digit number from another
		Y2	Calculating	• Count back in 1s, crossing a multiple of 10, beginning to partition

Week	Block		Strands	Objectives
9	Block E1.a: Know doubles for numbers up to 5 or 15	Y1	Knowing and using number facts	• Recognise doubling as the addition of two equal amounts • Begin to know by heart doubles for numbers up to at least 10 • Know by heart doubles for numbers up to at least 5
		Y2	Knowing and using number facts	• Know by heart doubles for numbers up to at least 15 and the corresponding halves • Recognise halving as the inverse of doubling
	Block E1.b: Y1 Add by identifying near doubles; Y2 Double and halve multiples of 5	Y1	Knowing and using number facts	• Add by identifying near doubles for numbers up to 10
		Y2	Knowing and using number facts	• Begin to derive doubles of multiples of 5 up to 100 and the corresponding halves • Begin to halve multiples of 10 up to 100
10	Block E1.c: Recognise and order coins, find totals of sets of coins	Y1	Using and applying mathematics	• Recognise coins of different values • Order coins according to their value
		Y2	Using and applying mathematics	• Recognise all coins and begin to use £·p notation for money • Find totals of sets of coins: relate to adding three or more numbers
	Block E1.d: Find totals of sets of coins, pay an exact sum using smaller coins	Y1	Using and applying mathematics	• Exchange coins for equivalent in 10p and 1p coins • Find total of sets of coins • Pay an exact sum using smaller coins up to 50p
		Y2	Using and applying mathematics	• Pay an exact sum using smaller coins up to £2 • Solve 'real-life' problems involving money (paying an exact sum)

Week	Block		Strands	Objectives
11	Block A2.a: Y1 Recognise zero, read numbers to 100; Y2 Count on/back in 1s, 10s, 100s	Y1	Counting and understanding number Knowing and using number facts	• Recognise zero • Count on and back in 1s to 100 • Write numbers up to 10 in words and up to 11 in figures • Begin to read numbers up to 100 in words and figures
		Y2	Counting and understanding number	• Count on and back in 1s or 10s from a 2- or 3-digit number • Count on and back in 100s from a multiple of 100
	Block A2.b: Y1 Count by grouping in 10s; Y2 Recognise odd and even numbers	Y1	Calculating Knowing and using number facts	• Count a large number of objects by grouping in 10s • Count on and back in 10s from a 1-digit number
		Y2	Counting and understanding number	• Count on in 2s (revise) • Begin to recognise odd and even numbers up to at least 50
12	Block A2.c: Understand and use ordinal numbers	Y1	Counting and understanding number	• Understand and use ordinal numbers up to at least 20th
		Y2	Counting and understanding number	• Understand and use ordinal numbers up to at least 100th
	Block A2.d: Compare and order numbers, and say a number between two numbers	Y1	Counting and understanding number	• Order numbers up to at least 20 • Begin to say a number lying between two numbers
		Y2	Counting and understanding number	• Compare two or more 2-digit numbers; introduce the greater than (>), less than (<) signs • Say a number lying between two numbers, up to at least 100
13	Block B2.a: Rehearse addition and subtraction facts for pairs that total up to 7 or 10	Y1	Calculating Knowing and using number facts	• Begin to recognise that addition can be done in any order • Know by heart addition facts for pairs of numbers that total up to 7 • Relate number bonds to an understanding of addition, including use of +, –, =
		Y2	Knowing and using number facts	• Rehearse addition and subtraction facts for pairs of numbers that total up to 10
	Block B2.b: Y1 Know addition facts for pairs that total up to 8; Y2 Add three 1-digit numbers	Y1	Knowing and using number facts Calculating Using and applying mathematics	• Know by heart addition and subtraction facts for pairs of numbers that total up to 8 • Relate addition facts for pairs of numbers to an understanding of addition, including use of +, –, = and missing numbers • Begin to use patterns of similar calculations (e.g. 10 – 0 = 10, 10 – 1 = 9, 10 – 2 = 8, …)
		Y2	Calculating	• Begin to add three 1-digit numbers mentally

Week	Block		Strands	Objectives
14	Block B2.c: Y1 Describe position; Y2 Recognise right angles	Y1	Understanding shape	• Describe position: above, below, beside, left, right
		Y2	Understanding shape	• Recognise whole, half and quarter turns • Know that a right angle is a measure of a quarter turn • Recognise right angles in simple shapes
	Block B2.d: Y1 Describe direction/movement; Y2 Recognise clockwise/anticlockwise turns	Y1	Understanding shape	• Describe direction and movement: forwards, backwards, up, down, left, right • Make whole turns, half turns and quarter turns • Talk about things that turn
		Y2	Understanding shape	• Recognise whole, half and quarter turns • Know that a right angle is a measure of a quarter turn • Recognise right angles in simple shapes • Give instructions for moving along a route in straight lines and round corners • Recognise clockwise and anticlockwise turns
15	Block C2.a: Estimate, measure and compare weights	Y1	Measuring	• Compare two or more weights by direct comparison
		Y2	Measuring	• Estimate, measure and compare weights using standard units: kilograms, grams • Begin to recognise the relationship between grams and kilograms • Begin to read simple weighing scales to the nearest labelled division
	Block C2.b: Y1 Measure weights; Y2 Read the time to the hour and half hour	Y1	Measuring	• Measure weights using uniform non-standard units (whole and half) • Estimate then measure weights, recording estimates
		Y2	Measuring	• Read the time to the hour and half hour on analogue and 12-hour digital clocks

Week	Block		Strands	Objectives
16	Block C2.c: Y1 Read time on an analogue clock; Y2 Create and interpret block graphs	Y1	Measuring	• Read the time to the hour on analogue clocks
		Y2	Handling data	• Sort, organise and interpret information in a block graph
	Block C2.d: Organise and interpret information in simple tables and pictograms	Y1	Handling data	• Organise information in simple lists, tables, pictograms or block graphs • Interpret information from simple lists, tables, pictograms or block graphs • Sort and organise information using objects or pictures
		Y2	Handling data	• Sort, organise and interpret information in a pictogram
17	Block D2.a: Use the names of common 3D shapes	Y1	Understanding shape	• Begin to relate solid shapes to pictures of them • Begin to use the names of common 3D shapes: cube, cuboid, cylinder, sphere, cone, pyramid
		Y2	Understanding shape	• Relate solid shapes to pictures of them • Use the names of common 2D shapes, including: cube, cuboid, cylinder, sphere, cone
	Block D2.b: Sort 3D shapes and describe their features	Y1	Understanding shape	• Describe features of familiar 3D shapes: number, shapes and types of faces
		Y2	Understanding shape	• Sort 3D shapes and describe their features: number of faces and corners
18	Block D2.c: Y1 Add by counting on; Y2 Add/subtract 9/11 by adding/subtracting 10	Y1	Calculating	• Add by counting on, not bridging a multiple of 10 other than 10 or 20
		Y2	Calculating	• Add and subtract 9 and 11 by adding and subtracting 10 • Begin to add and subtract 19 and 21 by adding and subtracting 20
	Block D2.d: Add or subtract multiples of 10 by counting on or back in 10s	Y1	Calculating	• Add two multiples of 10 by counting on in 10s
		Y2	Calculating	• Subtract a multiple of 10 from a 2-digit number by counting back in 10s

Week	Block		Strands	Objectives
19	Block E2.a: Y1 Count on/back in 10s; Y2 Count on in 2s/5s/10s, recognise odd/even numbers	Y1	Knowing and using number facts	• Count on and back in 10s from any number up to 100
		Y2	Counting and understanding number	• Count in 2s, 5s or 10s up to 100 • Begin to recognise odd and even numbers up to 100
	Block E2.b: Y1 Count on/back in 1s/10s; Y2 Understand multiplication as 'lots of'	Y1	Counting and understanding number Knowing and using number facts	• Say the number that is 1 or 10 more or less than a given number • Count on and back in 1s or 10s from any number up to 100
		Y2	Calculating	• Introduce multiplication as 'lots of' • Introduce the × sign
20	Block E2.c: Y1 Subtract 1-digit numbers; Y2 Multiply by adding repeatedly	Y1	Calculating	• Count a number of objects by grouping 5s or 10s
		Y2	Counting and understanding number	• Read and write numbers up to 100 in words • Begin to partition 3-digit numbers into H, T and U • Begin to read and write numbers up to 1000 in figures
	Block E2.d: Y1 Subtract by counting back to a multiple of 10; Y2 Divide by grouping	Y1	Counting and understanding number Calculating	• Say the number that is 10 more or less than a given number • Begin to add a multiple of 10 to a 2-digit number by counting on in 10s
		Y2	Counting and understanding number	• Begin to round numbers less than 100 to the nearest 10

Week	Block		Strands	Objectives
21	Block A3.a: Y1 Count by grouping in 5s or 10s; Y2 Partition numbers into H, T, U	Y1	Calculating	• Count a number of objects by grouping 5s or 10s
		Y2	Counting and understanding number	• Read and write numbers up to 100 in words • Begin to partition 3-digit numbers into H, T and U • Begin to read and write numbers up to 1000 in figures
	Block A3.b: Y1 Add multiples of 10 to 2-digit numbers; Y2 Begin to round to nearest 10	Y1	Counting and understanding number Calculating	• Say the number that is 10 more or less than a given number • Begin to add a multiple of 10 to a 2-digit number by counting on in 10s
		Y2	Counting and understanding number	• Begin to round numbers less than 100 to the nearest 10
22	Block A3.c: Y1 Partition into T and U; Y2 Add by bridging a multiple of 10	Y1	Counting und understanding number	• Begin to partition 2-digit numbers into T and U
		Y2	Calculating	• Add a 1-digit number to a 2-digit number, crossing a multiple of 10 (rehearse) • Begin to add by bridging a multiple of 10 (36 + 8 = 36 + 4 + 4)
	Block A3.d: Y1 Order numbers; Y2 Find the difference between two numbers	Y1	Counting and understanding number	• Order numbers up to at least 30 • Say a number lying between two numbers up to at least 50
		Y2	Calculating	• Extend understanding of relationship of subtraction to difference • Find the difference between two numbers by counting on
23	Block B3.a: Y1 Know addition/subtraction pairs up to 9; Y2 Describe 2D and 3D shapes	Y1	Knowing and using number facts Calculating	• Know by heart addition and subtraction facts for pairs of numbers that total up to 9 • Record addition and subtraction facts for pairs of numbers that total up to 9, using +, – and = in number sentences
		Y2	Understanding shape	• Classify and describe common 2D and 3D shapes • Make models, shapes and patterns and describe their features
	Block B3.b: Y1 Know addition/subtraction pairs up to 10; Y2 Recognise halves and quarters	Y1	Knowing and using number facts Calculating	• Know by heart addition and subtraction facts for pairs of numbers that total 10 • Record addition and subtraction facts for pairs of numbers that total 10, using +, – and = in number sentences
		Y2	Counting and understanding number	• Begin to recognise halves and quarters of shapes • Recognise fraction notation • Begin to recognise halves and quarters of small numbers of objects

Week	Block		Strands	Objectives
24	Block B3.c: Y1 Add TU + U; Y2 Know pairs of multiples of 10 that total 100	Y1	Calculating	• Add a 1-digit number to a 2-digit number, not crossing a multiple of 10 • Add a 1-digit number to a 2-digit number, crossing a multiple of 10
		Y2	Knowing and using number facts Calculating Using and applying mathematics	• Know by heart addition and subtraction facts for pairs of numbers that total up to 10 • State the subtraction corresponding to a given addition, and vice versa • Know by heart pairs of multiples of 10 that total 100 • Use patterns of similar calculations
	Block B3.d: Y1 Find the difference between two numbers; Y2 Add to the next multiple of 10	Y1	Calculating	• Find a small difference between two numbers by counting on
		Y2	Knowing and using number facts	• Know by heart addition and subtraction facts for pairs of numbers that total 20 • Use pairs that total 10 to make the next multiple of 10
25	Block C3.a: Estimate and compare capacities	Y1	Measuring	• Compare two or more capacities by direct comparison: pouring
		Y2	Measuring	• Begin to read a simple capacity scale to the nearest labelled and unlabelled division • Estimate a capacity, recording estimates • Measure capacities using uniform non-standard units (revise)
	Block C3.b: Measure capacities in standard and non-standard units	Y1	Measuring	• Measure capacities using uniform non-standard units (whole and half) • Begin to estimate then measure capacities, recording estimates
		Y2	Measuring	• Estimate, measure and compare capacities using standard units: litres, millilitres • Read a simple capacity scale to the nearest labelled and unlabelled division

Week	Block		Strands	Objectives
26	Block C3.c: Read the time to the hour, half hour or quarter hour	Y1	Measuring	• Read the time to the hour and half hour on analogue clocks
		Y2	Measuring	• Read the time to the quarter hour on analogue and 12-hour digital clocks
	Block C3.d: Y1 Measure time in minutes; Y2 Use hours, minutes, seconds	Y1	Measuring	• Read the time to the hour and half hour on analogue clocks • Begin to use units to measure time: minutes
		Y2	Measuring	• Read the time to the quarter hour on analogue and 12-hour digital clocks • Use units of time and know the relationship between them: hours, minutes, seconds
27	Block D3.a: Add or subtract a 1-digit number to or from a 2-digit number	Y1	Calculating	• Subtract a 1-digit number from a 2-digit number by counting back, not crossing 10 • Subtract a 1-digit number from a 2-digit number by counting back, crossing 10
		Y2	Calculating	• Add a 1-digit number to a 2-digit number, bridging a multiple of 10 without crossing 100 • Add two 2-digit numbers using an appropriate strategy • Partition additions into T and U, then recombine
	Block D3.b: Subtract multiples of 10 or 2-digit numbers	Y1	Calculating	• Subtract one multiple of 10 from another
		Y2	Calculating	• Subtract one 2-digit number from another using an appropriate strategy • Understand that subtraction is the inverse of addition, using missing number sentences
28	Block D3.c: Y1 Add two 'teens' numbers; Y2 Add 1-digit numbers to multiples of 10 and 100	Y1	Calculating	• Begin to add two 'teens' numbers, not crossing a multiple of 10
		Y2	Calculating	• Add and begin to subtract a 1-digit number to and from multiples of 10 and 100
	Block D3.d: Y1 Add/subtract 9, solve real-life problems; Y2 Create and interpret tables	Y1	Using and applying mathematics	• Add and subtract 9 by adding and subtracting 10 • Solve 'real-life' problems involving money (change)
		Y2	Handling data	• Organise information in a table • Interpret information from a table

Week	Block		Strands	Objectives
29	Block E3.a: Y1 Count on in 2s or 5s; Y2 Understand multiplication as repeated addition	Y1	Knowing and using number facts	• Count on in 2s or 5s up to 100 • Begin to count on in 3s from zero
		Y2	Calculating	• Begin to understand multiplication as repeated addition or as describing an array • Begin to understand division as the inverse of multiplication
	Block E3.b: Y1 Begin to recognise odd and even numbers; Y2 Know ×2, ×5 and ×10 tables	Y1	Using and applying mathematics	• Begin to recognise odd and even numbers up to at least 20
		Y2	Knowing and using number facts	• Know by heart the multiplication facts for 2, 5 and 10 times tables • Begin to recognise 2-digit multiples of 2, 5 and 10
30	Block E3.c: Y1 Exchange coins for smaller coins; Y2 Double/halve multiples of 5/10	Y1	Using and applying mathematics	• Exchange coins up to 10p for equivalent in smaller coins
		Y2	Knowing and using number facts	• Double multiples of 5 up to 50 • Halve multiples of 10 up to 100 • Add by identifying near doubles for multiples of 5
	Block E3.d: Y1 Add sets of coins; Y2 Know relationship between halves and quarters	Y1	Using and applying mathematics Calculating	• Find totals of sets of coins and give change • Begin to recognise that more than two numbers can be added together
		Y2	Counting and understanding number	• Recognise that two quarters and one half are equivalent • Begin to recognise that two halves or four quarters make one whole • Begin to position halves on a number line

Maths Weekly Plan: Year 1 and 2

Block A1.a: Count on or back in 1s or 10s; read and write numbers in words and figures
Block A1.b: Estimate a number of objects and count by grouping in 5s or 10s

	Mental oral starter	Objectives	Main teaching	Activities: Group 1 Y1	Activities: Group 2 Y1	Activities: Group 3 Y2	Activities: Group 4 Y2	Plenary	Outcomes
Day 1	**Count in 1s along the 100-square, marking the 5s.** *We will **count** to 100 using the 100-square and our fingers. When we say a number ending in five, we will wave our left hand in the air. When we say a number ending in 'ty', we will wave our right hand in the air.* Chn count in unison.	**Y1** • Count on in 1s to 20 and on to 100 • Read numbers up to 20 in words and figures • Estimate a number of objects up to 30 • Count on and back in 10s from a multiple of 10	**All** Read *The Quangle Wangle's Hat*. Chn hold up 1 finger for each creature. Build a tower using 1 linking cube for each creature. ***How many** creatures **altogether**?* Chn look at tower and **estimate**. *How will we know whose **guess** is correct?* Count the cubes. **[ITR Y1 Al.a]** **Y2** Introduce Pobble. Use Pobble to **count in 1s** to 27 on 100-square. *What is the **next** number?* Model writing 28. *What is **1 more**? What is **1 less**?* Point to 14. Identify 1 more and 1 less. Match to addition sentences eg 27 + 1 = 28. Encourage chn to count backwards. **[ITR Y2 Al.a]**	Y1 A1.a.3 Matching cubes to card numbers TA	Y1 A1.a.2 Creating a number line with number cards 1–20	Y2 A1.a.1 Identifying numbers 1 more and 1 less on a 100-square T	Y2 A1.a.7 Making 2-digit numbers and writing numbers 1 more and 1 less	Shuffle number cards 30–45. Ask chn to put them in order. Count in 1s **forward** and **back**. Ensure chn understand that 1 more is the 'next number' in the count, and 1 less is the 'number **before**'.	**Y1** • Count a number of objects using cubes (to 10) • Estimate a number of cubes (to 10) **Y2** • Identify numbers 1 more, 1 less (up to 99) • Estimate a number of cubes (to 10)
Day 2	**Write numerals 10 to 30.** Peg number cards 10–30 on washing line. Chn close their eyes while someone hides a few cards. Chn open their eyes and identify numbers missing. They write these on whiteboards. Repeat many times.	**Y2** • Count on and back in 1s or 10s from a 2-digit number • Read and write numbers up to 100 in figures	**All** Read last 3 verses of *The Quangle Wangle's Hat*. Show some 10p **coins**. *If each creature brought 10p, **how much money** in total?* Drop 10p into a mug for each creature, **counting in 10s**. Re-read 4th verse and repeat coin activity. Ask Y2s to write the totals on whiteboards. **Y1** Peg number cards 1–10 on washing line. Hand out **number name** cards **one–ten** to 10 chn. Count along the line, pausing to allow chn to peg their number up. Ask a child to cover up one number. Others find it by counting along the line.	Y1 A1.a.1 Counting to 10, matching numerals T	Y1 A1.a.4 Playing Pelmanism with number names and numerals	Y2 A1.a.3 Saying the number 10 more and 10 less TA	Y2 2.1 p4 Practising writing numbers 1 more/less and 10 more/less	Use number name cards one–ten. Choose a child to take a card without showing it to the class. The child shows the class that number of fingers. The other chn say the number. The child then reveals the card. Repeat.	**Y1** • Count in 10s from a multiple of 10 • Match number names to numerals **Y2** • Count on and back in 10s • Say the number 10 more/less
Day 3	**Count forwards and backwards in 10s from a multiple of 10.** Play 'Team counting'. Divide class into 2 teams to count in 10s. Say start number (30). Point to 1 team who say the next number together (40). Teams alternate in saying the next number. Repeat several times.		**All** Show 0–99 grid and ask how it differs from 100-square. *It starts with 0. How much do I have if I have **zero** sweets? **Nothing**.* Place Bisky Bat on 0 and count on in 10s. Ask chn to place him on a multiple of 10 and practise counting on and back. **Y2** Ask child to place Bisky on any number on 100-square. Count on and back in 10s. Match to addition sentences, eg 63 + 10 = 73. Choose different numbers and ask chn to use Bisky to add 10 to these numbers. Write as addition sentences. Rpt for subtracting 10.	Y1 A1.b.1 TM 1.1 1 Counting in 10s TA	Y1 A1.b.6 Selecting number cards and counting on in 10s up to 100	Y2 A1.a.4 Adding 10p coins to 6p by putting coins in a mug and counting in 10s	Y2 A1.a.5 Investigating counting in 10s above 100 T	Hand out number cards 6, 16, 26, 36, …96. Ask chn to count slowly in 10s from 6 to 96. As each number is said, the child holding that number stands up. Rpt counting back with chn sitting down at their number.	**Y1** • Count on and back in 10s from a multiple of 10 **Y2** • Count on and back in 10s from any number (1–100) • Say the number 10 more/less

	Mental oral starter	Objectives	Main teaching	Activities: Group 1 Y1	Activities: Group 2 Y1	Activities: Group 3 Y2	Activities: Group 4 Y2	Plenary	Outcomes
Day 4	**Estimate quantities less than 30 and write numerals.** Place about 25 small bricks in a colander, shake it and show it to class. Chn discuss possible total and write estimates on their whiteboards. Find out who is **closest** by counting the bricks, **grouping in 5s**. Remove handful of bricks from colander and repeat.	**Y1** • Estimate a number of objects up to 30 • Estimate a number of objects and count by grouping in 10s **Y2** • Estimate a number of objects up to 50 • Begin to count up to 100 objects by grouping in 5s or 10s	**All** *Can you remember how many creatures visited the Crumpetty Tree?* Read the poem; chn count the creatures on their fingers. Fill a hat with 30–40 seedless grapes, pass the hat round the class, and ask them to write in figures an estimate of the total number of grapes. Model writing some of their estimates in words. Match these to estimates in figures, asking chn to read them. *How do we count the grapes?* Group them into 5s and count. Stress it is easier to keep track if we group the grapes. Repeat using more grapes (eg 40–50), reminding chn to write their estimates. Ask different chn to come and count by grouping in 5s. **[ITR Y1 A1.b]**	Y1 1.1 p2 Counting to 10	Y1 A1.a.5 Estimating and counting objects T	Y2 A1.b.1 Taking turns to estimate and count objects, grouping in 10s TA	Y2 A1.b.2 Taking turns to estimate and count cubes	Flick through the pages of a favourite storybook. *Can you estimate how many pages are in this book?* Chn make a quick guess. Note some guesses on the board. Count the pages, stressing the 5s.	**Y1/Y2** • Estimate and count objects by grouping in 5s/10s **Y2** • Recognise and write numbers 1–20 **Y2** • Count up to 100, grouping in 5s/10s
Day 5	**Recall addition facts for numbers up to 10.** Play 'Quick on the Draw'. Say an addition fact for a number up to 10. On command of *Fire!* or *Go!* chn hold up their fingers to match the answer as quickly as possible. Rpt for diff addition facts.		**All** Show chn a pile of about 45 pebbles. *The Quangle Wangle wants to know how many pebbles there are. How should we count them?* Chn estimate how many pebbles. Ask chn to come and count the pebbles by **grouping in 10s**. Stress that it is easier to keep track if we count in groups. Show the chn a pile of 26 1p coins. *How can we count these?* Ask chn to come and group them in 5s. *We count by grouping, often in 5s or 10s.* **[ITR Y2 A1.b]**	Y1 1.1 p5 Counting in 10p coins	Y1 A1.b.2 Using a 100-square, estimating and counting in 10s TA	Y2 A1.b.2 Taking turns to estimate and count cubes	Y2 A1.b.3 Investigating counting in 2s using coins T	Put chn in 2 teams. Show a jar of marbles. Teams make 3 estimates of the number of marbles. Record them. Count the marbles together, grouping in 10s. The team with the closest estimate wins!	**Y1** • Estimate and count objects by grouping in 5s/10s • Count in 10s **Y2** • Estimate and count objects by grouping in 5s/10s • Count up to 100, grouping in 5s/10s

Vocabulary
count
how many?
altogether
estimate
guess
count in 1s, 5s, 10s
next
before
after
1 less/more
10 less/more
count forward, back
coins
how much
money
number names
one, two, three, … twenty
zero
nothing
closest
group in 5s, 10s

Resources
100-squares
The Quangle Wangle's Hat by Edward Lear
about 100 linking cubes
picture of Pobble
number cards 0–100
extra set of number cards 1–10
counters
Post-it notes
empty 10-space number tracks
washing line
pegs
individual whiteboards
about 20 10p coins
mug
number name cards one–ten
large number cards 1–10
cloth bag
nine small soft toys
0–99 grid
picture of Bisky Bat
a tin
about 25 small bricks
colander
hat
30–50 seedless grapes
about six sealable transparent plastic bags
20–40 small objects per bag, e.g. conkers, bottle tops, corks, marbles or shells
sticky labels
up to 100 pebbles
a favourite storybook
26 1p coins
about 15 2p coins
jar
about 60 marbles

Year 1 Block A1.a Activities

A1.a.1 A group of up to 8 children

Count along the line of large number cards 1-10 two or three times. Show children a bag of nine toys; let them feel it and discuss. Ask each to guess how many toys and take a small number card to match. Match children's numbers to the number line. *Who guessed the most/least?* Remove the toys one at a time. *How many? Find that number on the line. Who was closest?* Replace some of the toys and repeat, noting that this time there will be fewer.

Adult support may be useful in running this activity.

large 1–10 number cards; cloth bag; nine small soft toys; 1–20 number cards

A1.a.2 Two groups of 3 children

Place the shuffled 1–20 number cards in a pile face down. Explain that children will create a number line. In turn, children pick a card and read the number out loud; the group agrees. They place the card face up on the table. The next children do the same, placing their cards to the right or left along the line, until it is complete.

Adult support may be useful in running this activity.

1–20 number cards

A1.a.3 A group of 5 children

Place the shuffled 1–10 number cards in a pile face down. In turn, children pick a card and say the number, other children helping if necessary/appropriate. When all have cards, they place matching towers of cubes on them. Children repeat with a second card, then with another set of 1–10 cards.

Adult support may be useful in running this activity.

two sets of 1–10 number cards; linking cubes

A1.a.4 A group of up to 12 children, working in fours

Shuffle both sets of cards and spread them face down on the table: numbers and names on different sides. In turn, children turn over one number and one name card. If they match (and the child recognises this) they place them face up as a pair in front of them. If they do not match, the child turns them back over in their original places. Play until all the cards have gone. Who has the most pairs? Each child says the numbers of their pairs. Shuffle, replace and play again.

Adult support may be useful in running this activity.

1–10 number cards; set of number name cards one–ten

A1.a.5 A group of 3 children

Children look at a bag and guess how many objects it contains, choosing number cards. They unseal the bag, count the objects, and group in 5s. They agree on the total and label the bag, replacing the objects. Groups repeat with a new sealed bag.

Adult support may be useful in running this activity.

sealed transparent bags of 20–40 conkers, marbles, etc. (two different bags per group); 1–50 number cards; sticky labels

Year 1 Block A1.b Activities

1.1 1 Counting in 10s

A1.b.1 A group of 6 or more children

Drop five 10p coins into the tin one at a time, counting aloud with children: *ten, twenty, thirty, forty, fifty.* Ask: *How much is in the tin?* Take the coins out and repeat, this time asking children to close their eyes as they count with you. Drop in three coins while the children count in their heads with eyes closed: *How much is in the tin?* Repeat, dropping in other amounts.

Where on the 100-square are the numbers that we said when we counted in tens? What do you notice about them?

Adult support is needed to run this activity.

nine 10p coins; a tin; 100-square

A1.b2 A group of 6 or more children

Show children a pile of 50–60 pebbles. Ask them each to make a careful estimate, and take a matching number card. Record their estimates. Then choose a child to count the pebbles, with the whole group helping them to group in 10s. Take a card to match the total. Look on the 100-square. *Whose estimate was closest?* Repeat.

Adult support may be useful in running this activity.

50–60 small objects such as pebbles; 0–100 number cards; 100-square

A1.b.6 A group of 3 or 4 children

Shuffle the multiple of 10 cards and place them in a pile face down. One child takes a card from the pile and says the number out loud, for example *forty.* The other children take turns to count on in 10s: *fifty, sixty* … They continue until one child reaches *one hundred*. That child keeps the card and the counting stops. Repeat and continue until all the cards have gone.

10–100 multiple of 10 cards

Year 2 Block A1.a Activities

A1.a.1 A group of 6 children

Give each child a 100-square and place a shuffled set of 1–100 number cards face down in a pile. In turns, children pick a card and read the number aloud, and the group agrees. The child then places a counter on their grid on the number 1 more than the card number, or writes the number 1 more on a Post-it and sticks it on the card. Repeat to include finding the number 1 less.
Adult support may be useful in running this activity.

100-square and counter for each child; 1–100 number cards; Post-it notes

A1.a.3 A group of 12 children in pairs

Give each pair of children a 100-square. One child chooses a number on the grid, e.g. 55, but does not tell their partner. They say the number 10 more, e.g. *Sixty-five*. Their partner must find this number on the grid, and count back one 10 to identify the original number. If correct, they write the two numbers in order, e.g. *55, 65*. Repeat the activity at least six times, monitoring all pairs.
Adult support is needed to run this activity.

100-square per pair

A1.a.4 A group of 6 children

Take out 1–9 from the set of 1–100 number cards. Shuffle and place face down in a pile. One child takes the top card and puts the matching number of 1p coins in a mug. Children then take turns to add a 10p coin to the mug and count on 10p to find the total; e.g. start with 6p and count 16p, 26p, 36p… Make a line of cards, e.g. 6, 16, 26, 36…, to match the count. Empty the mug and repeat.
Adult support may be useful in running this activity.

mug; 1p and 10p coins; 1–100 number cards

A1.a.5 A group of 6, 7 or 8 children

Shuffle a pile of number cards 70–100 and place in a pile face down. One child takes a card: this is their starting number. They pass it to the second child, who writes the number 10 more on a Post-it note and sticks it next to the number on the number card. The third child does the same and so on. When they reach over 100, they agree as a group what the next number must be. Play continues until they have 20 Post-it notes in order from their first card number. The children recite each number as it is pointed out. Repeat the activity, choosing a different starting number.
Adult support is needed to run this activity.

Post-it notes; 70–100 number cards

A1.a.7 Groups of 3 children

Place a set of shuffled 0–9 digit cards face down in a pile. Child 1 takes the top two cards and arranges them as a 2-digit number. Child 2 writes this at the centre of an empty 10-space number track. Child 3 writes on the track the number before or the number after. Children continue in turn to write the number before or the number after until the track has a line of 10 consecutive numbers. Repeat with a new starting number on a new track.

0–9 digit cards; empty 10-space number tracks

Year 2 Block A1.b Activities

A1.b.1 A group of 6 or more children

Place 1–100 number cards face up in order in rows of 10. Show children a collection of pebbles or similar objects. Children estimate how many pebbles are in the collection and take a matching number card to display their estimate. Choose a child to count the pebbles. Make sure that the whole group helps to group the pebbles in 10s. Take the card that matches the actual number of pebbles. Look on a 100-square to see whose estimate was closest to the actual number. Repeat, letting a different child do the counting.
Adult support may be useful in running this activity.

up to 100 pebbles or similar objects; 1–100 number cards; 100-square

A1.b.2 Groups of 3 children

Give each group a pile of up to 100 cubes. Each child writes on their whiteboard an estimate of the number in the pile. One child counts the cubes. The others make sure that the cubes are grouped in 10s so that they can all see that the count is correct. They discuss whose estimate was closest, and that child records the actual number. Children take a new pile of cubes and repeat the activity, letting a different child do the counting. The child whose estimate is closest always writes the actual number. *Are your estimates getting closer?*
Adult support may be useful in running this activity with several groups.

cubes; individual whiteboards

A1.b.3 A group of up to 8 children

Show children a large pile of 1p and 2p coins. Ask them to estimate **how many** coins (not how much) there are. Record each child's sensible estimate. Consult the group. *How shall we count these? Shall we group in ones? (No) In twos? (No) In fives or tens? (Yes!)* Count the coins grouped in 10s. Compare how many there are with their estimates. *Who was closest?* Discuss how much there is. Point out that some of the coins are larger than others. *These are the 2p coins. They are worth 2p – two of the 1p coins. To find out how much we have, we shall have to count in twos.* First let the children sort the coins into two piles: 2p coins and 1p coins. Then help them to count the 2p coins, counting in 2s: *two, four, six, eight, …* Write the total, e.g. 26p. Now count on, counting the 1p coins. *How much in all?* Record the amounts in each type of coin as well as the total.
Adult support is needed to run this activity.

1p and 2p coins

Maths Weekly Plan: Year 1 and 2

Block A1.c: Partition numbers into T and U and recognise the value of each digit
Block A1.d: Compare and order numbers

	Mental oral starter	Objectives	Main teaching	Activities: Group 1 Y1	Activities: Group 2 Y1	Activities: Group 3 Y2	Activities: Group 4 Y2	Plenary	Outcomes
Day 1	**Count back in 1s from different numbers.** Place number cards 10–20 in a hat. Choose a child to select a card. Chn **count back** together from this number, as you point at the numbers on a 100-square. Repeat for other numbers.	**Y1** • Recognise the value of each digit in a 'teens' number **Y2** • Know what each digit in a 2-digit number represents, including 0 as a place holder • Partition 2-digit numbers into T and U	**All** Introduce Blue Baboon from *The Quangle Wangle's Hat. He likes blue things.* Count 10 blue pegs onto a coat hanger. Add 3 yellow pegs. Write *10 + 3 = 13. Now we want 15 pegs on the hanger.* Add 2 yellow pegs as you count. Write *15 = 10 + 5*. Rpt for other **'teens' numbers**. **Y1** Show 5 towers of 10 blue linking cubes. **Count** the cubes **in 10s**. Show 4 yellow cubes and count on from 50 to 54. Write *50 + 4 = 54*. Write *69*. ***How many** blue towers do we need? How many yellow cubes?* Write *69 = 60 + 9*. Stress all **2-digit numbers** are a number of **tens** and some **units**.	Y1 A1.c.1 TM 2.1 2 Making amounts TA	Y1 1.1 p8 Matching cubes to 2-digit numbers	Y2 A1.c.1 Finding 2-digit numbers on a 100-square T	Y2 2.1 p9 Matching amounts to 10p and 1p coins	Place 10 yellow pegs and 10 blue pegs on a coat hanger. Hide them behind a card. Reveal some blue pegs. Challenge chn to say how many pegs are hidden and how many of each colour.	**Y1** • Recognise the value of each digit in a 'teens' number **Y2** • Recognise how many tens and units are in a 2-digit number
Day 2	**Write numerals up to 20 (Y1) or 100 (Y2).** Use set of 1–20 cards for Y1s, and 1–100 cards for Y2s. Choose a child to select a card and say the number out loud. Write number in the air together. Chn write number on whiteboards and show you. Repeat for other numbers.		**All** Show Blue Baboon. *He collects 10s.* Point at 14 on the number line and place Olympian Bear there. *Bear has 14p. How can we make this amount? We can use a 10p coin and four 1p coins.* Show the chn the coins and write *10p + 4p = 14p*. Rpt for 19p. **[ITR Y1 Al.c]** **Y2** Show Blue Baboon and a pot. *Baboon saves 10p coins.* Drop 7 10p coins in pot. *How much is that? 70p.* Stick the coins to the board. Show five 1p coins. Stick them to the board. Write *70p + 5p =*. **Count** from 70 **in 1s** to get answer. Rpt for 37p and 66p.	Y1 1.1 p7 Matching hangers/ pegs to teen numbers	Y1 A1.c.3 TM 2.2 2 Making amounts TA	Y2 2.1 p8 Matching towers to 10s, cubes to 1s	Y2 A1.c.3 Investigating combinations of tens and units cards T	Show chn 2 towers of 10 blue bricks. They write numbers that have two towers of 10 and some loose bricks. Eg 25: two towers of 10 and 5 loose bricks.	**Y1** • Split 'teens' numbers into a ten and some units **Y2** • Partition 2-digit numbers into tens and units
Day 3	**Estimate and count a set of objects.** Choose a child to take two handfuls of cubes and drop them into a jar. Hold up the jar and ask each child to write two **estimates** on their whiteboard. Count the cubes one by one. Repeat.		**All** On a 100-square, colour the multiples of 10 in blue. Count in 10s from 10 to 100. Write *27* on the board. *Baboon likes the tens part of each number.* Show **place-value** cards 20 and 7. Write *20 + 7 = 27*. Repeat to show 16 = 10 + 6 and 32 = 30 + 2. **Y1** *Let's help Baboon make 'teens' numbers using p-v cards and cubes. Let's make 15.* Ask chn to find correct T & U cards. Make tower of 10 blue cubes and 5 yellow. Ask different chn to come and make other 'teens' numbers. Write number sentences on the board, eg *15 = 10 + 5*.	Y1 A1.c.4 Using towers of 10 cubes to make 2-digit numbers T	Y1 1.1 p9 Matching 10p and 1p coins to 2-digit numbers	Y2 A1.c.4 Playing a tens and units card game TA	Y2 A1.c.5 Matching 2-digit numbers on calculator with coins and cubes	Give each pair a place-value card (tens or units). They have to find a partner to make a 2-digit number. Go round the class asking chn to read their number and say how many tens and how many units are in their number.	**Y1** • Split 'teens' numbers into a ten and some units **Y2** • Partition numbers into tens and units

	Mental oral starter	Objectives	Main teaching	Activities: Group 1 Y1	Activities: Group 2 Y1	Activities: Group 3 Y2	Activities: Group 4 Y2	Plenary	Outcomes
Day 4	**Count in 10s, forwards and backwards.** Explain to class they are going to do some silent counting. Each child writes a multiple of 10 on their whiteboard. Child shows and says their multiple of 10. Ask them to **count** either **forwards** or backwards in 10s from their multiple.	**Y1** • Say which is more or less of two numbers **Y2** • Order numbers up to at least 100 and position them on a 100-square	**All** Write *27* and *43*. *Which is **larger**? Look at number of 10s.* Below 27 stick 20 card, below 47 stick 40 card. Count in 10s using fingers and show 20 is 2 tens, 40 is 4 tens. Stick units cards next to the tens cards. Look at 10s card to see which number is larger. **[Y2 ITR A1.d]** **Y1** Shuffle number cards 0–20. Hold face down and ask 2 chn to choose a card each. *Which number is larger?* Show number line. *Which number is **further along**?* Chn match numbers with fingers. Rpt for different pairs of cards. **[Y1 ITR A1.d]**	Y1 1.1 p10 Comparing two numbers using cubes	Y1 A1.d.4 Comparing and ordering numbers 1–20 T	Y2 A1.d.2 Investigating 2-digit numbers with consecutive digits TA	Y2 A1.d.2 Investigating 2-digit numbers with consecutive digits TA	Put chn in 2 teams, A and B. Give each team a set of shuffled 0–20 cards. A child from each team chooses a card. *Which is the larger number?* The team with the larger number collects a point. Repeat many times.	**Y1** • Find the larger and the smaller of two numbers **Y2** • Order numbers from smallest to largest using the tens digit
Day 5	**Double numbers 1–6, and halve corresponding numbers.** Play 'Thumbs up, thumbs down'. Write numbers 1–6 on the board. Point to a number randomly and say its **double**. Chn show whether they think it is right or wrong using thumbs. Repeat for doubles of different numbers.		**All** Show place-value cards 20 and 4, and 40 and 2. Place the pairs together and read. *Which number is larger? Baboon likes the tens.* Remove units to compare tens to see which number is larger. Look at 100-square to identify numbers, reminding chn that numbers get larger as they go down the square. Show chn three numbers, eg 38, 27 and 15. Discuss which is the **largest**. *How do we know?* Remind chn that, like Blue Baboon, we should look at the tens. Put the three numbers in **order**. Repeat for 26, 13 and 19.	Y1 A1.d.2 Comparing two numbers using cubes T	Y1 A1.d.3 Comparing two numbers using a 100-square TA	Y2 2.1 p10 Writing prices in order	Y2 2.1 p11 Combining tens and units	Send 3 chn out of the class. The remaining chn choose a number from the 100-square and remember it. The 3 chn come back and identify the number by asking six questions with yes or no answers.	**Y1** • Find the larger and the smaller of two numbers **Y2** • Order numbers from smallest to largest using the tens digit

Vocabulary
count forward/ backward
'teens' number
count in 1s, 10s
how many?
2-digit number
tens
units, ones
one ten and … more/extra
digit
estimate
place value
larger/smaller than
largest/smallest
more/less than
further along the line
order
between
double

Resources
number cards 0–100
extra set of number cards 0–20
hat
100-squares
picture of Blue Baboon
10 blue pegs
10 yellow pegs
coat hanger
60 blue linking cubes
9 yellow linking cubes
six counters
large piece of card
individual whiteboards
1–20 number line
picture of Olympian Bear
nine 10p coins
nine 1p coins
a pot
Blu-tack
place-value cards (T, U)
20 blue bricks
two handfuls of cubes
a jar
blue colouring pencil/pen
calculators

Year 1 Block A1.c Activities

2.1 2 Making amounts

A1.c.1 A group of 6 or more children working in pairs

Show children the coins. *What amount of money could we make using some of these coins?* Show one amount of money, for example two 10p and three 1p coins. *How much money do the 10p coins make? And the 1p coins? How much altogether? How do we write that number?* Help children to write 23p. Pairs then choose 10p and 1p coins to make different amounts of money. Help them to record the amounts. Discuss which digit tells them the number of 10p coins and which tells them the number of 1p coins.
Adult support is needed to run this activity.

three 10p and three 1p coins per pair

2.2 2 Making amounts

A1.c.3 A group of 6 or more children working in pairs

Show children the coins. *What amount of money could we make using some of these coins?* Show one amount of money, for example two 10p and three 1p coins. *How much money do the 10p coins make? And the 1p coins? How much altogether? How do we write that number?* Ask each pair to make a different amount of money using 10p and 1p coins. Help them to record the amounts. Discuss which digit tells them the number of 10p coins and which tells them the number of 1p coins.
What's the smallest amount we could make using 10p and 1p coins? What digit would be in the tens place? And the ones place? What's the biggest amount we could make using 10p and 1p coins? What digit would be in the tens place? And the ones place?
Adult support is needed to run this activity.

three 10p and three 1p coins per pair

A1.c.4 Pairs of children

Shuffle the place value cards and place them face down in two piles, one for tens and one for units. Children each take a card, one child from each pile. They show each other their cards and create a 2-digit number, for example 40 and 5 make 45. Check each pair's number and read it together. Each pair now matches their number to towers of 10 cubes and loose cubes. Check these, and support pairs where necessary. Children replace the cards and repeat the activity.
Adult support may be useful in running this activity.

lots of linking cubes: towers of 10 and loose cubes; tens and units place value cards

Year 1 Block A1.d Activities

A1.d.2 Up to 10 children working in pairs

Give out two 2-digit number cards to each pair. They lay their cards face up in the middle of the table. They must identify and discuss the two numbers and put a counter on the larger number. Each pair makes their numbers using towers of 10 cubes and loose cubes. Each pair in turn then shows their numbers created in cubes. The other children say which of these two numbers is more cubes: *That one is larger.* Does the pair have the counter on the correct number? Go round each pair in turn in this way, then repeat the activity with different cards.
Adult support may be useful in running this activity.

linking cubes, towers of 10 cubes and loose cubes; 1–20 2-digit number cards; counters

A1.d.3 Up to 10 children working in pairs

Give out two 2-digit number cards to each pair. They lay their cards face up in the middle of the table. They must identify and discuss the two numbers and put a counter on the larger number. Each pair in turn then goes to the 100-square. They identify their numbers on the square. The other children say which of these two numbers is further along: *That one is larger.* Does the pair have the counter on the correct number? Go round each pair in turn in this way, then repeat the activity with different cards.
Adult support may be useful in running this activity.

10–100 2-digit number cards; counters; 100-square

A1.d.4 A group of 6 children working in pairs

Shuffle the cards and spread them out on the table. Each pair reveals one card. The pair with the larger number keeps both cards. Continue like this until all cards have been chosen. *Who has the most cards?* Each pair creates a line of their cards in order, from smallest to largest. Reshuffle the cards and repeat.
Adult support may be useful in running this activity.

1–20 number cards, or extend to 1–50

Year 2 Block A1.c Activities

A1.c.1 A group of up to 6 children

Write or show a multiple of 10. Children count down their 100-square to that multiple. Each child then chooses a single-digit number and moves along the grid that number of spaces, for example start on 60 and choose 4, so count four more and place a counter on 64. Children record their movements like this: *64 = 60 + 4*. Repeat several times, giving a different multiple of 10 to start with. Extend by comparing the chosen numbers.

Whose counter is on the largest/smallest number?

Adult support is needed to run this activity.

100-square and counter per child

A1.c.3 A group of 4 children

Place tens and units place value cards face down in separate shuffled piles. Child 1 takes a tens card, child 2 takes a units card, child 3 takes a tens card and child 4 takes a units card, for example 40, 8, 60 and 6. Children try to pair up their cards to make the smallest and the largest number possible, for example 46 and 68. They then use the cards to make all the possible numbers and list them from smallest to largest, for example 46, 48, 66, 68. Repeat the activity, replacing the cards at the bottom of the piles.

Adult support may be useful in running this activity with several groups of children.

place value cards (T, U)

A1.c.4 A group of up to 6 children

Children each think of a 2-digit number and write it secretly on a piece of paper. Place tens and units place value cards face down in separate shuffled piles. Turn up the top tens card. Any child with that number of tens may ask for a 10p coin. Turn up the top units card. Any child with that number of units may ask for a 1p coin. Keep playing like this until each child has two coins and then ask children to reveal their numbers. Together put their numbers in order. Play again.

Adult support is needed to run this activity.

place value cards (T, U); 10p and 1p coins

A1.c.5 Two groups of 4 children

Child 1 enters a 2-digit number into a calculator and shows it to child 2 and child 3 but not child 4. Child 2 matches the number with 10p and 1p coins. Child 3 matches the number with interlocking cubes. Child 4 looks at the coins and cubes and selects the matching number card. They check it against the calculator display. Repeat the activity, swapping roles.

1–100 number cards; interlocking cubes in towers of 10; loose cubes; 1p and 10p coins; calculator

Year 2 Block A1.d Activities

A1.d.2 A whole class investigation with children working in pairs

Explain that you want to make a list of all the 2-digit numbers where the tens digit is 1 more than the units digit. Ask children to guess how many numbers like this there are between 10 and 100. Record the guesses. Give pairs time to look for and list on their whiteboards all such numbers. *Are you sure you have found all the numbers?*

When a pair has found all the numbers, ask them to predict how many numbers there are between 10 and 100 where the tens digit is 1 **less** than the units digit. They record their prediction and then find and list the numbers. Extend the activity in stages by predicting how many numbers there are between 10 and 100 where the tens digit is 2, 3… more/less than the units digit. Encourage the more able children to be systematic in their search, checking and convincing you that they have found all the possible numbers at each stage.

Adult support is needed to run this activity.

individual whiteboards

Maths Weekly Plan: Year 1 and 2

Block B1.a: Y1 Say the number 1 more; Y2 Add by counting on in 1s
Block B1.b: Y1 Say the number 1, 2, 3 or 4 more; Y2 Add three numbers by counting on

	Mental oral starter	Objectives	Main teaching	Activities: Group 1 Y1	Activities: Group 2 Y1	Activities: Group 3 Y2	Activities: Group 4 Y2	Plenary	Outcomes
Day 1	**Count back in 1s from different numbers.** Peg number cards 0–20 along a washing line. Choose a child to select one of the cards from the line and remove it. Use a puppet to touch the pegs as chn **count back** from the chosen number. Replace the card and repeat.	**Y1** • Say the number that is 1 more than a given number • Count on 1 from a given number **Y2** • Recognise addition as counting on • Add by counting on in 1s from the larger number, crossing a multiple of 10	**All** **Count** along number line to 20. Point at 6. *What number comes **next**?* Encourage chn to use number line to help them say correct number. Rpt for several numbers. Show chn that 6+1=7, a number + 1 = the **next number**. Stress the next number is **1 more** than the number. **Y2** Point to 16 on number line. Point to next number. Whisper next 2 numbers. Write *16+3=*. Point to 16 in the addition. Put Midgard on 16. Point to +3. *Midgard will fly 3 spaces. Where will he land?* Put Midgard on 19 and complete **number sentence**. Rpt for 12+5 and 34+4.	Y1 B1.a.1 Counting to 10, identifying the next number TA	Y1 B1.a.3 Building towers of cubes and finding the next number	Y2 B1.a.3 Using card number lines to model adding by counting on T	Y2 2.1 p13 Practising addition by counting on using a number line	Re-read the last page of *Whatever next!* by Jill Murphy. *What does Baby Bear's mum say?* Say a number and then ask: *Whatever next?* The child has to say the next number. Help by whispering the count from the number before.	**Y1** • Say the next number **Y2** • Say the next number • Know that counting on 1 is addition
Day 2	**Count in 10s to and from a multiple of 10.** Ask chn to shut their eyes and turn around so they can't see you. Drop seven 10p coins one at a time into a ceramic mug. Chn **count in 10s** when they hear the clinks. ***How much** is in the mug?* Repeat several times.		**All** Remind children how to find the next number. Show photo of a celebrity. Say their age. *How old will they be next birthday?* Write a number sentence, eg *28+1=*. Pairs work out answer. Complete number sentence and read together. Rpt. *How old will you be next birthday?* Write number sentences, eg 5+1=6. How old will they be in 3 years' time? *What is 5 **and 3 more**?* Chn **put 5 in their heads** and use fingers to **count on** 3. What about when they are in Y6? Rpt for Bear, who could be 9 or 19 or 29 to target different chn. *How old is Bear in 4 years' time?* Count along number line. Write matching addition sentence on board, eg 19+4=23.	Y1 1.1 p13 Identifying the next number	Y1 B1.a.2 Finding the next number using number cards 1–50 T	Y2 2.1 p13 Practising addition by counting on using a number line	Y2 B1.a.2 Adding 5 to number cards, and writing totals on sticky notes TA	Ask a child to point to a number less than 10 on the number line. Ask another child to use fingers to count on 2. *What number do you get to?*	**Y1** • Count on 1 to find the next number • Count on up to 10 **Y2** • Count on up to 10 • Know that counting on is addition
Day 3	**Say the number 1 more than a given number.** Play 'Ping-Pong'. Say a number. Chn say number that is 1 more. Start slowly then gradually increase the pace. Occasionally say 'Ping', to which the response is 'Pong'.	**Y1** • Count on 1, 2, 3 or 4 from a given number • Begin to use the + and = signs to record addition sentences • Relate counting on to addition and to addition sentences	**All** Recap how to count on. Show 1–40 number line. *Midgard the dragon likes flying.* Write *36+7=*. Put Midgard on 36. *He rests on 10s.* Point to +7. Show 7 fingers. Count on from 36, folding down fingers. Land Midgard on 30, then on 43. Complete addition sentence. Rpt for 38+6=. **Y1** Show large colander with 8 small potatoes. *This is Midgard's supper!* Count the potatoes. ***How many** if he **adds 4 more**?* Write *8+4=*. Chn hold up 4 fingers, put 8 in their heads and count on. Add potatoes as you count. Complete the number sentence. Rpt for 13+4.	Y1 B1.b.1 Adding three cubes to a tower, counting on T	Y1 1.1 p15 Counting on using fingers	Y2 B1.b.1 Using coins to make an amount, and adding two small amounts to it by counting on TA	Y2 2.1 p16 Practising adding three numbers, identifying the largest and counting on	Give each pair a 2-digit number card with a small sticky note on it. Throw a dice several times. Ask chn to **add** each dice number to their card number by counting on. They write the answers on the sticky note.	**Y1** • Count on up to 10 from 1-digit numbers • Work out additon by counting on **Y2** • Count on up to 10 from 1-digit numbers • Work out additions by counting on

	Mental oral starter	Objectives	Main teaching	Activities: Group 1 (Y1)	Group 2 (Y1)	Group 3 (Y2)	Group 4 (Y2)	Plenary	Outcomes
Day 4	**Say the next number to a given number.** Pass a ball to a child. Say a number; they say the next number. If they are successful they pass the ball to another child. The first child says a number and the second child says the next number. Continue like this.	*(Continued)* **Y2** • Add three numbers by putting the largest number first • Recognise that addition can be done in any order • Use the + and = signs to record addition sentences	**All** Make large dice numbered 6, 8, 10, 13, 15, 20. Cover 6 on an ordinary dice with a 4. Throw both dice. *We will add the small number to the large number.* Write the addition sentence. Chn put large number in their heads and count on using fingers. Check using number line and ask a child to complete the addition sentence. Rpt for three numbers: roll the large dice; then roll the small dice and count on from the larger number using fingers; then roll the small dice again and count again. Write number sentence, eg *14+3+4=21*, asking a child to write answer. Rpt several times, making sure chn always start by putting the larger number in their heads.	Y1 1.1 p15 Counting on using fingers	Y1 B1.b.2 Adding 3 to a number between 7 and 30 TA	Y2 2.1 p15 Practising adding three numbers	Y2 B1.b.2 Taking cards from two piles and throwing a dice to make an addition T	Ask a child to pick a number less than 50 on 100-square. Ask chn to write this. They then write an addition sentence using the number and two 1-digit numbers. Chn swap whiteboards and complete the additions.	**Y1** • Put large number in head and count on using fingers **Y2** • Add three numbers by counting on • Find answers to additon sentences
Day 5	**Count on in 10s from any 1-digit number.** Play 'Pass the bear'. Chn sit in a circle. Give bear to a child and say a start number. The child counts on 10 and passes the bear. Continue in this way. Repeat several times.		**All** Chn recall how to find **total** of 3 numbers. Practise for several additions, with Y1s adding 2 numbers, eg 8+5=, 13+6=, and Y2s adding 3 numbers, eg 8+5+4=, 12+6+7=. Emphasise starting by putting the large number in your head. Ensure chn can count on using fingers. **Y2** Show 3 items with prices: pencil 25p, rubber 4p and sticker 2p. *What is the total cost?* Write *25p+4p+2p=*. Put 25 in your heads. Count on 4, then count on 2, holding up fingers if it helps. Complete the number sentence. Rpt for 5p+1p+36p.	Y1 B1.b.4 Adding two 1p coins to an amount TA	Y1 B1.b.5 Adding on dice numbers to number cards 1–10	Y2 B1.b.4 Practising adding two numbers by counting on in 10s T	Y2 p8 Practising adding three numbers	Give each child a 1p, 2p or 5p **coin**. Choose card at random from a pile of number cards 10–50. Write the card number on the board as an **amount** in pence. Choose chn in turn to add their coin to the amount on the board.	**Y1** • Count on using fingers from large no. in head • Know that counting on is addition; match to addition sentences **Y2** • Add three numbers by counting on • Solve additons

Vocabulary
count
count on/back
next
next number
1 more
number sentence
count in 10s
how much?
how many?
add
add 4 more
and 4 more
put this number 'in your head'
total
altogether
coin
amount

Resources
number cards 0–100
pegs
washing line
puppet
0–20 number line
0–100 number line
picture of Midgard the dragon
about 100 linking cubes
Post-it notes
Whatever Next! by Jill Murphy
about nine 10p coins
ceramic mug
photo of a celebrity
large 100-square
1–40 number line
large colander
up to 20 small potatoes
individual whiteboards
about twelve 1p coins
about twelve 2p coins
dice numbered 1–6
ball
large dice numbered 6, 8, 10, 13, 15, 20
extra set of number cards 1–10
100-square
teddy bear
pencil labelled *25p*
rubber labelled *4p*
sticker labelled *2p*
1–20 number tracks
about twelve 5p coins

Year 1 Block B1.a Activities

B1.a.1 A group of up to 8 children

Sit children in a circle. Together lay the 1–10 cards in order to make a number line. Count along the line together, pointing at each number. One child chooses a card and takes it. *What number is it?* If necessary, count along the line to the space: *five*. The next child then says the next number. If necessary whisper the number before and point at the number line: *four, five, …* The child says *six*. The first child puts their card back, and the next child round the circle now takes a card. Their neighbour says the next number, and play continues. Everyone finger claps to give praise for the next numbers!
Adult support is needed to run this activity.

1–10 number cards

B1.a.2 A group of up to 6 children

Shuffle the 1–50 number cards and place them in a pile face down. Each child takes a card. They look at each other's and agree what number each child is holding. Each child then says the next number, if necessary looking at the 100-square. They write it on a Post-it note and stick it on their card. Each child should support the others so that they all do this correctly. Then they take another card each, and continue.
Adult support may be useful in running this activity.

1–50 number cards; Post-it notes; large 100-square

B1.a.3 A group of up to 12 children

Children sit in a circle. Provide lots of linking cubes for each pair. Shuffle the 1–20 number cards and place them in a pile face down. Choose a child to take a card from the pile. Show all the children. Together, identify the number and say it aloud, for example, *ten*. In pairs, children build a tower of ten cubes. Then, working in unison, everyone adds another cube to their tower and says the next number: *eleven*. When everyone agrees, write 11 on a Post-it note and stick it on the card. Then choose a child to take another card and play continues.
Adult support may be useful in running this activity.

1–20 number cards; linking cubes; Post-it notes

Year 1 Block B1.b Activities

B1.b.1 A group of up to 12 children working in pairs

Choose a starting number and write it on the flip chart, for example 8. Each pair makes a tower of this many cubes. Explain that we shall add 3. As children add the three cubes, they count on one number for each cube. Write the addition on the flip chart. Repeat, starting with a different number. If appropriate, children can write the additions on individual whiteboards, which may then be photocopied to record their work.
Adult support may be useful in running this activity.

linking cubes; individual whiteboards (optional)

B1.b.2 A group of 3 children

Shuffle the 7–30 number cards and spread them out face down. Children take it in turns to turn over two cards. If one card is 3 more than the other (and the child recognises this), they take the pair and place them face up in front of them. They show that they can start at the smaller card, count on 3, and end at the larger card. *One card is three more than the other.* If the two cards are not in this relation, the child turns them back over, leaving them in the same place. Play until all the cards have gone. Who has the most pairs? Shuffle the cards and play again.
Adult support may be useful in running this activity. Two or three groups can be supervised at once.

7–30 number cards

B1.b.4 A group of up to 8 children working in pairs

Children sit in a circle. Shuffle the 1–20 number cards and place them in a pile face down. Choose a child to take a card from the pile and show it. Together identify the number and say it aloud, for example *twelve*. Write *12p* on the flip chart. In pairs, children match this to coins, using a 10p coin instead of ten 1p coins. Then, working in unison, everyone adds another two 1p coins and counts on to the new amount: *thirteen, fourteen pence*. Check that everyone agrees, and write the matching addition: $12p + 2p = 14p$. Read this together. Then choose a child to take another card and play continues.
Adult support may be useful in running this activity.

1–20 number cards; 1p and 10p coins per pair

B1.b.5 A group of 3 or more children

Shuffle the 1–10 cards and place them in a pile face down. One child takes a card, for example 5. Another child rolls the dice, for example 3. Children use their number track to help them add the two numbers, starting at 5 and counting on 3. They point at the answer: 8. Children check each other's answers. Repeat, swapping roles, for each card in turn.

1–10 number cards; dice; 1–20 number track per child

Year 2 Block B1.a Activities

B1.a.2 A group of 4, 6 or 8 children working in pairs

Place a set of shuffled 10–50 number cards face down in a pile. Pairs take a card each, read their number to their partner and show them the number card as a check. Each child adds 5 to their number, writes the answer on a Post-it and sticks it on their card. They each check their partner's answer. Repeat 10 times, then discuss any patterns in the additions as a group.

Which addition gave you the largest total? Which gave you the smallest?

10–50 number cards; Post-it notes

B1.a.3 A group of 6 or more children

Place a set of shuffled 20–60 number cards face down in a pile. Choose a child to take the top card, for example 36. Use the number to write an addition, for example $36 + 7 =$. Show children how to make a suitable number line (for example from 30 to 50) from an ordered set of 1–100 number cards to use with their fingers to help them count on. Each child records the addition. Repeat five times.

Adult support is needed to run this activity.

20–60 number cards; ordered set of 1–100 number cards; Post-it notes

Year 2 Block B1.b Activities

B1.b.1 A group of 6 or more children

Use 10p and 1p coins to make an amount, for example 34p. Ask children to write the amount on their whiteboards. Show a 2p coin and a 1p coin. Explain how to add both coins to 34p: ask children to identify the larger coin (2p) and add this first by placing 34 'in their heads' and counting on two using their fingers (or tapping the 2p coin twice); add the 1p coin by counting on one. Children write the total, for example $34p + 3p = 37p$. Check answers together by counting the total amount. Repeat several times, starting with a different amount each time. You may wish to photocopy children's recording on their whiteboards as a record of their work.

Adult support is needed to run this activity.

several 10p and 1p coins ('real' if possible); 2p coin ('real' if possible); individual whiteboards

B1.b.2 Groups of 3 children

Place a shuffled set of 20–50 number cards face down in a pile. Shuffle two sets of 1–10 number cards and place them face down in a pile. Child 1 takes a card from one pile, child 2 takes a card from the second pile and child 3 rolls the dice to make an addition of three numbers. They each record the addition on their whiteboard, for example $34 + 5 + 2 =$. The group works out the answer together, first agreeing which number is the largest and then starting to count on from the largest number. They write in the total to complete the recording. Repeat the whole process five times.

What numbers are easiest to add? Can you say why you think so?

Adult support may be useful in running this activity.

20–50 number cards; two sets of 1–10 number cards; 1–6 dice

B1.b.4 Pairs of children

Place a shuffled set of 20–60 number cards face down in a pile. One child takes the top card and both children then decide which tens number to add: 20, 30 or 40. They complete the addition together by using a 100-square to count on in 10s, writing the total on a Post-it and sticking it on the card. They repeat this 10 times.

Adult support may be useful in running this activity with several pairs of children.

20–60 number cards; 100-square; Post-it notes

Maths Weekly Plan: Year 1 and 2

Block B1.c: Know addition and subtraction facts for numbers that total up to 6 or 9
Block B1.d: Rehearse addition and subtraction facts and record number sentences

	Mental oral starter	Objectives	Main teaching	Activities: Group 1 Y1	Activities: Group 2 Y1	Activities: Group 3 Y2	Activities: Group 4 Y2	Plenary	Outcomes
Day 1	**Read and write numerals to match number words.** Peg number cards 0–20 on washing line. Take another set of cards that show number names from **zero–twenty**. Shuffle the cards and choose a child to select one of them. Show card to class. Chn write the matching numeral on their whiteboards. Match to numeral card.	**Y1** • Recognise a number of objects up to 6 without counting • Know by heart addition facts for pairs of numbers that total up to 6 **Y2** • Rehearse addition and subtraction facts for pairs of numbers that total up to 9 • Use the +, – and = signs to record addition and subtraction sentences	**All** Show picture of Bear. *He eats apples.* Draw 6 apples. Chn show 6 fingers. *Mrs Bear eats 1 apple, Mr Bear eats 5.* Match fingers to **addition sentence**: 1 + 5 = 6. Model other pairs to 6, eg 2 + 4 = 6. *Is it fair?* 3 + 3 is fair because both bears get same. Point out 6 + 0 = 6. **[ITR Y2 B1.c]** **Y1** Hold up 4 teddy bears. ***How many** are there?* Chn count. Write *4* on the board. Give one child 1 teddy and another 3. Match this to **number sentence** 3 + 1 = 4. Give two chn 2 teddies each. Match this to 2 + 2 = 4. Rpt for 3 + 1 = 4 and then 4 + 0 = 4. Discuss which one was fair: 2 + 2.	Y1 B1.c.6 Making towers of 5 cubes using two colours, and matching to additions T	Y1 1.1 p18 Adding to make 4 and 5	Y2 B1.c.5 Recalling pairs to 7 by rolling a dice and saying what number is on the bottom TA	Y2 B1.c.2 Making pairs to 6 using dominoes	Hand out one number card 0–5 to each child. Ask chn to find a partner whose card number goes with theirs to **make** 5. They can use their fingers to help them decide.	**Y1** • Make pairs that total 4 and 5 **Y2** • Make pairs that total 6 • Match these to addition sentences
Day 2	**Add two 1-digit numbers, not crossing 10.** Play 'Quick on the draw'. Say an addition, eg *Four **add** two.* Ask chn to hold up fingers to match the answer. Rpt for different **additions** with **totals** up to 10. Vary the vocabulary.		**All** Show a rabbit and 5 baby rabbits. *How many baby rabbits are there?* Count 5. *How many different ways of making 5 are there?* Chn use fingers to show the ways of making 5. Each time colour the rabbits brown and white to match and write an addition sentence, eg *4 + 1 = 5*. **Y2** Show Bear. Draw 7 fish. **Partition** fish with a line: 1 for Mrs Bear and 6 for Mr Bear. *One and six make seven.* Write matching **subtraction**: *7 – 1 = 6*. Write addition and **subtraction sentences** for each pair to 7. *Can we share 7 fish fairly?* Repeat for sharing 8 nuts.	Y1 1.1 p18 Adding to make 4 and 5	Y1 B1.c.2 Playing Pelmanism, making pairs to 5 TA	Y2 B1.c.3 Playing Pelmanism, making pairs to 7 or 8 T	Y2 2.1 p19 Adding pairs to make 9	Write ***Monday*, *Tuesday*, … *Friday*** on board. *How many **days** are there in the **week**? Seven.* Count along to today. *How many days have gone this week? How many days are there to go?* Write number sentence, eg 4 + 3 = 7.	**Y1** • Make pairs that total 5 • Begin to match these to addition sentences **Y2** • Make pairs that total 7 • Match these to addition sentences; begin to match to subtraction
Day 3	**Recall addition pairs to 5, 6, 7.** Play 'Ping-pong'. Say a number, eg 2. Children say its partner to 5. Start slowly, then increase the pace. Extend pairs to other numbers, eg 6 and 7.	**Y1** • Begin to know by heart addition facts for pairs of numbers that total up to 7 • Relate addition facts for pairs of numbers to an understanding of addition, including use of + and = signs	**All** Across the centre of the carpet area, lay out number track made of 7 large tiles numbered 1–7. Arrange chn on either side. Place a toy cat on 1 and a toy dog on 7. *How many hops will cat need to make to get to dog?* Move cat, counting the hops. Write a matching number sentence: *1 + 6 = 7*. Put cat on 2 and repeat for all pairs to 7. Put chn into pairs with whiteboards and give each pair a number (4–9) to partition into **addition pairs**. Ask Y2s to write matching **subtraction pairs**. Check these as a class.	Y1 B1.c.5 Investigating ways to match ends of dominoes to make 6 T	Y1 B1.c.5 Investigating ways to match ends of dominoes to make 6 T	Y2 2.1 p19 Adding pairs to make 9	Y2 B1.d.3 Finding pairs of dominoes adding to 10 TA	Hand out one number card 0–7 to each child. Ask children to choose a partner whose card goes with theirs to make 7. They can use fingers to help them.	**Y1** • Make pairs that total 6 • Begin to match these to addition sentences **Y2** • Make pairs that total 7 • Create subtraction facts from pairs totalling 7

	Mental oral starter	Objectives	Main teaching	Activities: Group 1 Y1	Group 2 Y1	Group 3 Y2	Group 4 Y2	Plenary	Outcomes
Day 4	**Learn and recite number rhymes; count on from a given number.** Recite together the number rhyme 'Seven fat fishermen', or similar. Encourage children to hold up one finger for each item caught. *If we catch two* ***more*** *objects, how many things will we have caught?* **Count on** from 7.	*(Continued)* **Y2** • Recognise the use of a symbol to stand for an unknown number • Rehearse addition and subtraction facts for pairs of numbers that total 10 • Relate addition and subtraction facts to missing number sentences	**All** Recite the rhyme used in mental oral starter. Remind chn how many things were caught and write *7* on board. *How many ways can we make 7?* Write _+_=7. Pairs find ways of making 7 using fingers on both hands. Ask Y2s to make matching subtraction sentences, eg 7−_=4. **Y1** Show chn missing number sentence, eg _+4=5, and ask them to use fingers to work out answer. Show another sentence, eg 3+_=6. Use number line to find answer by counting on. *How many spaces do we need to count on?*	Y1 1.1 p21 Completing pairs to make 7	Y1 B1.d.5 Playing card game 'Fish', making pairs to 7 T	Y2 B1.d.1 Playing card game 'Fish', making pairs to 10 TA	Y2 2.1 p21 Making 10 with missing numbers	Give out digit cards 6, 7, 8 and 9, one to each pair. Ask pairs to think of a way of making their number, eg 2+4=6. They can say it, use digit cards or write it on their whiteboards.	**Y1** • Make pairs that total 7 • Match these to addition sentences **Y2** • Complete missing number sentences • Work out bonds to 9
Day 5	**Recognise coins up to £2.** Peg a large 1p **coin** onto a washing line. Children hold up fingers to match the number of pence. Repeat for 2p, 5p, 10p, 20p, placing them in **order**. Point out that you need two children to show 20 fingers! Extend to 50p and £1 coins.		**All** Write *10*. Ask chn to use fingers on both hands to work out all the addition pairs that make 10. Write these on the board: *1+9=10, 2+8=10, … 10+0=10*. Explain these are the **number bonds** to 10. *Our handy calculator (our fingers) will help us remember them.* **[ITR Y2 b1.d]** **Y2** Look at bonds to 10. Use fingers to work out subtractions. *10−1=?* Fold down 1 finger. *How many left? 9.* Ask a child to complete the subtraction. Ask chn to write all subtractions: *10−2=8, 10−3=7, …* Look at both lists. *Subtraction is the opposite of addition.*	Y1 B1.d.1 TM 3.1 3 Addition facts TA	Y1 1.1 p22 Completing additions to make 7	Y2 2.1 p21 Making 10 with missing numbers	Y2 B1.d.6 Generating subtraction sentences to match bonds to 10 T	Make 2 teams. Chn in team A fold down some fingers. A child from team B takes a no. card (0–10) and chooses the chn with the matching fingers to get to 10. Team A scores that number of points. Rpt.	**Y1** • Begin to find bonds to 10 • Begin to match bonds to 10 to addition sentences **Y2** • Calculate bonds to 10 • Match bonds to 10 to addition and subtraction sentences

Vocabulary
zero, one, two, … twenty
add, addition
subtract, subtraction
addition sentence
subtraction sentence
number sentence
how many?
make
… and … is …
… and … make …
take away
leaves
how many more to make …?
equals
total
partition
Monday, Tuesday, … Friday
day
week
addition pair
subtraction pair
number pair
number bond
more
count on
coin
order

Resources
number cards 0–20
pegs
washing line
number name cards zero–twenty
individual whiteboards
picture of Mr Bear
four teddy bears
lots of linking cubes in two colours
large dice numbered 1–6
about ten 10p coins
lots of 1p coins
dominoes
five extra sets of number cards 0–10
picture of a rabbit with five baby rabbits
large number tiles 1–7
toy cat
toy dog
copy of number rhyme 'Seven fat fishermen', or similar
0–10 number line
large pictures of coins: 1p, 2p, 5p, 10p, 20p, 50p, £1
coat hanger
cloth, e.g. tea towel
about four towers of 10 linking cubes

Year 1 Block B1.c Activities

B1.c.2 A group of 3 to 5 children

Children play Pelmanism: shuffle all the cards and spread them out face down. Children take turns to turn over two cards. If the pair adds to 5, they keep them. If not, they turn them back over in the same place. Continue until all the cards are taken. *Who has the most pairs?* Ask children: *How many pairs have you collected?* Children could record the possible additions at the start to remind them of the pairs.

Adult support may be useful in running this activity.

four sets of 0–5 number cards

B1.c.5 A whole-class investigation, children working in 3s or pairs

Groups make a line of four dominoes, matching ends that add to 6. Point out all the possible additions written on the flip chart from whole-class teaching. For example, a line might go 5/4, 2/0, 6/1, 5/6. Once most groups have done this (with support if necessary), make the task harder. For example, they might make a square with each matching edge adding to 6. Ask particularly able groups to make a square where the total number of dots is 6 and all the domino edges match (e.g. four dominoes arranged 0/2, 2/1, 1/0, 0/0). Some groups might make a long line using all the dominoes, matching ends that add to 6.

Adult support is needed to run this activity.

lots of dominoes per group

B1.c.6 Pairs of children

Children build as many different towers from five cubes as they can using only two colours, for example 5 red cubes and no blue cubes; 4 red cubes and 1 blue cube. Ask them to lay out number cards to match each tower, for example 5 and 0; 4 and 1. Repeat for a different number of cubes.

Adult support may be useful in running this activity.

sets of 0–5 number cards; linking cubes of two colours

Year 1 Block B1.d Activities

B1.d.1 A group of 6 or more children

Hang six pegs on the coat hanger. *How many pegs?* Children close their eyes. Cover up the last peg with the cloth. *How many pegs can you see? How many have I hidden?*

Five and what makes six? Write $5 + 1 = 6$.

Repeat, covering up the last two pegs. *What number sentence could I write? How many pegs do you think I might cover up next?* Repeat the activity, covering three pegs, then four, five and all six.

Ask children to close their eyes while you cover a number of pegs. *Open your eyes. How many pegs do you think I've covered up? How do you know?*

Adult support is needed to run this activity.

coat hanger; six pegs; a cloth (for example tea towel)

B1.d.5 A group of 4 to 6 children

Shuffle the cards and deal four to each player. Place the rest in a pile face down. Play a version of 'Happy Families' called 'Fish'. Each player takes turns to choose another player and ask for a card which will pair with one of their cards to make 7. For example, if a player has a '4' they may ask for a '3'. If the person they ask has that card, they must pass it over. If not, they say 'fish'. The first player takes a card from the middle. Players keep pairs which make 7 face up in front of them. Play continues clockwise around the group. When all the cards have been taken, carry on until nobody has cards left in their hand. Count the number of pairs each.

Adult support may be useful in running this activity.

four sets of 0–7 number cards

Year 2 Block B1.c Activities

B1.c.2 A group of 4, 6 or 8 children working in pairs

Pairs place dominoes so that the adjoining ends add to 6; for example if a child places a 4/4 domino, the one touching it must have two dots next to the four dots. They record all four additions: $0+6=6$, $1+5=6$, $2+4=6$, $3+3=6$.

How long a line can you make?

dominoes

B1.c.3 Groups of 3 or 4 children

Take cards 0–7 (or 0–8) from four sets of digit cards for each group of 3 or 4 children to play Pelmanism. Children can record the possible additions at the start as a reminder of all the number pairs that make 7 (or 8). Shuffle the cards and spread them out face down. Children take turns to turn over two cards. If the pair of cards adds to 7 (or 8) they may keep it. If not, they turn the cards face down again in the same place. Continue playing until all the cards are taken. Adult support may be useful in running this activity with several groups of children.

four sets of digit cards

B1.c.5 Pairs of children

Children take turns to roll a large dice. Looking at the number of spots on the top face, they say how many spots are hidden on the bottom face and pick up the dice to check. If correct, they take a matching number of 1p coins. You may need to remind children how to find the answer by counting on from the dice number up to 7. When a child has more than ten 1p coins, they can be exchanged for a 10p coin. The winner is the first player to reach 20p or 30p.

large 1–6 dice; 10p and 1p coins

Year 2 Block B1.d Activities

B1.d.1 A group of 4, 5 or 6 children

Deal four cards to each player from a shuffled pack of four sets of 0–10 number cards. Place the remaining cards face down in a pile. Play 'Fish' (a version of 'Happy families'). Each player takes turns to name another player and request a number that is the complement to 10 for one of the cards in their own hand, for example if a player has a 4 they may ask for a 6. The named player **must** pass the card over if they have it. If not they tell the first player to 'fish', i.e. take a card from the central pile. As players collect pairs that make 10, they put them face up in front of them. When all the cards from the central pile have been taken, play continues with one request at a time from each player in turn until no player has any cards left in their hand. The winner has the most pairs.
Adult support is needed to run this activity.

four sets of 0–10 number cards

B1.d.3 Pairs of children

Children work with a partner to find pairs of dominoes with numbers of spots that add to 10, for example 2/3 and 5/0, or 2/4 and 2/2. They find all the pairs they can and record the matching additions, for example *5 + 5 = 10*, or *6 + 4 = 10*.

How many pairs can you find?

Do any different pairs of dominoes match the same addition? (for example 3/3 and 2/2, and 5/1 and 3/1 both match $6+4=10$)

a set of dominoes per pair

B1.d.6 Pairs of children

Pairs shuffle their set of number cards 0–9 and place them in a pile face down. They take a card from the top of the pile, for example 4. They take this number of cubes off their tower. Then they each write the matching subtraction sentence, for example $10-4=6$. Pairs repeat this until they have used all the cards, and written 10 subtraction sentences.

one tower of 10 linking cubes per pair; one set of number cards 0–9 per pair

Maths Weekly Plan: Year 1 and 2

Block C1.a: Compare lengths and heights, and estimate and measure in centimetres
Block C1.b: Estimate and measure lengths in non-standard units or metres

	Mental oral starter	Objectives	Main teaching	Activities: Group 1 Y1	Activities: Group 2 Y1	Activities: Group 3 Y2	Activities: Group 4 Y2	Plenary	Outcomes
Day 1	**Count on or back in 1s from different numbers.** Give each child a large number card 0–30 (or more if more than 30 chn). Start with the **largest** number. The child holding that card says their number. The child with the number **1 less** says their number. Continue like this.	**Y1** • Compare two or more lengths or heights by direct comparison **Y2** • Estimate, measure and compare lengths using standard units: centimetres • Use a ruler to draw and measure lines to the nearest centimetre	**All** Hold up 2 scarves. *Which is* ***longer****? We can find out by placing them* ***side by side****.* Chn stretch out both scarves on floor, ends **lined up**. *Which is* ***shorter****?* Extend to **comparing** 3 scarves. Use the vocab. *longer,* ***longer than****, shorter,* ***shorter than****.* **[ITR Y1 C1.a]** **Y2** Show a straw. Show **smallest** scarf. *Longer or shorter than the straw?* Compare. Ask chn to choose other objects to compare to **length** of straw. Show a 10cm rod. *The* ***markings*** *are* ***cm****.* Count them. **Measure** objects with the rod. Find objects that are longer/shorter than the rod.	Y1 C1.a.1 Finding objects longer and shorter than a leaf TA	Y1 C1.a.1 Finding objects longer and shorter than a leaf TA	Y2 C1.a.1 Finding objects longer and shorter than a shoe	Y2 C1.a.2 Measuring objects using a 10cm rod and writing lengths T	Each child collects an object. You choose another object, eg a paintbrush. Select one of the chn's objects. *Is this longer or shorter than the paintbrush?* Test it. Rpt for other objects.	**Y1** • Compare lengths of objects using appropriate vocab. **Y2** • Compare lengths using appropriate vocab. • Measure using a 10 cm rod
Day 2	**Estimate and count a set of objects.** Place 100-square on surface. Spread handful of 1p coins on surface. Children **estimate** number of coins and put a counter on the matching number on the 100-square. **Count** the coins, asking chn to hold sets of 10p. *Who was close?* Rpt with other numbers of coins.		**All** Stand 2 books on table. *Which is* ***taller****?* Put side by side. Compare. A child chooses a 3rd book. *Taller or shorter than the others?* Encourage chn to compare using ***short****(er),* ***tall****(er)*, etc. Put book next to others to compare. **Y2** Show 10cm rod. Write *10* ***centimetres*** and *10 cm*. Explain that cm is a shorter way to write centimetres. Measure **width** of a book using rods placed **end to end**. Write down *width of book = _ cm*. Ask a child to measure the width of another book. *Is it* ***wider*** *than the first book?*	Y1 1.1 p24 Identifying longer and shorter objects	Y1 C1.a.2 Ordering a set of leaves by length TA	Y2 C1.a.2 Measuring objects using a 10cm rod and writing lengths T	Y2 2.1 p22 Measuring objects in cm	Put children in 2s and 3s and give each group a 10 cm rod. Each group tries to find an object that is 1 cm, 2 cm, … 5 cm **long**. Discuss results.	**Y1** • Compare lengths of objects using appropriate vocab. **Y2** • Compare lengths using appropriate vocab. • Measure using a 10 cm rod
Day 3	**Add two small numbers with totals below 10.** Make 2 teams. A 'owns' even numbers; B 'owns' odd. A child from each team stands, 1 hand hidden. On count of 3, chn show hand with some fingers standing and some folded down. Chn find **total** of fingers standing. The team who 'owns' this number gets a point. Repeat.	**Y1** • Estimate then measure lengths, recording estimates • Measure lengths using uniform non-standard units (whole, half and quarter)	**All/Y1** Ask 2 chn to come to the front and stand either side of you. *Which child is taller?* Encourage a discussion using appropriate vocab. Stand the chn back to back to compare them. Show the class a box of pencils. *We are going to measure these two using pencils.* ***How many*** *pencils long do they think each child will be?* Write down some estimates on the board. Clear some space on the carpet and ask each child to lie down. Place pencils end to end to see how many pencils long each child is. Compare results to chn's estimates.	Y1 C1.b.1 Measuring the length of a book in cubes T	Y1 C1.b.1 Measuring the length of a book in cubes T	Y2 C1.a.3 Measuring lengths of string using 10 cm rods TA	Y2 C1.a.3 Measuring lengths of string using 10 cm rods TA	Ask chn to estimate how many pencils long they think you are. Write estimates on the board. Lie on the carpet and let the chn measure you by placing pencils end to end. Compare result to estimates.	**Y1** • Begin to estimate lengths and measure in non-std units • Use language of measuring incl. tall(er), short(er) **Y2** • Measure using a 10 cm rod • Order objects by length

	Mental oral starter	Objectives	Main teaching	Activities: Group 1 (Y1)	Activities: Group 2 (Y1)	Activities: Group 3 (Y2)	Activities: Group 4 (Y2)	Plenary	Outcomes
Day 4	**Name 2D shapes.** Make 4 teams: **Squares**, **Circles**, **Triangles**, **Rectangles**. Play 'Behind the wall'. Use a puppet to take a 2D shape from behind a 'wall'. Slowly reveal part until half is showing. Chn try to name it. Discuss its properties. Reveal shape and give to appropriate team. Rpt for other shapes.	*(Continued)* **Y2** • Estimate, measure and compare lengths using standard units: metres • Recognise relationship between metres and centimetres	**All** Place 3 pens end to end. Ask some chn to find 3 objects that are longer than 3 pens. Ask other chn to find 3 objects that are shorter than this. Compare objects by placing them next to the pens. Discuss results using *short(er)*, *long(er)*, *length*. **Y2** Show 30cm **ruler**. *A ruler is used to measure.* Show spaces and marks. *The space between each mark is 1cm.* Count along marks to 30cm. Measure some objects with the ruler. Give chn rulers and objects to measure. *Place the bottom of the object at 0cm.* Record results on board.	Y1 C1.b.3 Measuring their forearms using crayons TA	Y1 1.1 p26 Measuring objects on the page using cubes	Y2 C1.a.4 Measuring books using rulers	Y2 C1.a.5 Measuring lengths of string using rulers T	Play 'Guess the length'. Choose a long object. Choose a unit, eg straws. Children each write an estimate of the object's length in the chosen unit. *Whose estimate is **closest**?*	**Y1** • Estimate lengths and measure using non-standard units **Y2** • Use rulers to measure in cm. • Compare lengths using appropriate vocab.
Day 5	**Add by counting on, starting with the larger number.** Children have number lines in front of them. Write an **addition**, eg *4 + 7 =*. Children add mentally by putting a counter on the larger number, **counting on** the smaller number, and placing the counter on the answer. Repeat for other additions.		**All** *Remember we measured 2 chn using pencils? How many pencils tall were they? Let's measure other objects in the room. How many pencils long is the table?* Record estimates. 2 chn measure the table by laying pencils end to end. Compare with estimates. Rpt for the carpet. **Y2** Show a **metre stick**. *It measures a metre.* Show the gaps (1 cm) and count along. Write *1 **m** = 100 cm, 1 **metre** = 100 centimetres. How many metres long is the table?* Record estimates. Measure using metre stick. Compare with estimates. Rpt for the carpet.	Y1 1.1 p25 Measuring objects using crayons	Y1 C1.b.2 Measuring the circumference and diameter of a plate in cubes TA	Y2 C1.b.1 Using strips to mark metres and estimate heights T	Y2 2.1 p25 Estimating in m and cm	Compare a 30 cm ruler with the unmarked side of a metre stick. Place three rulers end to end along the stick and count up in 10s to 90. Use a 10 cm rod to show that the stick is 100 cm long.	**Y1** • Estimate lengths and measure using non-standard units **Y2** • Measure in metres • Understand 1 m = 100 cm

Vocabulary
largest, smallest
length, long, longer than, longest
height, high, higher than, highest
width, wide, wider than, widest
tall, taller than, tallest
short, shorter than, shortest
less/more than
compare
estimate
closest estimate
about, nearly, almost
whole, half, quarter
measure
line up
side by side
end to end
alongside
markings
centimetres, cm
metres, m
ruler
metre stick
tape measure
how many?
1 more/less
count, count on
total
addition
circle
square
triangle
rectangle

Resources
large number cards 0–30 (or more if more children)
three scarves of different lengths
drinking straws
10 cm rods (e.g. base-10 rods)
a large leaf
a shoe
objects 2–20 cm long
small Post-it notes
large 100-square
two handfuls of 1p coins
counters
four books of different heights
seven or eight large leaves of different sizes
felt-tipped pens
box of pencils
about 50 linking cubes
four or five picture books
different lengths of dampened string
set of 2D shapes: squares, rectangles, circles, triangles
a 'wall', e.g. a big book
a puppet
three identical pens
four 30 cm rulers marked in cm
A4 paper
crayons
glue
0–20 number lines
metre stick
lots of non-linking 1 cm cubes
about five different sized paper plates

Year 1 Block C1.a Activities

C1.a.1 A group of 6 to 8 children working in pairs

Place a large leaf in the middle of the table. Children suggest things that they can see around the classroom that are longer. Then they suggest things that are shorter. Children work in pairs to find specific things, for example: *Go and find one thing a bit longer* or *Go and find one thing a bit shorter.* Children draw the leaf and then draw something a bit longer and something a bit shorter. Repeat, giving pairs new instructions.
Adult support may be useful in running this activity.

large leaf

C1.a.2 Groups of 2 to 3 children

Each group sorts their leaves in order from shortest to longest. They work together and discuss this as they do it, making lots of direct comparisons. Then they label each leaf with a felt-tipped pen, writing 1 on the shortest, 2 on the next shortest, etc.
Adult support may be useful in running this activity.

seven or eight large leaves of different sizes; felt-tipped pens

Year 1 Block C1.b Activities

C1.b.1 A group of 8 or 10 children working in pairs

Each pair first estimates how many cubes will fit along the length (the longer side) of their book. Record each pair's estimate. Then each pair builds a line of cubes the same length as their book. *How many cubes in the line? Is it exact? Do we actually need to add half a cube?* Record the actual number beside each pair's estimate. *Whose guess was closest?* Repeat, estimating and measuring the shorter side.
Adult support may be useful in running this activity.

linking cubes; picture book per pair

C1.b.2 A group of 8 or 10 children working in pairs

Each pair first estimates how many cubes will fit all around their plate. Record each pair's estimate. Then each pair arranges a line of cubes which goes all the way round their plate. *How many cubes in the line? Is it exact? Do we actually need to add half a cube?* Record the actual number beside each pair's estimate. *Whose guess was closest?* Repeat, estimating and measuring a straight line across the middle of their plate (the diameter).
Adult support may be useful in running this activity.

non-linking 1 cm cubes; paper plate, preferably a different size for each pair

C1.b.3 Pairs of children

One child lays their arm, bent at the elbow, on a piece of paper. The other child marks the fingertips and the elbow, so marking the length of the arm. They both lay a line of crayons or rods along this length. They discuss whether they need half a crayon, or even a quarter of a crayon, to make the line exactly the same length as their arm. They count the crayons together, and agree how many crayons long the arm is, including the half or quarter crayon if necessary. Then both children draw their arms and write the number of crayons long they are.
Adult support may be useful in running this activity.

A4 paper; crayons or 10 cm rods

Year 2 Block C1.a Activities

C1.a.1 A group of 4, 6 or 8 children working in pairs

Place a shoe in the middle of the table. Ask children to suggest things that are longer than the shoe. Then ask them to suggest things that are shorter than the shoe. Give specific commands to pairs of children, for example *Go and find something a bit longer; Go and find something a lot shorter.* Children should draw the shoe and then draw something a bit longer, something a bit shorter… Adult support may be useful in running this activity.

a shoe

C1.a.2 A group of 4, 6 or 8 children working in pairs

Provide different objects with lengths between 2 cm and 20 cm, for example plastic animals, paint brushes, glue spatulas, pencils. Each pair takes an item and measures its length using a 10 cm rod. They write the length on a Post-it and stick it on the item. Each child in the pair checks their partner's measurement. Children group the items according to their length.

objects with lengths between 2 cm and 20 cm; 10 cm rods; small Post-it notes

C1.a.3 A group of 4, 6 or 8 children working in pairs

Pairs use 10 cm rods to measure lengths of string. Provide different lengths of cotton string that have been slightly dampened for ease of handling. Children take turns to measure a length or check their partner's measurement. They write their agreed length on a Post-it and wrap the Post-it round the string so that the measurement is visible. Children group the items according to their length.

different lengths of dampened string; 10 cm rods; small Post-it notes

C1.a.4 A group of up 4, 6 or 8 children working in pairs

Each child takes a book and uses their ruler to measure its dimensions. They write the length and the width on a Post-it and stick it on the book. Children then swap books with their partner, repeat the exercise and compare measurements. Discuss how to use a ruler to measure accurately, for example line up the zero mark (or end of the ruler) exactly with the edge of the book, hold the ruler and book still once the ruler is positioned correctly. Adult support is needed to run this activity.

books of different sizes; rulers marked in centimetres; Post-it notes

C1.a.5 Pairs of children

Pairs use rulers to measure lengths of string. Provide different lengths of cotton string that have been slightly dampened for ease of handling. Children take turns to measure a length or check their partner's measurement. Then they coil the string and use a little glue to stick it next to the written measurement. Check that children are using their rulers correctly. Adult support may be useful in running this activity with several pairs of children.

different lengths of dampened string; glue; rulers

Year 2 Block C1.b Activities

C1.b.1 A group of 6 or 8 children working in pairs

Stand by the door. Choose a pair of children to use a metre rule to measure 1 m from the floor up the door. Use Blu-tack to stick a strip of coloured paper horizontally to mark the 1 m measurement. Choose another pair of children to measure 2 m from the floor up the door by holding another metre rule above the first metre rule. Stick a strip of paper in a second colour horizontally to mark the 2 m measurement. Talk about and estimate how tall children in the group are (between the 1 m and the 2 m marks but closer to the 1 m mark). Discuss heights of other animals, for example giraffe (above the 2 m mark), dog (below the 1 m mark), cat (below the 1 m mark), horse (above the 1 m and below the 2 m marks)… Make labels to mark the estimated heights of the animals on the door.
Adult support is needed to run this activity.

metre rule; two strips of paper in different colours; labels

Maths Weekly Plan: Year 1 and 2

Block C1.c: Know days of the week and hours in a day, and order events in time
Block C1.d: Know the months and seasons of the year

	Mental oral starter	Objectives	Main teaching	Activities: Group 1 Y1	Activities: Group 2 Y1	Activities: Group 3 Y2	Activities: Group 4 Y2	Plenary	Outcomes
Day 1	**Partition 'teens' numbers into 10 plus units.** Give each child a number card 0–10. Count in unison along 0–20 number line until you reach 17. *What number is this?* Chn show you 10 toes and 7 fingers. *Take away 10 toes, how many are left?* Any child with a 7 card gets a cube. Rpt.	**Y1** • Order familiar events in time • Know the days of the week **Y2** • Use units of time and know the relationship between them: hours in a day, days in a week	**All** Read *The Very Hungry Caterpillar*. Recite **days** of **week** in order. Open book at day other than **Saturday** or **Sunday**. *What's the day? What does the caterpillar eat? What day comes* ***next****?* Continue like this, turning to different pages in the book and repeating the questions. **Y2** *How many* ***hours*** *in a day?* Show clock. *12 in a day, 12 in a* ***night****: 24 hours.* Show hands. *Short hand shows hours; long hand* ***minutes***. Set to 12 o'clock. *What do we do at 12? Lunch.* Move hands round, asking what we do at each hour. Back to 12: ***Midnight*** *and* ***midday***. **[ITR Y2 C1.c]**	Y1 C1.c.1 Ordering day of the week cards TA	Y1 C1.c.5 Making a zig-zag book of pictures to represent days of the week	Y2 C1.c.1 Setting a clock to o'clock times and drawing pictures to represent hours of the day T	Y2 C1.c.2 Drawing pictures and matching to clock stamp to show hours of the day	Seat chn in circle. 1st child says ***Monday***, next says ***Tuesday***, … 7th says *Sunday*. *One week.* Continue on from Monday. *Two weeks.* Continue. *How many weeks have passed now that everyone has had a turn?*	**Y1** • Learn the days of the week in order **Y2** • Learn the days of the week in order • Learn that there are 24 hours in a day, made up of two sets of 12 hours
Day 2	**Find totals of two or three coins.** Blu-tack a large cardboard 5p coin and 2p coin onto board. Chn show **total** number of pence using their number fans: 7. Rpt with totals up to 20p and progressing to larger totals. Extend to **adding** three coins.		**All** Write days in **order**. Recite. Say what caterpillar ate each day. Write *The Very Hungry Child*. Chn say food for each day. Set clock to 12 o'clock. *Midday is* ***lunchtime***. *What do we eat?* Set to breakfast and dinner times. *What do we eat?* Discuss hours in a week. **[ITR Y1 C1.c]** **Y1** Teach chn rhyme to remember days of the week in order, eg *Solomon Grundy born on Monday, christened on Tuesday* etc. (You can make up a class rhyme). Practice rhyme, giving individual chn day of the week cards. As they say the rhyme they order themselves correctly.	Y1 C1.c.5 Making a zig-zag book of pictures to represent days of the week T	Y1 1.1 p27 Ordering days of the week	Y2 2.1 p26 Identifying and ordering days of the week	Y2 C1.c.7 Writing a poem for days of the week TA	Shuffle a set of number cards 1–12. Reveal one, eg 9. Choose 2 chn to say what they might be doing at that time in the **evening**, eg 9 o'clock: ***Bedtime***. Repeat for other numbers.	**Y1** • Learn the days of the week in order **Y2** • Learn the days of the week in order • Learn that there are 24 hours in a day, made up of two sets of 12 hours
Day 3	**Say a number 1 more or 1 less than a given number.** Give some chn number cards 1–100. Divide class into two teams: A is **1 more**; B is **1 less**. One child holds up their card. Chn in each team write their answers on whiteboards. Give teams 5 points if correct. Rpt.	**Y1** • Begin to know and order the months of the year • Know the seasons of the year	**All** Draw four columns on the board headed ***Winter***, ***Spring***, ***Summer***, ***Autumn***. *In Britain we have four* ***seasons***. *Each one has different* ***weather***. *Other countries have a different number of seasons, eg Indonesia has two: a wet season approx. Nov–Apr and a dry season approx. May–Oct.* Discuss. Point to winter. *What is the weather like in winter?* Draw clothes that we might wear in winter. Rpt for other seasons. Stress the weather to identify each season. **[ITR Y2 C1.d]**	Y1 1.1 p28 Matching pictures to seasons	Y1 1.1 p28 Matching pictures to seasons	Y2 C1.d.1 Relating months to seasons TA	Y2 C1.d.2 Ordering months with descriptions T	Give each pair a card with a season on it (use Y1 PCM 126). Draw weather symbol on board, eg sun. Chn holding the season card to match the weather stand up. Rpt for other symbols.	**Y1** • Learn the seasons and associate them with weather **Y2** • Learn the seasons and associate them with weather

	Mental oral starter	Objectives	Main teaching	Activities: Group 1 Y1	Activities: Group 2 Y1	Activities: Group 3 Y2	Activities: Group 4 Y2	Plenary	Outcomes
Day 4	**Give a number between two numbers.** Play 'Stand up'. Give a number card 10–50 to each child. *Stand up if your number is* ***between*** *25 and 32.* Check their numbers. Extend: *Stand up if your number is* ***more than*** *18 and* ***less than*** *35.*	*(Continued)* **Y2** • Use units of time and know the relationship between them: months in a year, seasons in a year • Order the months of the year	**All** Use **month** cards **January–December**. Choose child to find January card and peg it to a washing line. Continue until line shows all 12 months. Point to and say months together. *How many months in a* ***year****?* Remind chn that spring, summer, autumn and winter are called seasons. Ask the class to remind you of the weather in each season. Group the months into seasons. Practise reciting months. Discuss whose **birthdays** are in which month. *Which season is your birthday in?* **[ITR Y1 C1.d]**	Y1 1.1 p29 Ordering the months of the year	Y1 C1.d.1 Identifying seasons and months T	Y2 C1.d.3 Saying the month that comes after a given month TA	Y2 C1.d.4 Playing a card game, finding the month that comes before or after a given month	Show chn 'knuckle method' for remembering months of year. Close fists, thumbs hidden. Start with the knuckle of the left-hand little finger. Each knuckle is a long month; each dip is a short month.	**Y1** • Learn the months of the year in order **Y2** • Learn the months of the year in order • Group months of the year into seasons
Day 5	**Add a 1-digit number to a 2-digit number, not crossing a ten.** Write five **additions** of 1-digit numbers to 2-digit numbers on board. Make sure that two of these are incorrect, eg 12 + 5 = 19. Chn work in pairs to 'mark' your work. Allow 5 mins for this then discuss their decisions.		**All** Choose a pair of chn to peg month cards January–December on a washing line in order. Discuss **current** month. *Who has a birthday in July?* Count the number of children and put that many pegs on that month. Repeat for the other months. *How many of us have a birthday in the summer months? Which month comes before November?* Ask chn to recite the months of the year, first looking at the line, and then without looking.	Y1 C1.d.2 Matching months and seasons T	Y1 C1.d.4 Sorting month cards by season TA	Y2 2.1 p27 Ordering the months of the year	Y2 2.1 p28 Ordering months	Chn born in Jan form a line. Chn born in Feb form line behind them, and so on. Shuffle month cards. Pick one and say it, eg *May*. All chn born in this month sit down. Winners are the last month standing.	**Y1** • Learn the months of the year in order • Group months of the year into seasons **Y2** • Identify each month in order; identify events and weather of that month

Vocabulary
day
week
Monday, Tuesday, … Sunday
next
last
after
before
current
hour
minute
hour hand
minute hand
night
midnight
midday
order
morning
afternoon
evening
lunchtime
bedtime
season
winter, spring, summer, autumn
weather
month
year
January, February, … December
birthday
how old …?
total
add
addition
1 more/less
between
more/less than

Resources
number cards 0–10 (one card per child)
cubes
The Very Hungry Caterpillar by Eric Carle
large analogue clock with moveable hands
number cards 1–100
clock stamp
Blu-tack
large cardboard coins
number fans (one per child)
day cards Monday–Sunday (Y1 PCM 123)
individual whiteboards
month chart (3 × 4 grid with month names written at top of each space)
about four sets of month cards January–December (Y1 PCMs 124 and 125)
season cards winter–autumn
number cards 10–50 (one card per child)
washing line
about 45 pegs
counters

Year 1 Block C1.c Activities

C1.c.1 A group of up to 8 children

Shuffle the cards and spread them out face down. Each child takes a card. (If there are eight children, one is your helper and does not take a card yet.) Ask children to identify their day. Give clues, for example starting sound/letter, length of name, etc. Recite the days of the week in order. Repeat this, and as you do so, the appropriate child offers their card for the helper to collect. Lay the cards face up in order and recite the days again.

Now spread the cards out face down. Going round the circle, children turn over a card. *Can you say what day it is?* If yes, they keep the card. If no, they turn it back over and leave it on the table.

Adult support is needed to run this activity.

set of day of the week cards

C1.c.5 A group of 3 or 4 children

Children draw a picture of something they have done or will do on each day of the week, Monday to Saturday, and label each picture. Stick the pictures in a zig-zag book. Extend the activity by asking the children to draw a picture for Sunday.

Year 1 Block C1.d Activities

C1.d.1 A group of up to 8 children

Children discuss the seasons and the months. Working with the children, fill in any known events in each month, for example Christmas and any other appropriate festivals, birthdays, school holidays, outings, etc. Discuss the four seasons of the year. Together devise a symbol for each season. Then ask children to write the months of the year in order and draw a season symbol beside each one.

Adult support may be useful in running this activity.

month chart

C1.d.2 Pairs of children

Children discuss the seasons and the months. They work together in their pairs to divide their month cards into four piles, one for each season. They then draw a descriptive picture for each season, and label it. These pictures can relate to personal things, for example a child's birthday party, or they can be general, for example dark evenings, fires lit, etc.

Adult support may be useful in running this activity.

set of month cards per pair

C1.d.4 A group of 3 children

Shuffle the month cards and place them face down on the table. Children arrange the four season cards in sequence in a line. They take turns to pick a month card, decide in which season it belongs, and place it underneath the appropriate season. Continue like this through all the months. Reshuffle the cards and repeat the activity.

set of month cards; set of season cards

Year 2 Block C1.c Activities

C1.c.1 A group of up to 8 children

Spread out a shuffled set of 1–12 number cards face down. Each child takes a card. Pass the clock round the group so that each child can set it to the o'clock time indicated by their number card and say what they might be doing at that time of day. For example, card 3 means 3 o'clock when they might be listening to a story before home-time.
Each child then draws a small cartoon picture of what they might be doing and labels it with the time, for example 3:00.
The point of this activity is to encourage a lot of discussion about what might be happening at each hour of the day.
Stress the fact that there are 12 hours of 'daytime' and 12 hours of 'night', making 24 hours in the day.
Adult support is needed to run this activity.

1–12 number cards; teaching clock

C1.c.2 Pairs of children

Each child chooses three different hours of the day, for example 1 o'clock, 4 o'clock, 7 o'clock, and tells their partner what they might be doing at each time. They talk about and agree their suggestion for each time with their partner. Each child then draws a cartoon picture of what they have decided they might be doing at each of the three times, leaving space to 'stamp' a clock-face next to each one.
The point of this activity is to encourage a lot of discussion about what might be happening at each hour of the day.
Stress the fact that there are 12 hours of 'daytime' and 12 hours of 'night', making 24 hours in the day.
Adult support may be useful in running this activity with a several pairs of children.

clock stamp

C1.c.7 A group of up to 8 children

Use name cards to rehearse the days of the week several times, either in a song or a rhyme (for example Solomon Grundy). Then each child writes their own rhyme to help remember the days of the week, starting each line with a day, for example *Monday is the moon's day, Tuesday is my fish-and-chips day…*
They can try to introduce some rhyming words if they want to and they can be as personal as they like! Encourage children to illustrate their rhymes and use them for display.
Adult support is needed at the beginning of this activity.

name cards for days of the week

Year 2 Block C1.d Activities

C1.d.1 A group of up to 8 children

Use a month chart to discuss seasons and months. First work with children to fill in any known events each month, for example Christmas and any other appropriate festivals, birthdays, school holidays, outings… Together talk about the four seasons of the year and devise a symbol for each one. Ask children to write the months of the year in order and draw a season symbol beside each one. They may not agree which months are in a particular season. This is fine, but children should argue their case, for example May could be in spring or summer but it is definitely not in the autumn or winter!
Adult support is needed to run this activity.

month chart

C1.d.2 Pairs of children

Ask pairs to discuss the seasons and months of the year. *Do you agree which months are in each season?* Give out name cards for the months of the year to each pair to put in order. Each child writes the months of the year in an ordered list and then adds a descriptive phrase beside each one. These phrases can relate to personal or general things, for example *It's my/Granny's birthday! Evenings get dark.*
Adult support may be useful in running this activity with several pairs of children.

name cards for months of the year

C1.d.3 A group of 8 children working in pairs

Children spread out one set of name cards in order in a straight line. They shuffle the other set and place them face down in a pile. They take turns to turn over the top card in the pile and, without looking at the line of name cards, say the month **after** the month on the card. All children look at the line to check. A counter is taken for a correct answer. Children continue until they have all had four turns. Repeat the activity, this time saying the month **before**. See who collects the most counters.

two sets of name cards for months of the year; counters

C1.d.4 A group of 8 children working in 4s

Children spread out one set of month cards in order. They shuffle the other set, deal three to each child and take turns to play a card. The first child begins the sequence by putting down either May or June or July. Children take turns to follow on with the month that comes just before or just after the cards already placed. They take a counter if they cannot place a card. When all the months are placed, the winner has the fewest counters.

two sets of name cards for months of the year; counters

Maths Weekly Plan: Year 1 and 2

Block D1.a: Use names of common 2D shapes and describe their features
Block D1.b: Rehearse features of 2D shapes and begin to recognise line symmetry

	Mental oral starter	Objectives	Main teaching	Activities: Group 1 Y1	Activities: Group 2 Y1	Activities: Group 3 Y2	Activities: Group 4 Y2	Plenary	Outcomes
Day 1	**Recognise coins.** Children work in pairs. Hold up a large cardboard **coin**, eg 20p. Children write the amount on their whiteboards. Repeat for other coins. Variation: describe a coin, eg *It's large and silver with seven sides.* Children write amount on whiteboards.	**Y1** • Begin to use the names of common 2D shapes; circle, square, rectangle, triangle • Describe features of familiar 2D shapes: number of sides and corners, types of sides	**All** Hold up a **square**. *What is this* ***shape*** *called?* Point at each **side** in turn. Discuss its **properties**. Rpt for **rectangle**, **circle**, **triangle**. Draw four large houses with shape names written below them. Choose a shape. Child sticks shape to correct house. Rpt for each shape. **Y2** Write shape names on board. Hold up a triangle. ***How many*** *sides?* Rpt for rectangle, square, **hexagon**, **pentagon**, **octagon**. Put shapes in bag. Take one, show and say name. Stick shape beside name. Rpt for all shapes in bag. Look at hexagons. Check same number of sides.	Y1 D1.a.1 Sorting 2D shapes (TA)	Y1 1.1 p30 Identifying circles, triangles, rectangles and squares	Y2 D1.a.1 Taking shapes from a cloth bag and describing properties (T)	Y2 2.1 p29 Joining shapes with the same name	Challenge chn to draw a rectangle, a triangle, a square and a circle.	**Y1** • Recognise and name 2D shapes: triangle, circle, square, rectangle **Y2** • Recognise and name 2D shapes including hexagon, pentagon, octagon
Day 2	**Say a number 1, 2, or 3 more than any number up to 100.** Make 4 teams. Divide each team into pairs. Give each pair a number card 1–100. Pairs work out the **next number**. Choose 2 pairs from each team to say their next number. If correct, their team scores 5 points. Rpt for numbers 2 or 3 more.	**Y2** • Use the names of common 2D shapes, including: pentagon, hexagon, octagon • Sort 2D shapes and describe their features: number of sides and corners	**All** Rehearse shape names. Place a shape behind a screen. Use a puppet to slowly reveal the shape. Chn name the shape. (Only Y2s need to know pentagon, hexagon and octagon). Rpt. Stick shapes to correct shape house. Count how many shapes are in each house. **[ITR Y1 D1.a]** **Y1** Put triangles, rectangles, circles in bag. Lay 3 hoops on floor. Label each hoop: *Circles, Triangles, Rectangles.* Play music and pass the bag round. When music stops, child holding bag takes out a shape, puts it in correct hoop, and says shape name and properties.	Y1 1.1 p30 Identifying circles, triangles, rectangles and squares	Y1 D1.a.2 Drawing circles, triangles, rectangles and squares (T)	Y2 2.1 p29 Joining shapes with the same name	Y2 D1.a.6 Identifying regular 2D shapes and drawing non-regular examples (TA)	Search for examples of 2D shapes around the room. *Can you see any rectangles? What about squares? What shape is the ceiling? How many sides does it have?*	**Y1** • Recognise and name 2D shapes: triangle, circle, square, rectangle • Begin to list properties **Y2** • Recognise and name 2D shapes incl. hexagon, pentagon, octagon
Day 3	**Recall addition pairs to 10.** Play 'Front and back'. Use a set of number cards 0–10, with each number's partner to 10 written on the back. Hold up 0. *What* ***adds*** *to this to make 10?* Turn card around to reveal answer: 10. Rpt for each card. If necessary model with fingers. Shuffle and repeat.		**All** Hold up rectangle. *What is this shape called?* Point at side of rectangle. *This is called a side. How many sides does the rectangle have? How many* ***corners*** *does it have?* Rpt for other shapes. (Only Y2s need to know names of pentagon, hexagon and octagon.) Write numbers 1–8 in order on board. Child selects a shape and sticks it under correct number of sides. Discuss number of corners. Rpt for other shapes. *A triangle has 3 sides and 3 corners. Which other shapes have the same number of corners and sides? Which shapes have an odd/even number of corners and sides?* Describe a shape, saying the number of sides and corners it has. Chn find the shape.	Y1 D1.b.1 Printing 2D shapes (T)	Y1 D1.b.1 Printing 2D shapes (T)	Y2 D1.a.5 Drawing shapes on square dotty paper (TA)	Y2 D1.a.8 Making shapes on pin board and copying onto square dotty paper	Lay a hoop on the carpet and give it a label, eg ***More than*** *3 sides* or ***Fewer than*** *4 sides.* Ask chn to sort shapes, putting them inside or outside the hoop as appropriate.	**Y1** • Name and list properties of 2D shapes **Y2** • Name and list properties of 2D shapes

	Mental oral starter	Objectives	Main teaching	Activities: Group 1 (Y1)	Activities: Group 2 (Y1)	Activities: Group 3 (Y2)	Activities: Group 4 (Y2)	Plenary	Outcomes
Day 4	**Estimate and measure lengths using non-standard units.** Choose an object, eg a big book. Choose **units**, eg glue-sticks. Chn **estimate** how many glue-sticks will fit end to end alongside the book. Chn show estimates on their number fans. **Measure** the **length**. Rpt for lengths of other objects.	**Y1** • Begin to use the names of common 2D shapes; circle, square, rectangle, triangle • Describe features of familiar 2D shapes: number of sides and corners, types of sides	**All** Hold up a circle. *How many sides? Are the sides **straight** or **curved**?* Repeat for triangle and **semi-circle**. Place two hoops on the floor so they overlap. Label one hoop *Straight sides* and the other *Curved sides.* Chn sort shapes into the correct sections. **Y2** Fold paper in **half**, forming a sharp crease. Cut out pattern. Show one half **exactly matches** the other. *If one half fits exactly onto other, the shape has **symmetry**.* Write *symmetry*. *The **fold line** is called the **line of symmetry***. Repeat for other **symmetrical** patterns.	Y1 D1.b.2 TM 4.1 4 Sorting shapes TA	Y1 1.1 p32 Counting corners and edges	Y2 D1.a.4 TM 3.1 3 Symmetry T	Y2 2.1 p32 Drawing lines of symmetry	Use number cards 3, 4, 5, 6, 8. Hold up a card. Ask chn to say the name of a shape with that number of sides. Repeat, sometimes asking for shapes with that number of corners.	**Y1** • List properties of 2D shapes • Sort 2D shapes by properties **Y2** • Sort 2D shapes by properties • Begin to recognise symmetry in 2D shapes
Day 5	**Estimate lengths in centimetres.** Choose an object that can be measured in **cm**. Hold up a ruler, and show cm markings. *How **long** is the object?* Chn show their estimates using number fans. Ask a child to measure the object using the ruler. *Whose estimate was closest?*	**Y2** • Begin to recognise line symmetry • Make symmetrical patterns by folding and cutting • Begin to sketch the reflection of a simple shape in a mirror line	**All** Child chooses a shape from the shape bag and describes it to the class (without showing it to them) by saying how many sides and corners it has, and whether it has straight or curved sides. Rest of the class have to say the name of the shape. Repeat for several shapes. **Y2** Show paper shape, eg isosceles triangle. *Does it have symmetry?* Fold it in half to show that one half exactly matches the other. Form sharp crease along the fold line. Rpt for rectangle. Show lines of symmetry. *The rectangle has 2 lines of symmetry.* Rpt for other shapes.	Y1 1.1 p32 Counting corners and edges	Y1 D1.b.2 TM 4.3 4 Sorting shapes TA	Y2 2.1 p32 Drawing lines of symmetry	Y2 D1.b.7 Making paper 2D shapes and folding to find lines of symmetry T	Place edge of a book alongside edge of a large mirror. Adjust the angle so that chn can see the symmetrical image. Show how one will fold exactly onto the other. Rpt for other objects.	**Y1** • Describe 2D shapes and sort them according to properties **Y2** • Sort 2D shapes according to properties • Recognise symmetry in 2D shapes

Vocabulary
shape
square
rectangle
triangle
circle
hexagon
pentagon
octagon
semi-circle
side
property
how many …?
corner
more/fewer than
straight, curved
half
exactly matches
symmetry, symmetrical
line of symmetry
fold line
coin
next number
add
unit
estimate
measure
length, long

Resources
large cardboard coins 1p–£2
plastic/card 2D shapes: circles, squares, rectangles, triangles, pentagons, hexagons, octagons
Blu-tack
cloth bag
red cubes
number cards 1–100
screen, e.g. a large book
puppet
three hoops
music CD
square dotty paper
shape name cards: triangle, rectangle, square, circle, pentagon
number cards 0–10 with partners to 10 written on back
poster of powder paints mixed with PVA glue
3D shapes to use for printing
four pin boards, rubber bands
objects to measure
set of identical glue-sticks
number fans (one per child)
plastic/card semi-circle
scissors
about six sheets of A3 paper folded in half, halves labelled *Three sides* and *Four sides*
regular paper shapes folded in half: triangle, square, rectangle, hexagon, octagon
30 cm ruler
large paper symmetrical 2D shapes
large mirror

Year 1 Block D1.a Activities

D1.a.1 A group of up to 8 children

Place one set of shapes in the cloth bag and spread out the other set on the table. Point to each shape and say its name. Rehearse this several times, testing that children know the names.
One child secretly chooses a shape from the bag. They describe it, giving the number of sides, corners, etc. Each child decides which shape on the table matches the description, and points to it. When everyone has decided, the child reveals the shape. *Who pointed at the matching shape?* Give each child who did a red cube. Agree the shape's name.
Repeat this, choosing a different child to take a shape from the cloth bag.
Adult support is needed to run this activity.

red cubes; two sets of plastic shapes; cloth bag

D1.a.2 Pairs of children

One child takes a card and reads the name, for example *circle*. The pair discuss its properties, for example how many sides, corners, etc. Both children draw an example of that shape. They label it with its name, copying from the card. They repeat this with the other cards.
Adult support may be useful in running this activity.

dotty paper; cards with shape names (triangle, rectangle, square, circle)

Year 1 Block D1.b Activities

D1.b.1 A group of up to 8 children

Children make prints of the end faces of 3D shapes. Before printing each one they must say what the shape is: circle, square, oblong (rectangle but not square) or triangle. After they have printed it, it can be labelled for them.
Adult support may be useful in running this activity.

poster or powder paints mixed with PVA glue to make them glossy and sticky; 3D shapes

4.1/4.2/4.3 4 Sorting shapes

D1.b.2 A group of 6 or more children

Children draw a shape with four sides on the left-hand side of their paper, and a shape with three sides on the right-hand side. Compare the shapes. *What's the same about them? What's different?*
Challenge children to draw as many different-looking three-sided shapes and as many different-looking four-sided shapes as they can. They can use straight or curved sides.
Point to the three-sided shapes. *Can you name one of these shapes? Are there any other triangles? Are there any three-sided shapes that aren't triangles?*
Agree that three-sided shapes with one or more curved sides are not triangles.
What's special about triangles? How many corners? How many sides? What are the sides like?
Repeat the discussion for four-sided shapes, drawing out the properties of squares and rectangles.
Adult support is needed to run this activity.

sheet of A3 paper per child, folded in half, the left-hand side labelled 'Three sides' and the right-hand side labelled 'Four sides'

Year 2 Block D1.a Activities

D1.a.1 A group of up to 8 children

Place one set of 2D shapes in the cloth bag and spread out a matching set on the table. Number each shape on the table and label them. One child chooses a shape from the bag without showing the others. They describe it, referring to the number of sides, how many of the sides are the same… Each child decides which of the shapes on the table matches the one being described and writes that shape's number. Then the shape from the bag is revealed and each child who wrote the matching number gets a point. Agree the shape's name and write it. Repeat several times.
Adult support is needed to run this activity.

a set of 2D shapes in a cloth bag; a matching set of 2D shapes

3.1 3 Symmetry

D1.a.4 A group of 6 or more children

Hold up the folded triangle. Children discuss and then sketch what they think the shape will look like when unfolded.
Could it be a square? Why not?
Encourage children to talk about the properties of squares and triangles, for example a square has square corners. Open out the shape and ask children to describe it using precise vocabulary.
Repeat with other shapes.
Adult support is needed to run this activity.

regular paper shapes each folded in half: triangle, square, rectangle, hexagon, octagon

D1.a.5 Pairs of children

One child takes a shape card and reads the name. They discuss its properties with their partner, for example how many sides. Both children draw an example of that shape and label it. Repeat for at least four shapes.

square dot grid paper; cards with shape names: *triangle, rectangle, square, pentagon*

D1.a.6 Pairs of children

One child chooses a regular shape. Both children identify it by name and each draws a different example of the shape, for example two different non-regular hexagons. Then they each try to draw more different examples of the same shape. Repeat with a different shape.
How many different examples of a hexagon/triangle/4-sided shape… can you draw?

regular 2D shapes

D1.a.8 Pairs of children

Child 1 creates a shape on a pin board. Child 2 copies the shape onto a piece of square dot grid paper. They reverse roles. When they have drawn at least five shapes each child writes down the names of their shapes.
Adult support may be useful in running this activity with several pairs of children.

pin board and rubber bands per pair; square dot grid paper

Year 2 Block D1.b Activities

D1.b.7 Pairs of children

Children draw around different 2D shapes on plain paper and cut out paper copies. They fold the paper shapes to investigate any lines of symmetry and then use a ruler to draw in any lines of symmetry.

2D shapes; scissors; paper

Maths Weekly Plan: Year 1 and 2

Block D1.c: Say the number 1 less, and count back in 1s
Block D1.d: Subtract a 1-digit number by counting back

	Mental oral starter	Objectives	Main teaching	Activities: Group 1 Y1	Group 2 Y1	Group 3 Y2	Group 4 Y2	Plenary	Outcomes
Day 1	**Count back in 1s from different numbers.** Play 'Team counting'. Divide class into 3 or 4 teams. Say a start number, eg *17*. 1st group start counting back in 1s, then after 3 or 4 counts, another team takes over. Rpt, starting at different numbers.	**Y1** • Say the number that is 1 less than a given number • Count back 1 from a given number **Y2** • Count back in 1s, not crossing a multiple of 10 • Extend understanding of subtraction as taking away	**All** **Count** in 1s to 30 using fingers, stressing multiples of 5. **Count back** to 1. *Hold up 8 fingers. Fold 1 finger down. 8 take away 1* ***leaves*** *…?* Write 8 − 1 = 7. Write 6 − 1 = . Chn find answer using fingers. Ask a child to complete the **subtraction**. Model 15 − 1 by counting back 1. Rpt. **Y2** Show a 20–40 number line. Write *26 − 4 =* on the board. *To work this out, you have to count back 4 from 26.* Point to 26 on the number line. Hold up 4 fingers. Count back from 26, folding down 1 finger for each number. ***Taking away*** *is the same as counting back.* Rpt for 35 − 3.	Y1 D1.c.2 Finding 1 less using number track and towers of bricks TA	Y1 1.1 p35 Finding 1 less using number tracks	Y2 D1.c.1 Using number track to subtract 1-digit numbers T	Y2 2.1 p34 Counting back to take away	Play 'The **number before**'. Give each child a number card 1–20. The child holding 20 starts, saying: *Twenty. Where is the number before?* The child holding 19 responds. Continue.	**Y1** • Count back 1 from a given number • Find the number 1 less than a given number **Y2** • Count back in 1s • Subtract a 1-digit number from a given number
Day 2	**Write numerals 1–20.** Say a sequence, eg *5, 6, 7, 8*. When you stop, children must write the **next number** on their whiteboards, eg *9*. For children who are unsure, use number cards 1–20 pegged along washing line to help. Chn show their numbers. Rpt for different sequences.		**All** Count back along a 1–20 number line, ending with *3, 2, 1, Blast off!* Say a number, eg *16*. Ask a child to say the number before. Write the matching **number sentence** on the board, eg *16 − 1 = 15. Taking away 1 is the same as counting back 1.* Rpt for several numbers. **Y2** Show 47p in 10p and 1p coins. *I have 47p. I want to buy a sticker for 5p.* ***How much*** *will be* ***left****?* Write *47p − 5p =*. Stick p-v cards 40 and 7 to board. Show 5 fingers. Point to 7 in 47. Count back 5, folding down fingers. *42p*. Check money left over. Rpt for other amounts.	Y1 1.1 p34 Finding 1 less using fingers	Y1 D1.c.1 Finding 1 less using number track and number cards TA	Y2 2.1 p33 Counting back using number tracks	Y2 D1.c.2 Exploring patterns in subtraction T	Ask 10 chn to stand up. ***How many*** *will be left if we take away 2?* Chn predict. 2 chn sit down. Check how many are left standing. Ask the 2 chn to stand back up. *How many left if we take away 3?* Chn predict, and so on.	**Y1** • Count backwards • Subtract 1 by counting back 1 **Y2** • Subtract a 1-digit number from a given number • Understand subtraction as counting back and taking away
Day 3	**Partition numbers into tens and units.** Play 'Number partners'. Give each child a T or U p-v card. Chn form pairs with one T and one U, to make a 2-digit number. Ask pairs to say their number and point to it on a 100-square. Pairs then arrange themselves in order from smallest to largest number.	**Y1** • Subtract a 1-digit number from a 'teens' number by counting back, not crossing 10 • Subtract one 1-digit number from another	**All** Show Frog. *He jumps back.* Write *8 − 3 =*. Put Frog on 8 on 1–20 number line. Jump back 3. Complete subtraction; read together: *8 take away 3 is 5*. Rpt for 9 − 4. Give each pair a subtraction, eg 9 − 2 = (Y1), 38 − 6 = (Y2). Pairs count back using fingers. Check answers as a class. **Y1** *Counting back is same as taking away/****less*** *than.* Show 10p. A child makes 10p using 1p coins. Write *10p − 3p =*. Count back from 10p to 7p using fingers, folding one down each time. Write *7p*. Check by removing 3 of the 1p coins and counting what is left. Rpt for 10p − 6p.	Y1 D1.d.2 Counting back 1 or 2 using cube towers T	Y1 1.1 p37 Counting back using a number track	Y2 2.1 p34 Counting back to take away	Y2 D1.d.1 TM 4.3 4 Subtraction TA	Write a subtraction on the board, eg 8 − 3. Children select the answer on their number fans and wave them in the air. Check the answer by counting back along a 1–20 number line. Repeat.	**Y1** • Subtract a 1-digit number • Understand subtraction as counting back **Y2** • Subtract 1-digit numbers • Understand subtraction as counting back and taking away

	Mental oral starter	Objectives	Main teaching	Activities: Group 1 Y1	Activities: Group 2 Y1	Activities: Group 3 Y2	Activities: Group 4 Y2	Plenary	Outcomes
Day 4	**Double multiples of 10 to 50, and halve corresponding numbers.** Play 'Front and back', using number cards 10–50 (multiples of 10 only) with **doubles** written on the backs. Hold up card, eg 10. *What is double 10?* Reveal answer. Demo with cube towers if needed. Rpt for each multiple of 10. Extend to **halving** numbers.	*(Continued)* **Y2** • Count back in 1s, crossing a multiple of 10, beginning to partition	**All** Give 10p–50p in 10p and 1p coins to each mixed-ability pair. *How much do you have?* Record, eg *37p*. *Now lose the 1ps! How much is left?* Write subtraction. Rpt with other pairs. *If we take away a no. that is the same as the no. of* ***units****, we're left with just the* ***tens****.* **Y1** Show one 10p and four 1p coins. Write *14p−4p=*. Chn count back 4p from 14p, using fingers. Complete subtraction: *10p*. Rpt for other **'teens' numbers**, making the amount from a 10p coin and some 1p coins, eg 17p−7p=10p. *When you take away the units you are left with 10.*	Y1 1.1 p36 Counting back using cube towers	Y1 D1.d.3 Subtracting to get specific answers T	Y2 D1.d.5 Subtracting 1-digit numbers from 2-digit numbers TA	Y2 2.1 p37 Subtracting, bridging 10	Each pair writes a 2-digit number ending in 7 on whiteboards, eg *47*. Roll dice, eg *5*. Chn **subtract** dice number and write answer on whiteboards, eg *42*. Chn hold up whiteboards to show you. *What do you notice?*	**Y1** • Subtract by counting back • Know that a 'teens' number take away the units leaves 10 **Y2** • Subtract by counting back • Know that a 2-digit number take away the units leaves the tens
Day 5	**Name 2D shapes, and recognise and extend a repeating pattern.** Show **circle**, **square** and **triangle**. *What are they called? How many sides and corners do they have?* Stick onto board in a **repeating pattern**. Read along the pattern together. Pairs draw the next 2 shapes on whiteboards. Rpt using different shapes.		**All** Together count 8 pegs onto one side of a coat hanger. *We are going to take away 2 pegs. How many will be left?* Slide 2 pegs over, 1 at a time. Write *8−2=*. Chn hold up 8 fingers and count back 2. Re-read the completed number sentence. Rpt for 16−3=. **Y2** Show chn 100-square with multiples of 10 coloured red. Write *25−7*. *How many 1s are we going to take away? 7.* Make 25 with place-value cards. Take away 5, leaving 20. *We need to take away 2 more.* Point to 20 on 100-square. Count back 2. Change cards to 18. Rpt for 34−6.	Y1 27 Taking 1p off prices between 1p and 10p	Y1 1.1 p38 Subtracting from amounts	Y2 D1.d.3 TM 4.2 4 Subtraction T	Y2 D1.d.4 Subtracting 1-digit numbers from a 3-digit number, looking at patterns TA	(Rpt from Day 4 to reinforce unit pattern) Pairs write 2-digit number ending in 7. Roll dice. Chn subtract dice number and write answer, holding up whiteboards to show you. *What do you notice?*	**Y1** • Subtract by counting back, understanding that this is taking away **Y2** • Count back in 1s, crossing a multiple of 10

Vocabulary
count on, count back
subtract, subtraction
take away
leaves
number before
next number, number after
number sentence
how much/many left
1 less/more
tens, units
'teens' number
double, halve
circle, square, triangle
repeating pattern

Resources
20–40 number line
large 1–20 number track
lots of wooden bricks
large 1–40 number track
individual whiteboards
number cards 1–10 (one card per child)
20 pegs
washing line
1–20 number line
lots of 1p and 10p coins
two sets of place-value cards (T, U)
place-value cards (H)
Blu-tack
up to eight sets of number cards 1–20
two sets of number cards 15–60
Post-it notes
large 100-square
Jumping-back Frog
linking cubes
about four 0–100 number lines
number fans (one per child)
number cards 10–50 (multiples of 10 only) with doubles written on backs
dice numbered 1–6
card 2D shapes: circle, square, triangle
coat hanger
large 100-square with multiples of 10 highlighted

Year 1 Block D1.c Activities

D1.c.1 A group of up to 8 children

Each child chooses a number on the number track, and then finds that number in their pile of cards. Ask each child to tell you the number they have chosen. Now children find the number in their pile of cards that is one less than their chosen card, for example if they chose 10, they now find 9. They can use the track to help them. Support those who need it by counting back, for example *eleven, ten, …?* Ask each child to identify their number and the number one less. Replace the cards and repeat several times. Give lots of praise.
Adult support may be useful in running this activity.

large 1–20 number track (this can be made from large cards); 1–20 number cards per child

D1.c.2 A group of up to 8 children working in pairs

Ask one child to choose a number on the track. Identify the number with all the children. Children now work in pairs to build this number as a tower of bricks. Then explain that we want to find the number one less. Encourage children to look at the number track and to count back one. They remove one brick from their tower, saying the number one less as they do so. They may then count to check. Repeat this six or seven times, with different children choosing different numbers on the track.
Adult support is needed to run this activity.

large 1–20 number track (this can be made from large cards); lots of wooden bricks

Year 1 Block D1.d Activities

D1.d.2 A group of up to 8 children

Shuffle the number cards and place them in a pile face down. One child takes a card. Identify the number and ask children to record it on their whiteboards. Then ask them to draw the subtraction sign. Decide whether to subtract 1 or 2. Children record this, for example $6-2=$. Each child now builds a tower of six cubes. Together, count back from a couple of numbers above the tower number, and as you say the number below the tower number, children remove a cube. For example, *eight, seven, six* (pointing at towers), *five* (removing one cube from the tower), *four* (removing a second cube). *We have four cubes left*. Ask children to complete their subtraction, for example $6-2=4$. Repeat this activity several times. At the end, photocopy some whiteboards to record their work.
Adult support may be useful in running this activity.

individual whiteboard per child; linking cubes; 2–12 number cards

D1.d.3 Pairs of children

The challenge is for pairs to write as many subtractions as possible that have an answer ending in 5. Give a couple of examples, for example $16-1=15$. Children should find different subtractions, some taking away large numbers and some taking away small numbers. Children work in pairs for a while, generating some examples, and then come back together to look at the patterns.
Adult support may be useful in running this activity.

large 100-square

Year 2 Block D1.c Activities

D1.c.1 A group of up to 8 children

Ask each child to write on their whiteboards a 2-digit number where the units are more than 5. Help as necessary. Write your own 2-digit number, for example 36. Say that you will all subtract four. Write your subtraction and encourage children to write theirs, for example *36 − 4 =*.
Discuss how to subtract by looking at the number track, holding up four fingers (everyone can do this together because everyone is subtracting four) and counting back by folding down one finger with each number spoken.
Use the number track to support any children who need it. Repeat this process until each child has written and completed five subtractions. Photocopy the whiteboards to keep a record in children's books.
Adult support is needed to run this activity.

large 1–40 number track (can be made from cards); individual whiteboards

D1.c.2 A group of up to 8 children

Take out all the numbers with fewer than 5 units from two sets of 15–60 number cards. Place the remaining shuffled cards in a pile face down. Children each take a card, lay it face up on the table and say the number. They roll their dice and subtract the dice number from their card number. (If they throw a 6, and their number has less than 6 units, they may roll again.) They write the answer on a Post-it and stick it on the card. When all children have done this, take feedback and check their subtractions. Draw a large table to record their subtractions and look at the number endings.
Repeat another three or four times and then study the table together. *What do you notice about the units digits of the numbers in each subtraction?*
Adult support is needed to run this activity.

two sets of 15–60 number cards; Post-it notes

Year 2 Block D1.d Activities

4.3 4 subtraction

D1.d.1 A group of 6 or more children

Point to 50 on the number line. Establish how many to count back to get to 46. Draw a jump from 50 to 46 and agree that children could write *50 − 4 = 46*. Now write *60 − _ = 53*. Discuss how to work out the missing number. Agree that children could count on from 53 to 60. *What do we add to 3 to make 10?* Point to this jump on the number line. *What do we add to 23 to make 30?* Ask a child to draw this jump on the number line. *What do we add to 33 to make 40?* Encourage children to use their knowledge of pairs with a total of 10 to make up similar number sentences, and then to check them on the number line.
Adult support is needed to run this activity.

0–100 number line for each pair

4.2 4 subtraction

D1.d.3 A group of 6 or more children

Point to 47 on a 0–100 number line. Establish how many to count on to get to 50. Draw a jump from 47 to 50 and agree the number sentence: 47 + 3 = 50. Establish how many to count back from 50 to get to 47. Agree the number sentence: 50 − 3 = 47.
Write *40 − _ = 37*. Discuss how to work out the missing number, e.g. counting on from 37 to 40. Children make up their own number sentences subtracting a single digit from a multiple of 10, first drawing the jump from the lower to the higher number on a number line.
Adult support is needed to run this activity.

0–100 number line

D1.d.4 A group of 3 children

Remove 8 and 9 from the units place value cards. Put the remaining hundreds, tens and units cards in separate shuffled piles face down. Children take a card each and make the 3-digit number, for example 365. They all write this number and each create a different subtraction: child 1 subtracts the number one more than the units digit of their number, e.g. 365 − 6 =; child 2 subtracts the number two more than the units digit of their number, e.g. 365 − 7 =; and child 3 subtracts the number three more than the units digit of their number, e.g. 365 − 8 =.
Children complete their subtractions and note the patterns in the units digits. Repeat this at least six times.
Adult support may be useful in running this activity with several groups of children.

place value cards (H, T, U)

D1.d.5 A group of 2, 3, 4 or 5 children

Place a shuffled set of 20–50 number cards face down in one pile and a shuffled set of 1–9 number cards face down in another. One child chooses one card from each pile, then all children write a subtraction of the smaller number from the larger with its answer. They check by making the larger number with the cubes, and taking away cubes to match the small number. Check each other's answers. Repeat, taking turns to select the cards.
Adult support may be useful in running this activity.

20–50 and 1–9 number cards; interlocking cubes in towers of 10; loose interlocking cubes

Maths Weekly Plan: Year 1 and 2

Block E1.a: Know doubles for numbers up to 5 or 15
Block E1.b: Y1 Add by identifying near doubles; Y2 Double and halve multiples of 5

	Mental oral starter	Objectives	Main teaching	Activities: Group 1 Y1	Activities: Group 2 Y1	Activities: Group 3 Y2	Activities: Group 4 Y2	Plenary	Outcomes
Day 1	**Add two 1-digit numbers, not crossing 10.** Pairs each place a 0–20 number line in front of them. Write an addition on the board, eg *6+8*. Pairs place a counter on the number line to match the answer. Check answers. Rpt for other additions.	**Y1** • Recognise doubling as the addition of two equal amounts • Begin to know by heart doubles for numbers up to at least 10 • Know by heart doubles for numbers up to at least 5 **Y2** • Know by heart doubles for numbers up to at least 15 and the corresponding halves • Recognise halving as the inverse of doubling	**All** Show 2 towers of 3 cubes. *How many cubes in each? Both have 3. We will **add** the towers by putting them together.* Write *3+3=6. Two numbers the **same** is called a **double**. Double 3 is 6.* Model doubles to 5+5 on fingers. Write **additions**. Reinforce with cube towers. Rpt for 6+6. **Y2** Show 2 towers of 6 cubes. *What is double 6? 12.* Remove 1 tower. Write ***half** of 12=*. ***Halving** 12 is the **opposite** of doubling 6.* Rpt to show half of 2, 4, 8 and 10.	Y1 E1.a.2 Doubling card numbers, using fingers to help TA	Y1 1.1 p39 Doubling, using cubes to help	Y2 2.1 p38 Doubling numbers	Y2 E1.a.3 Doubling numbers up to 20, and halving corresponding numbers T	Play 'Double my number'. Say *1*. Chn must say its double: *2*. Continue in sequence for the numbers 1–5. If possible, extend to include doubles up to 10.	**Y1** • Recognise doubling as adding a number to itself **Y2** • Begin to know doubles up to 10 • Understand that halving is the opposite of doubling
Day 2	**Say the number 1 less than a given number.** Pairs each place a 0–20 number line in front of them. Say a number, eg *8*. Pairs place a counter on the number **1 less**, eg *7*. Rpt for different numbers, starting with numbers 1–10 and developing to 11–20. Extend to '2 less'.		**All** Rehearse the meaning of a double. Write *double 4=*. *What do we add?* Demonstrate by showing a coat hanger with 4 pegs on either side. *How many pegs **altogether**? 8.* Write *double 7=*. Rpt process. Draw table on board with headings *Number* and *Double*. Write numbers 1–10 in the left-hand column, and fill in the doubles on the right. Emphasise the pattern in the doubles. Remind Y2s that the opposite of doubling is halving. *All the numbers in the left-hand column are half of the numbers in the right-hand column, eg 4 is half of 8.*	Y1 1.1 p39 Doubling, using cubes to help	Y1 E1.a.1 Doubling card numbers, using fingers to help T	Y2 E1.a.2 Playing a card game involving doubles of numbers up to 10 TA	Y2 2.1 p39 Halving numbers	Show a double domino (ie one with the same number of dots on both halves). Cover half. Ask what the **total** is. Encourage fast answers. Repeat many times so chn get faster.	**Y1** • Recognise doubling as adding a number to itself • Begin to know doubles up to 5 **Y2** • Know doubles up to 10 • Begin to know doubles up to 15
Day 3	**Count in 5s and 10s.** Play 'Team counting'. Divide the class into 2 teams to **count back** in 10s. Say a starting number, eg *90*. Point to a team who say the next number: *80*. Teams alternate in saying the next number. Repeat, each team saying 2 or 3 numbers in the count.		**All** Make a 'double-your-money' machine. Put some coins inside. Give a child three 1p coins. *What is double 3p?* Child puts 3p into machine, you take 6p out. Rpt for other amounts, including double 10p. Take 14p out of the machine. *How much was put in? Half of 14=7.* Repeat. **Y2** Write *16. This came out of the machine. What number went in for the machine to make 16? Half of 16?* Write *16=10+6. We can halve 16 by halving both parts. Half of 10 is 5.* Write 5 below 10. *Half of 6 is 3. 5+3=8.* Check using cubes. Repeat to halve other numbers up to 20.	Y1 E1.a.5 Doubling numbers, using towers of bricks to help TA	Y1 1.1 p40 Doubling, using coins to help	Y2 E1.a.4 Investigating number chains made by halving numbers T	Y2 E1.a.4 Investigating number chains made by halving numbers T	Play 'What's my double?' Say a double, eg *8*. Chn say the number that has this as its double, eg *4*. Rpt for different numbers up to 20.	**Y1/Y2** • Know halving is the opposite of doubling. **Y1** • Begin to know doubles up to 10 **Y2** • Know doubles up to 15 • Begin to halve numbers up to 20

	Mental oral starter	Objectives	Main teaching	Activities: Group 1 (Y1)	Activities: Group 2 (Y1)	Activities: Group 3 (Y2)	Activities: Group 4 (Y2)	Plenary	Outcomes
Day 4	**Take away by counting back.** Put 12 objects on a tray. Count objects with chn. Write *12* on board. Remove two things from tray. Chn shut their eyes. ***How many*** *things are* ***left****? We put 12 in our head and count back 2.* Complete number sentence. Rpt, removing three things.	**Y1** • Add by identifying near doubles for numbers up to 10 **Y2** • Begin to derive doubles of multiples of 5 up to 100 and the corresponding halves • Begin to halve multiples of 10 up to 100	**All** Put 3 yellow pegs on one side of a coat hanger, and 4 blue pegs on the other. *How many yellow pegs? How many blue? Is it a double? Why not? It is a* ***near double****.* Slide 3 blue pegs to join the yellows. Write $3+4=\text{double } 3+1=6+1=7$. Rpt for other near doubles. **[ITR Y1 E1.b]** **Y1** A child says a number 1–10, eg *7*. Another child says the **next number**, or the **number before**, eg *8*. Write an addition sentence on the board, eg $7+8=$. *This is a near double. What is double 7? 14. Now add on* ***1 more****, this makes 15.* Rpt, asking different chn for numbers.	Y1 E1.b.1 Adding near doubles, using 1p coins to help T	Y1 1.1 p41 Adding near doubles (with help)	Y2 E1.b.2 Using 5p and 10p coins to find doubles TA	Y2 2.1 p41 Finding doubles of amounts	Give child a purse with 9p in, and tell them not to open it. Write *18p* on board. Tell chn the purse contains half this amount. Each pair uses 10p and 1p coins to work out half of 18p. Open purse to check. Repeat.	**Y1** • Begin to add by recognising near doubles **Y2** • Add by recognising near doubles
Day 5	**Write numerals up to 100.** Play 'Detective maths'. Give clues for children to solve, eg *The number is* ***more than*** *20 and* ***less than*** *30. It is* ***half-way between*** *them.* Children write number on their whiteboards and hold them up to show you. Repeat for different clues for numbers up to 100.		**All** Chn rehearse counting in 5s up to 50. Give each pair a multiple of 5 card up to 50. Choose pair with 15. *Let's double 15.* Remind chn about splitting 'teens' numbers. Write $15=10+5$. Double T and U, then combine. *Double* $15=30$. Rpt for other multiples of 5. **Y2** Use dice numbered 3–8. A pair rolls it and takes that number of 10ps, eg roll 4, take 40p. ***Share*** *it* ***equally*** *between you.* ***How much each****? 20p.* Rpt. *What happens when we roll 7? How can we share the last 10p?* Demo splitting 10p into two 5ps. Repeat to halve 50p and 30p.	Y1 1.1 p41 Adding near doubles (with help)	Y1 E1.b.4 Adding near doubles TA	Y2 2.1 p41 Finding doubles of amounts	Y2 E1.b.1 Playing doubling and halving race T	Write a double on the board, eg *Double* $4=8$. Ask children to say two related near double additions, eg $3+4=7$ or $4+5=9$.	**Y1** • Begin to double larger numbers • Add by recognising near doubles **Y2** • Double multiples of 5 up to 100 • Begin to halve multiples of 10 up to 100

Vocabulary
add, addition
same
double
half, halve
opposite
altogether
total
near double
next number, number before
share equally
how much?
each
tens, units
1 more
1 less
count back
how many left?
more/less than
half-way between

Resources
0–20 number lines (one per pair)
counters (one per pair)
up to 40 linking cubes
four sets of number cards 1–20
small Post-it notes
coat hanger
up to 10 yellow pegs
up to 10 blue pegs
a 30-second sand timer
dominoes
'double-your-money' machine (cardboard box with 'in' slot and 'out' hole)
10p, 5p and 1p coins
about 40 wooden bricks
tray of 12 different objects
two sets of number cards 5–50, multiples of 5 only
purse
individual whiteboards
dice numbered 3–8
number cards 50–100, multiples of 10 only

Year 1 Block E1.a Activities

E1.a.1 A group of 4 children

Spread the cards out face down.
Children take turns to turn over a card. They say the double of that number, using fingers to help them if appropriate. If correct, they keep the card, write the double on a Post-it note and stick it on the card. If they are not correct they replace the card, turning it back face down. Children continue taking turns until all the cards have been taken and have Post-it notes on them. Who has most cards?
Adult support may be useful in running this activity. Two or three groups can be supervised at once.

four sets of 1–6 number cards; small Post-it notes

E1.a.2 A group of up to 8 children

Spread the cards out face down.
Children take turns to turn over a card. All the children show that number of fingers on one hand. They double it by showing a matching number of fingers on the other hand. Agree the double and record this for children on the flip chart. Children continue taking turns until all the cards have been taken.
Adult support may be useful in running this activity.

four sets of 1–5 number cards

E1.a.5 A group of 3 children

Spread out the 1–20 cards face up.
Shuffle the 1–10 cards and place them in a pile face down. One child takes a card from the pile, lays it down, and reads the number. The second child builds a tower with a matching number of bricks. The third child builds another tower the same size. The first child puts the two together, counts how many bricks there are altogether and finds the matching card from those face up on the table. The children put both cards and bricks together. They swap roles and repeat the activity, using each card in the pile.
Adult support may be useful in running this activity.

1–10 number cards; 1–20 number cards; wooden bricks

Year 1 Block E1.b Activities

E1.b.1 A group of up to 8 children working in pairs

Shuffle the cards and place them in a pile face down. One child in each pair takes a card and matches it to 1p coins. For example, they take the card 5, and match it to five 1ps, counting as they do so. The second child takes the same number of 1p coins. Both children together work out the double of the number on the card. Now they add 1p to the second child's amount. Children work out the total and record the addition, for example $5p + 6p = 11p$.
They repeat the activity, swapping roles. Continue until each pair has written at least four calculations.
Adult support may be useful in running this activity.

two sets of 1–10 number cards; 1p coins

E1.b.4 A group of 4 children working in pairs

Shuffle the cards and spread them out face up. Children take turns to take a card. Each pair has to collect two consecutive numbers. They write them down and double the smaller one. They then work out the total; for example they take 2 and 3, write $2 + 2 = 4$, and then write $2 + 3 = 5$. The pairs show each other and check. Repeat. Extend the activity by doubling the larger number instead.
Adult support may be useful in running this activity.

1–10 number cards

Year 2 Block E1.a Activities

E1.a.2 A group of up to 6 children

Spread four sets of 1–10 number cards out face down. Children take turns to turn over a number card and say its double within 30 seconds. They use a sand timer to measure the time limit. If they are correct, they write the double on a Post-it, stick it on the card and keep it. If they are not correct, they replace the card face down. Children continue taking turns until there are no cards left face down.
Adult support may be useful in running this activity.

four sets of 1–10 number cards; a 30-second sand timer; small Post-it notes

E1.a.3 Pairs of children

One child takes the top card from a pile of shuffled 1–20 number cards placed face down. Without showing the card to their partner, they write its double on a Post-it and show their partner the Post-it. The partner has to say half of the Post-it number. If this matches the number on the card, both children record the calculation they did, for example *double 18 = 36* and *half 36 = 18*. If the spoken number does not match the card number, the child with the card replaces it on the bottom of the pile without showing their partner. Swap roles to continue. Keep playing until all the cards have Post-its and all the calculations have been recorded.

1–20 number cards per pair; small Post-it notes

E1.a.4 A whole-class investigation with children working in pairs

Explain that you are all going to make number chains and look for the longest one. Demonstrate how to make a chain. Choose a 2-digit number less than 25. If it is odd, add 1, then halve it. If the answer is odd, do the same again, i.e. add one and halve it. If it is even, halve it straight away. Keep going until you reach the number 1. Give an example:

17 (odd) 17 + 1 = 18
half of 18 = 9 (odd)
9 + 1 = 10
half of 10 = 5 (odd)
5 + 1 = 6
half of 6 = 3 (odd)
3 + 1 = 4
half of 4 = 2 (even)
half of 2 = 1 (the end)

This chain is 9 steps long.
Challenge children to find and record different length chains, counting the steps. Extend the investigation by trying larger numbers. Ask children to try to predict the length of a chain if you give them a number.
Do you think 30 will have a long or a short chain? Does it make any difference if you start with an even or an odd number?
Challenge very able children to list the numbers less than 30 with 5 or fewer steps (1, 2, 4, 8, 16). *What do you notice about these numbers? Can you predict the next chain number with fewer steps than those around it?*
Adult support is needed to run this activity.

counters or cubes for support

Year 2 Block E1.b Activities

E1.b.1 A group of 4 children

Play a doubling and halving race. Spread out 1–10 number cards, 5–50 multiple of 5 cards and 50–100 multiple of 10 cards face down. Children take three cards each and choose whether to halve or double each number. They race to see who can write the three answers first. Note the order of finishing. Then each child lays their cards face up on the table in front of them. Everyone checks each other's answers. If the person who was fastest does not have them all correct, then it is the next fastest with correct answers who wins. Play again.
Adult support is needed to run this activity.

1–10 number cards; 5–50 multiple of 5 cards; 50–100 multiple of 10 cards

E1.b.2 A group of 4, 6 or 8 children working in pairs

Place a shuffled set of 5–50 multiple of 5 cards face down in a pile. Child 1 in each pair takes a card and counts in 5s to match it to 5p coins, for example match 25 to five 5p coins. Child 2 takes the same number of 10p coins counting in 10s as they do so. Child 2 now doubles the amount on the card. Children record both amounts, for example double 25p is 50p. They repeat the activity, swapping roles. Continue playing like this until each pair has written at least four calculations.

two sets of 5–50 multiple of 5 cards; 5p and 10p coins

Maths Weekly Plan: Year 1 and 2

Block E1.c: Recognise and order coins, find totals of sets of coins
Block E1.d: Find totals of sets of coins, pay and exact sum using smaller coins

	Mental oral starter	Objectives	Main teaching	Activities: Group 1 Y1	Activities: Group 2 Y1	Activities: Group 3 Y2	Activities: Group 4 Y2	Plenary	Outcomes
Day 1	**Double numbers 1 to 10.** Write six numbers and their **doubles** on the board. Two of these should be incorrect, eg *2 and 6*, *5 and 11*. Chn work in pairs to mark your work, then discuss what they decided.	**Y1** • Recognise coins of different values • Order coins according to their value **Y2** • Recognise all coins and begin to use £·p notation for money • Find totals of sets of coins: relate to adding three or more numbers	**All** Read *The Owl and the Pussy-Cat. They took one of each **coin***. Show large card coins. Identify/discuss coins and **values**. Chn identify coin that is **worth** the **most**. Line chn up with £2 at one end and 1p at the other. Stress chn are in order of how much their coin is worth. **Y2** *Cat likes silver coins. Owl likes brown and gold.* Separate the coins into silver and brown/gold. Write $50p+20p+10p+5p=$. Encourage chn to count in 10s from 50 to 70p, then **add** 5p. Complete **addition** sentence: *75p*. Add Owl's coins in the same way: $£2+£1+2p+1p=£3{\cdot}03$.	Y1 E1.c.1 Identifying coins TA	Y1 1.1 p43 Recognising coins	Y2 E1.c.1 Sharing and adding sets of coins up to 50p T	Y2 2.1 p43 Adding two or three coins	Place one of each coin in a cloth bag. Ask a child to take out a coin without showing it to the rest of the children. They describe it. The other chn try to guess which coin they are holding. Rpt, choosing other chn to take a coin.	**Y1** • Recognise coins to £2 • Begin to order coins according to value **Y2** • Recognise coins and know their value • Add coins to find the total
Day 2	**Estimate and measure lengths using non-standard units.** Choose a **length**, eg a table top. Hold up the **units** you will use to **measure** the length, eg a pen. *How many pens will fit end to end along the table?* Chn write their **estimates** on whiteboards, and then reveal them. Measure. Rpt for other lengths.		**All** Show children large cardboard pictures of the different coins. Stick the £2 coin on the board. *Think of things that you could **buy** with this coin.* Discuss. Repeat for the other coins in order, £1–1p. Point at each coin in turn and ask children to name them. Draw 4 things on the board, eg ice cream, crisps, comic, apple. Ask chn to think about **how much** these things usually **cost**. Write a suitable **price** by each item, eg *comic £1·20, ice cream 80p, crisps 45p, apple 20p*. Ask Y2s to come and choose coins to **pay** for each item. Stress which coins are used and which are worth the most.	Y1 1.1 p43 Recognising coins	Y1 E1.c.3 Matching coins to properties T	Y2 2.1 p43 Adding two or three coins	Y2 E1.c.2 Sharing and adding sets of coins up to £2, trying to get two equal amounts TA	Show a coin, eg 10p. Ask a child to say something about it, eg *It is silver*. Choose a 2nd child to say something different, eg *It is round*. Ask a 3rd child to say something else, eg *It has a rough edge*. Repeat for another coin.	**Y1** • Recognise coins and know their value • Match coins to physical properties **Y2** • Add two or three coins to find total amount • Make amounts using coins
Day 3	**Recognise coins up to £2.** Peg a large cardboard picture of a 1p coin to a washing line. Chn hold up fingers to show **amount** in **pence**. Repeat for 2p, 5p, 10p and 20p, placing them in order along the line. Extend to include 50p, £1 and £2.	**Y1** • Exchange coins for equivalent in 10p and 1p coins • Find total of sets of coins • Pay an exact sum using smaller coins up to 50p	**All** Draw a pancake. *How much might a pancake cost? Maybe 20p. What coin would we use to pay 20p? Suppose we didn't have a 20p coin. Are there any other coins we could use?* Show two 10ps and count in 10s to 20p. Rpt to show how to make 10p, 5p and 2p using 1p coins. **Y2** Ask two chn to act out a shopping transaction. *Pancakes have gone up to 50p each.* Give one child a £1 coin to buy a pancake. *How much **change** does she need?* Write $50p+\_p=£1$. Show that two 50p coins make £1. Ask chn to make £1 using 20p, 10p and 5p coins.	Y1 E1.d.1 Matching 10p or 1p coins to make the value of other coins TA	Y1 E1.d.1 Matching 10p or 1p coins to make the value of other coins TA	Y2 E1.d.4 Writing the sum of three coins, then asking a partner to work out which coins were used T	Y2 E1.d.2 Working out the 'value' of names using coins	Give one child a 50p coin. Ask pairs to find another way to pay 50p. They write it on their whiteboard as an addition sentence, eg $10p+10p+10p+10p+10p=50p$. Discuss different suggestions.	**Y1** • Match 10p and 1p coins to make different amounts up to 50p **Y2** • Add amounts to find the total • Make amounts using coins

	Mental oral starter	Objectives	Main teaching	Activities: Group 1 Y1	Group 2 Y1	Group 3 Y2	Group 4 Y2	Plenary	Outcomes
Day 4	**Recall and order the months of the year.** Recite sequence of **months**. Peg month cards to washing line in order. Point to each in turn and recite, counting as you point. Discuss hot/cold months. Remove a card and discuss which one is missing. Extend to swapping two months.	*(Continued)* **Y2** • Pay an exact sum using smaller coins up to £2 • Solve 'real-life' problems involving money (paying an exact sum)	**All** Show coins 50p–1p. *An orange costs 14p. How can we pay 14p* ***exactly****?* Point to 10p. *We will need this and some more.* Write *14p = 10p + _p*. Ask chn to count on from 10p to 14p using fingers. *Four fingers; we need 4p more.* Discuss how to make 4p using 1p and/or 2p coins. **Y1** *An apple costs 7p. What coins will we need to make 7p?* Point to 10p. *This is too much*. Point to 5p. *We will need this and some more.* Write *7p = 5p + _p*. Count on from 5p to 7p using fingers. *We need 2p more.* Discuss how to make 2p using a 2p coin or two 1ps. Rpt to make 12p.	Y1 E1.d.2 Identifying coins and making amounts using 10p and 1p coins T	Y1 E1.d.2 Identifying coins and making amounts using 10p and 1p coins T	Y2 E1.d.1 TM 5.1 5 Money problems TA	Y2 2.1 p47 Investigating ways of making amounts	Draw ticket on board. *This is a bus ticket. It costs 25p. Can anyone suggest the coins that we would need to use to pay for it?* Chn work in pairs to suggest different ways of paying 25p.	**Y1** • Identify coins and know their value • Make amounts using 10p and 1p coins **Y2** • Solve 'real-life' money problems • Make amounts using different coins
Day 5	**Find totals of sets of coins.** Blu-tack a large cardboard 2p coin and a large cardboard 1p coin to the board. Chn show **total** pence using number fans. Repeat for other sets of coins with totals up to 10p. Extend to three coins.		**All** Give child 2p, 5p and 10p. Draw these on board. Help them to identify the three coins. *Which is worth most? How much altogether? 10 and 5 makes?* Write *10 + 5*. Chn count on using fingers. Rpt to count on another 2p. Complete addition. Rpt to add 10p, 2p and 1p. **[ITR Y1 E1.d]** **Y2** Put 10p, 10p, 5p in purse. *3 silver coins inside, 2 the same, 1 different.* Chn write possible total. Reveal coins. Put £1, 20p, 10p, 5p in purse. *25p* ***more than*** *before. £1·35. Which 4 coins?* Reveal them. Replace £1 with 50p. *How much now?* Model addition: *50p + 20p + 10p + 5p = _p*.	Y1 1.1 p45 Matching identical amounts	Y1 E1.d.3 Making amounts up to 50p using different coins TA	Y2 2.1 p45 Matching amounts	Y2 E1.d.5 TM 5.3 5 Money problems T	Show apple, orange, grapefruit. *Apple is 16p, orange is 5p more, grapefruit is 6p more than orange.* Some chn work out price of orange, others find price of grapefruit. Ask which coins to use.	**Y1** • Identify coins and know their value • Make amounts using different coins **Y2** • Solve 'real-life' money problems • Make amounts using different coins

Vocabulary
money
coin
value
worth
most, least
add, addition
buy
pay
sell
cost
price
amount
how much?
pound, £
penny, pence, p
change
exact, right money
total
more/less than
double
length
unit
measure
estimate
months

Resources
The Owl and the Pussy-Cat by Edward Lear
large cardboard coins 1p–£2
lots of real coins 1p–£2
cloth bag
individual whiteboards
Blu-tack
labels that describe coins, e.g. *silver, milled edges, round, gold*
12 pegs
washing line
month cards January–December
about 20 red cubes
three blank cards
vocabulary cards: *total, altogether, cost, change, left, total cost, costs more than, costs less than, how much*
number fans (one per child)
two purses
number cards 5–50
apple
orange
grapefruit

Year 1 Block E1.c Activities

E1.c.1 A group of up to 8 children working in pairs

Lay out one of each coin, discussing with the group which is the most valuable, which is the least, and so on. Point out how we recognise the two most valuable (£1 and £2) and the two least valuable (1p and 2p). Then give each pair a set of coins. You say a coin, for example *ten pence.* They must immediately show you that coin. If they are correct, you take it. The first pair to get rid of all their coins wins. Play again. Adult support may be useful in running this activity.

set of real coins up to and including £2 per pair

E1.c.3 Pairs of children

Read a label and ask each pair to show you the matching coins. For example, if you read 'writing round the edge' then children have to show you the £1 and £2 coins. Identify these coins. Repeat for another label. Add up some of the coins, for example 'brown coins' add up to 3p. Adult support may be useful in running this activity.

set of real coins up to and including £2 per pair; labels that describe the coins, for example 'silver', 'milled edges', 'round', 'gold', 'writing round the edge', etc.

Year 1 Block E1.d Activities

E1.d.1 Pairs of children

Show children a number of large 10p or 1p coins to make the value of one of their coins, for example five large 10p coins. Each child or pair must show you the matching coin in their set, for example 50p. Repeat this, showing the children five 1p coins. They must show you the 5p coin. Continue like this. Adult support may be useful in running this activity.

set of coins up to and including £2 per child or pair; large 10p or 1p coins

E1.d.2 A group of up to 10 children working in pairs

Pairs sort their 10p and 1p coins into separate piles. Hold up a coin, for example 50p. Do not say what it is! Children have to identify the coin and make that amount using 10p or 1p coins. Give a red cube to each pair who does this correctly. Hold up a different coin and repeat. Adult support may be useful in running this activity.

red cubes; set of coins for the teacher; large pile of real 10p and 1p coins per pair

E1.d.3 A group of up to 10 children working in pairs

Shuffle the 5–50 number cards and spread them out face down. Each pair takes a card, for example 34. They make that amount of money using their coins, for example one 20p, one 10p and two 2p coins. Give each pair 2 or 3 minutes to do this, offering support if necessary. Look at their amounts: do they match the card? If so, the pair keep their card. If not, then the card is returned face down to the table. Continue playing until all the cards have been taken. Adult support may be useful in running this activity.

5–50 number cards; a set of 20p, 10p, 1p, 2p and 5p coins per pair

Year 2 Block E1.c Activities

E1.c.1 A group of 4, 6 or 8 children working in pairs

Ask all children in the group to help you find one of each coin up to 50p to place in a row. Find the total amount together (88p). Each pair then works with a matching set of coins, one as the Owl and one as the Pussy-Cat. They divide the coins between them and work out how much Owl has and how much Cat has. Help pairs record as an addition each way they find of partitioning the coins, for example Owl has 1p, 5p and 20p; Cat has 2p, 10p and 50p; *26p + 62p = 88p.*

Adult support may be useful in running this activity.

enough real coins for each pair to have a set of one of each of 1p, 2p, 5p, 10p, 20p, 50p

E1.c.2 Pairs of children

One child in each pair is the Owl, the other is the Pussy-Cat. Pairs try out various ways of partitioning a set of one of each denomination of coin. They record each way as an addition, for example Owl has 1p, 5p, 20p and £2; Cat has 2p, 10p, 50p and £1; *£2·26 + £1·62 = £3·88.* After a few examples ask children to try to give Owl and Cat as nearly equal amounts as possible. They should record all their attempts.

enough real coins for each pair to have a set of one of each denomination

Year 2 Block E1.d Activities

5.1 5 Money problems

E1.d.1 A group of 6 or more children

Ask children for an addition fact that they know, for example 6 + 4 = 10. Write the number sentence on one of the blank cards. Repeat for a subtraction. Then ask them to think of three small numbers and their total. Record this as a number sentence on the third card. Read the vocabulary cards and use them to make up a money problem together, for example Ben has 6p in one pocket and 4p in the other. Altogether he has 10p. Ask pairs to write another word problem for the same addition and then two word problems for each of the other two number sentences.

Adult support is needed to run this activity.

three blank cards; vocabulary cards for: *total, altogether, cost, change, left*

E1.d.2 Pairs of children

Pairs work out the cost of having names engraved or printed. The letters of the alphabet are priced like this:

a, e, i, o and u are 20p
c, g, m, p, y are 2p
d, h, r, s, t are 10p
j, k, q, v, x, z are 1p
b, f, l, n, w are 5p

Children should experiment, pricing both their names first, then the names of friends and celebrities, for example Wayne Rooney costs:

5p + 20p + 2p + 5p + 20p + 10p + 20p + 20p + 5p + 20p + 2p = £1·29.

1p, 2p, 5p, 10p and 20p coins

E1.d.4 Pairs of children

Each child looks at three coins and works out the amount they would have if they took those three coins. They each write the amount on a piece of paper and swap pieces of paper with their partner. Each child tries to work out which three coins their partner was looking at and record the addition, for example 2p + 5p + 10p = 17p.
Were you right?

one of each coin from 1p to £2 per pair

5.3 5 Money problems

E1.d.5 A group of 6 or more children

Ask children for an addition fact that they know, for example 60 + 20 = 80. Write the number sentence on one of the blank cards. Repeat for a subtraction. Then ask them to think of three small numbers and their total. Record this as a number sentence on the third card. Read the vocabulary cards and use them to make up a money problem together, for example *A packet of plain biscuits costs 60p. The chocolate biscuits cost 20p more than the plain ones. How much do the chocolate biscuits cost? They cost 80p.* Ask pairs to write another word problem for the same addition and then two word problems for each of the other two number sentences.

Adult support is needed to run this activity.

three blank cards; vocabulary cards for: *total cost, altogether, change, costs more than, costs less than, how much*

Maths Weekly Plan: Year 1 and 2

Block A2.a: Y1 Recognise zero, read numbers to 100; Y2 Count on/back in 1s, 10s, 100s
Block A2.b: Y1 Count by grouping in 10s; Y2 Recognise odd and even numbers

	Mental oral starter	Objectives	Main teaching	Activities: Group 1 Y1	Activities: Group 2 Y1	Activities: Group 3 Y2	Activities: Group 4 Y2	Plenary	Outcomes
Day 1	**Recognise coins up to £2.** Place **coins** in a bag (1p, 2p, 5p, 10p, 20p, 50p). Ask a child to take a coin and hold it up. Chn show fingers to match amount in **pence** (show sequences of fingers for large amounts). Rpt. When all coins have been chosen, ask chn with coins to stand in a line in order of **value**.	**Y1** • Recognise zero • Count on and back in 1s to 100 • Write numbers up to 10 in words and up to 11 in figures • Begin to read numbers up to 100 in words and figures **Y2** • Count on and back in 1s or 10s from a 2- or 3-digit number • Count on and back in 100s from a multiple of 100	**All** Count to 100, matching units to fingers. Show chn book with monsters in it. ***How many** monsters are there?* Count them. Draw 10 monsters. *What happens if 1 runs away?* **Count back** from 10. Rpt until you reach 0. ***Zero** means nothing.* Count down from 20 to 0. **Y2** Show 100-square. *Which is the largest number? 100.* Point to 46. Identify **next number**: 47. Point to 73. Write *73+1=* and *73-1=*. Chn write answers. Show 101–200 grid. Count along 1st 3 rows. *What is similar about the two grids?* Say numbers larger than 200. Chn write them.	Y1 A2.a.1 Matching written numerals to numbers of cubes TA	Y1 1.2 p3 Writing numerals, matching names to numbers (up to 100)	Y2 2.2 p2 Practising counting in 1s	Y2 A2.a.2 Working out numbers from the numbers before and after (101–200) T	Count back together from 18 to 0. Write *0* on board. Say a different start number, and ask a child to count back to 0. When child finishes the count, they write *0* on the board. If they are correct, they choose a new start number.	**Y1** • Count on and back in 1s • Understand that 0 means 'nothing' **Y2** • Identify numbers 1 more and 1 less
Day 2	**Add two 1-digit numbers, crossing 10.** Pairs place their 1–20 number lines in front of them. Write an **addition** on the board, eg *8+3=*. Pairs place a counter on their number line to match the answer. Rpt for different additions. Vary the activity by saying the addition rather than writing it.		**All** Write **digits** 0–9 on board. Write the **number names** below digits. Show 100-square. Point to 25. *25 is written using which digits?* Point at 2 and 5. Rpt for 35, 45, 55. Point at 76. *Seven-ty-six.* Write *seven* then add *ty,* then write *six* to complete. Rpt for other numbers. **Y1** Look at one of the monsters from yesterday's book. *What is its name? How many letters in its name?* Count together. *How do we write this number in words?* Write number and number name next to each other. Rpt for other numbers. **[ITR Y1 A2.a]**	Y1 A2.a.3 Investigating patterns made by counting the letters in children's names and number names T	Y1 A2.a.3 Investigating patterns made by counting the letters in children's names and number names T	Y2 A2.a.1 Counting in 10s from a 1-digit number TA	Y2 p3 Practising counting in 1s, 10s, 100s	Show number names one at a time, not in any order. Chn write the matching numeral on their whiteboards. Repeat this for several number names, one to twenty-five.	**Y1** • Recognise number names and match to numerals • Begin to write number names 0–10 **Y2** • Write number names 0–10 • Count on and back in 1s, 10s, 100s
Day 3	**Order days of the week; recognise the day before and after.** Recite the **days** of the **week**, **Monday** to **Sunday**. Peg day cards in order along washing line. Point at each in turn, counting the number of days. Play 'Say the day **after**'. You say a day, and chn say the next day. Extend to 'Say the day **before**'.		**All** Show 100-square. *Bisky Bat counts in 10s.* Put Bisky on 0. **Count on** in 10s to 100. Put Bisky on 7. Count in 10s. *The **units** stay the same. Bisky also counts back.* Count back in 10s from 43 to 3. Count on from 3 to 93. Rpt for other numbers. Discuss **patterns**. **[ITR Y1 A2.b]** **Y2** Write *100, 200, 300* on board. *We're counting in **hundreds** (**multiples of** 100).* Show Turkey from *The Owl and the Pussy-Cat. Turkey likes to count in hundreds.* Draw 1–1000 number line with multiples of 100 labelled. Write *146*. Count on in 100s. Discuss patterns. Rpt for 162.	Y1 A2.b.3 TM 5.1 5 Counting in 10s TA	Y1 A2.b.2 TM 5.2 5 Counting in 10s	Y2 2.2 p3 Practising counting in 10s	Y2 A2.a.5 Investigating patterns in sequences T	Count back in 10s from any 2-digit number. Choose different groups of children to repeat this. Y2s count on in 100s from any multiple of 100.	**Y1** • Count on/back in 10s • Know that units digit stays the same when counting in 10s **Y2** • Count on/back in 1s, 10s and 100s • Know that units digit stays the same when counting in 10s

	Mental oral starter	Objectives	Main teaching	Activities: Group 1 Y1	Activities: Group 2 Y1	Activities: Group 3 Y2	Activities: Group 4 Y2	Plenary	Outcomes
Day 4	**Estimate and count a set of objects.** Show chn a jar of marbles or a box of puzzle pieces. Ask chn to work in pairs to **estimate** how many objects there are. Each pair can have three guesses. Count the objects, **grouping** them in 10s. *Which pair had the **closest** estimate?*	**Y1** • Count a large number of objects by grouping in 10s • Count on and back in 10s from a 1-digit number **Y2** • Count on in 2s (revise) • Begin to recognise odd and even numbers up to at least 50	**Y2** Peg number cards 1–20 in order along a washing line. Count along line in 1s. Remove **odd** numbers. *We will whisper the missing numbers.* Count along line. Continue past 20, writing the 'loud' (**even**) numbers on the board. Keep going, creating a list of even numbers up to 100. Look at the units patterns. Put odd numbers back on line. Remove the even numbers, and repeat. Look at the units patterns of the odd numbers. Write *67* on board. *Is this odd or even? It ends in 7, so it's an odd number.* Repeat to identify 38 and 94. *We can find out by looking at the units digit.*	Y1 1.2 p4 Counting in 10s	Y1 A2.b.4 Playing a card game involving 10 more TA	Y2 A2.b.1 Listing even and odd numbers T	Y2 p4 Identifying even and odd numbers	Divide class into 2 teams: Lions and Tigers. One team collects even numbers, other collects odd. Throw a dice to generate a 2- or 3-digit number. *Is it odd or even?* Give the appropriate team a cube. Rpt.	**Y1** • Know number names • Count on/back in 10s **Y2** • Begin to recognise even and odd numbers • Identify odd and even numbers by units digit
Day 5	**Counting on/back in 10s and 1s.** Play 'Team counting'. Divide the class into 4 or 5 teams to count on in 1s. Say a starting number, eg *28*. Point to one team who say next number: *29*. Point to another team who say next number: *30*. And so on. Repeat, counting forwards and back.		**Y1** Show children a set of 35-40 leaves on a tray. *How many leaves do you estimate there are? How will we find out how many leaves there are? We can count the leaves, grouping them in 10s.* When the leaves have been counted, check whose estimate was closest. Repeat using 20–30 marbles in a jar: ask children to write an estimate, then help you to count by grouping in 10s.	Y1 A2.b.1 Counting objects, grouping in 10s T	Y1 A2.b.1 Counting objects, grouping in 10s T	Y2 2.2 p6 Counting in 2s	Y2 A2.b.3 Investigating ways of positioning odd and even numbers on a grid TA	Show children a small branch from a bush or tree. *Can you estimate the number of leaves?* Without picking each leaf, count them, grouping in 10s. *Whose estimate was closest?*	**Y1** • Estimate a number of objects • Count a large number of objects by grouping in 10s **Y2** • Identify odd and even numbers

Vocabulary
how many?
count on, back
zero
next number, number before
1 more, 1 less
before, after
digit
hundreds, tens, units
one, two, three, … one hundred
multiple of
pattern
estimate
closest
grouping
odd
even
coin
pence
value
addition
day
week
Monday, Tuesday, … Sunday

Resources
bag
coins 1p–50p, plus extra 10p coins
Where the Wild Things Are by Maurice Sendak, or other monster book
large 100-square
large 101–200 grid
number cards 0–100
linking cubes
small 101–200 grids (Y2 PCM 108)
1–20 number lines (one per pair)
counters (one per pair)
individual whiteboards
day cards, Monday–Sunday
20 pegs
washing line
picture of Bisky Bat
picture of Turkey
100-bead string or bead bar
jar of marbles or box of puzzle pieces
small Post-it notes
35–40 leaves
tray
a small branch covered in leaves
about 12 blank 5 × 5 grids
coloured pencils

Year 1 Block A2.a Activities

A2.a.1 Pairs of children

Children build a set of rods using linking cubes, one rod to match each number 1–10. They arrange the rods in order. The number cards are shuffled and placed in a pile face down. Children take turns to take a card. They read the number aloud, keep the card and place the matching rod on it. If a child takes the 0 card, they both say *zero!* After this they count how many cubes they each have, and the one with more cubes takes a 10p coin. They replace the rods, put the cards back in the pile, shuffle them and repeat, again totalling their scores when someone takes the 0 card.
Adult support may be useful in running this activity.

0–10 number cards; linking cubes; 10p coins

A2.a.3 A whole-class investigation with children working in pairs

Each pair writes one of their names, for example *Sam*. They count the letters and write the numeral, for example *3*. They then write this number as a name, for example *three*. Children count the letters in this name and write this as a numeral, for example *5*. They then write that number as a name, and continue like this until they reach a loop (four, 4, four, 4, …). The pair t hen try the other child's name and repeat the activity.
Which names lead to the longest chains? Can some pairs put into words any general rules?
Adult support is needed to run this activity.

number names to twelve displayed for children

Year 1 Block A2.b Activities

A2.b.1 A group of up to 8 children working in pairs

Pairs write estimates of the number of leaves on their branch, then count by pulling them off and grouping them in 10s, noting the number left over, e.g. *Five piles of ten leaves and three leaves left over*. They locate this number, e.g. 3, on the 100-square, and count on in 10s to match the piles of 10 leaves: *Three, thirteen* (pointing at one pile of 10), *twenty-three* (pointing at the next pile of 10), *thirty-three*, etc. Children record the total, e.g. 53. Compare the numbers of leaves with the estimates. Which pair made the best estimate?
Adult support may be useful in running this activity.

a small branch covered with leaves; 100-square

5.2 5 Counting in 10s

A2.b.2 A group of 6 or more children

Hide the last five beads on the bead string in your hand, leave the previous five showing and slide the remaining 90 away. Hold up the string, displaying the five visible beads. *How many?* Slide groups of ten beads to join the five, counting on in 10s: *Fifteen, twenty-five, …, ninety-five*. Children watch and count along. *The five on the right stay the same; only the number of tens changes.*
Repeat, gaining speed. Ask: *How many will be showing after another 10 beads?* Then slide back the beads and count back in 10s.
Adult support is needed to run this activity.

100-bead string or bead bar

5.1 5 Counting in 10s

A2.b.3 A group of 6 or more children

Hide the last five beads on the bead string in your hand, leave the previous five showing and slide the remaining 90 away. Hold up the string, displaying the five visible beads. *How many?* Slide 10 beads along to join them. *How many now? Do you need to count them one by one?* Point out the group of 10. Elicit that 10 and 5 makes 15, if necessary counting on 5 from 10. Slide another 10 beads along. *How many now? How many groups of ten?* Count them in 10s: *Ten, twenty. I've still got five here, making twenty-five.*
Repeat, gaining speed. Remind children that the five at the right-hand side remain the same. Ask: *How many will be showing after another 10 beads?*
Adult support is needed to run this activity.

100-bead string or bead bar

A2.b.4 A group of 3 children

Shuffle the number cards and pile them face down. Deal six cards each. Children take turns to place a card and say the number 10 more. The others must agree, if necessary using the 100-square. The child writes this number on a Post-it, sticks it on their card and places it face up on the table. They take a card from the pile. If it matches a number on a Post-it, they take the card and Post-it with their matching card and place them down, then take another card. Who can collect the most card pairs?
Adult support may be useful in running this activity.

1–100 number cards; 100-square; small Post-it notes

Year 2 Block A2.a Activities

A2.a.1 A group of up to 8 children

Place a shuffled set of 10–100 number cards face down in a pile. Each child takes four cards and keeps them secret. Roll a 0–9 dice. Show the number and write it up. Say that you are all going to count in 10s from this number but first children must look at their four cards to see if they have any of the numbers you will say in the count. If they think they have they say 'Me-in-the-count!' and lay the matching card(s) face down on the table. Give each child a chance to say 'Me-in-the-count', then perform the count in 10s from the single-digit starting number. Stop counting when you pass 100. Children who laid down a card reveal the numbers. If they were correct and the number was in the count, they hand in their card. If not, they not only keep that card but must take another. Play on till one child wins by getting rid of all their cards. Play again.

Adult support is needed to run this activity.

10–100 number cards

A2.a.2 Pairs of children

Give both children a 101–200 grid (Y2 PCM 108). Child 1 circles a number on the grid, being careful **not** to show their partner, for example 117. They then **tell** their partner the number before and the number after their chosen number, for example *one hundred and sixteen, one hundred and eighteen*. Child 2 writes these two numbers and also the number that comes in the middle. They show child 1, who reveals their number and checks that the middle number matches it. Swap roles to play again. Repeat until each child has written six sequences of three numbers.

Adult support may be useful in running this activity with several pairs.

Y2 PCM 108

A2.a.5 Pairs of children

Pairs investigate the patterns within runs of three 'next door numbers' where the sum of all the digits is 20 or less; for example for 31, 32, 33, the digit sum $=3+1+3+2+3+3=15$. Set a challenge to find how many such runs of three exist between 1 and 100. Look for patterns. *Are there any runs like this over 100?*

Adult support may be useful in running this activity with several pairs of children.

Year 2 Block A2.b Activities

A2.b.1 Pairs of children

Each pair agrees a 2-digit starting number, for example 56, and whether it is a loud (even) number ending in 2, 4, 6, 8 or 0 or a whispered (odd) number ending in 1, 3, 5, 7 or 9. Together they start the count in the appropriate voice and count on, saying the even numbers in loud voices and whispering the odd numbers, while taking turns to write the numbers until each child has written at least 10 numbers. Then they discuss and agree who has written the even (loud) numbers and who has written the odd (quiet) numbers. They label the numbers in their list O and E accordingly. Repeat.

Adult support may be useful in running this activity with several pairs of children.

A2.b.3 Pairs of children

Pairs play this game on an empty 5 × 5 grid. They agree that one child will write even numbers only and the other will write odd numbers only. The 'even' child starts by writing an even number anywhere on the grid. The 'odd' child then writes an odd number anywhere on the grid. Children take turns to write numbers until the grid is full or neither child can write a number. The child who has written more numbers wins.

This sounds easy, but they must obey the following rules:

An even number **cannot** be written in a box above, below, or to either side of a box with an even number but **can** be diagonally next to an even number.

An odd number **cannot** be written in a box above, below, or to either side of a box with an odd number but **can** be diagonally next to an odd number.

Neither child may write a number they have already written!

If a child cannot write a number without breaking one of these rules, they miss their turn.

Before playing again on a new grid, ask children to count up how many squares are 'wasted', i.e. have no numbers in them, and to try to waste fewer squares next time. Children should keep their grids to refer to.

Adult support may be useful in running this activity with several pairs of children.

several empty 5 × 5 grids for each pair; different coloured pencils per child

Maths Weekly Plan: Year 1 and 2

Block A2.c: Understand and use ordinal numbers
Block A2.d: Compare and order numbers, and say a number between two numbers

	Mental oral starter	Objectives	Main teaching	Activities: Group 1 (Y1)	Activities: Group 2 (Y1)	Activities: Group 3 (Y2)	Activities: Group 4 (Y2)	Plenary	Outcomes
Day 1	**Write numbers 1–100.** Shuffle a pile of number cards 1–100. Ask a child to choose one at random. The child says the number. Everyone else writes that number on their whiteboards. The child shows their card to the class. Does it match with all the numbers on the whiteboards? Repeat.	**Y1** • Understand and use ordinal numbers up to at least 20th **Y2** • Understand and use ordinal numbers up to at least 100th	**All** Read *The Quangle Wangle's Hat. Who arrived **first**? Mr and Mrs Canary.* Draw them on left of board. *They are 1st in the queue.* Continue for other creatures. Discuss London Marathon. Write *45th*. Y2s: *What position was the runner who finished **before**/**after** this?* **[ITR Y1 A2.c]** **Y1** Point to the picture of the queue on the board. *Who came first? **Second**? **Third**?* Then say the names of different creatures and ask the children to say their **position** as they arrived at the Quangle Wangle's tree.	Y1 A2.c.1 Ordering coloured cubes in a line T	Y1 1.2 p7 Colouring cars in a position in a line	Y2 2.2 p7 Recognising ordinal numbers	Y2 A2.c.3 Noting position and recording it in a table TA	Make a queue of 10 children. Place a hat on the head of one of them. *What position is the child with the hat?* Repeat, giving the hat to different chn in the queue.	**Y1** • Understand and use 1st, 2nd, ... 10th • Describe positions using correct vocabulary **Y2** • Understand and use ordinal numbers to 50th
Day 2	**Subtract a 1-digit number from a 1-digit number.** Play 'Fan-tastic'. Write ten 1-digit **subtractions** on the board, eg *8–2=*. Point at a subtraction. Choose a child to read it. Chn show the answer using their fans. If they are not sure, they can imagine jumps along a number line. Repeat.		**All** Child stands at front. *You are first in the queue.* Give the child a label saying *first*. Ask another child to stand behind the first, and state their position. Continue until 10 chn are in position. They hide their cards. Ask the other chn questions as to their positions. **Y2** Show picture of London Marathon. Write *Tim came 17th. What number was 10 after Tim?* Write *27th. What is 10 after that?* Stress that 17th, 27th, 37th look nearly the same as 17, 27, 37. *The only difference is the 'th'. We call these **ordinal numbers**. They describe the **order**.*	Y1 1.2 p6 Finding characters by identifying position in a line	Y1 A2.c.2 Playing a card game based on card positions in a line TA	Y2 A2.c.1 Using ordinal numbers T	Y2 2.2 p8 Recognising ordinal numbers	Each child writes on their whiteboard a position 1st–10th. Throw dice 10 times. Each child notes what the result was on the throw they chose. Keep a record. Check their notes. Repeat.	**Y1** • Identify position up to 20th using correct vocabulary **Y2** • Identify position up to 100th using correct vocabulary
Day 3	**Recall doubles of numbers 1-10.** Pairs each place a 1–20 number line in front of them. Say a number. Pairs place a counter on their number lines to match the **double** of that number. Check their answers. Rpt for different numbers up to 10. Check answers and say corresponding **halves**.	**Y1** • Order numbers up to at least 20 • Begin to say a number lying between two numbers	**All** Hand out number cards 1–100. Write *45*. Point to 45 on 100-square. *Where are the numbers **smaller**/**greater than** 45? (Behind/above 45.) Hold up numbers greater than 45.* Rpt for cards below 45. Write *84* and *48. Which is smaller? How do we know?* Rpt for 125, 109 and 132, 151. **Y1** Shuffle number cards 1–10. 2 chn select a card each. *Which is **smaller**? Which is **larger**?* Demonstrate using number line. *Which numbers come between them?* Count from one to the other to check. Rpt for a different pair. **[ITR Y1 A2.d]**	Y1 A2.d.2 TM 6.1 6 Ordering numbers T	Y1 1.2 p9 Comparing two numbers using a track	Y2 A2.d.1 TM 7.1 7 Ordering numbers TA	Y2 2.2 p10 Comparing numbers	Make 2 teams: Lions and Tigers. Shuffle T and U place-value cards into 2 piles. Write *47*. Lion takes **tens** card, Tiger takes **units** card. If number is lower than 47, Lions get cube, if higher, Tiger gets a cube. Play until 1 team collects 10 cubes.	**Y1** • Order numbers up to 20 • Compare numbers: smaller or larger **Y2** • Order numbers to 100 • Identify numbers smaller/larger than a named 2-digit number

	Mental oral starter	Objectives	Main teaching	Activities: Group 1 Y1	Activities: Group 2 Y1	Activities: Group 3 Y2	Activities: Group 4 Y2	Plenary	Outcomes
Day 4	**Recall 1 more and 1 less than a 2-digit number.** Play 'Number pointing'. Chn place their number board (Y2 PCM 113) flat. *Show me **1 less** than 62.* Chn point at the number. Repeat many times, asking children to say the number 1 less and **1 more** than different numbers.	*(Continued)* **Y2** • Compare two or more 2-digit numbers; introduce the greater than (>), less than (<) signs • Say a number lying between two numbers, up to at least 100	**All** Give 4 chn a number card 1–20 each. Challenge them to put themselves in order from **smallest** to **largest**. *How will we know if they are correct?* Chn look at the number line to check. *Which of our numbers are **between** our smallest and largest numbers?* Repeat. **Y2** Write *68, 92*. *Which is larger?* Write *68<92*. *This is a crocodile's mouth! It faces the larger number.* Write *173, 137*. Cover 1s and read. Uncover and read whole numbers. *Which is larger? Both have 100.* Point to T digits. *Which is larger?* Write *173 > 137*. Rpt for 164 and 146.	Y1 A2.d.5 Choosing two numbers 1–20, and finding all the numbers in between TA	Y1 A2.d.5 Choosing two numbers 1–20, and finding all the numbers in between TA	Y2 2.2 p9 Looking for numbers more/less than a given number	Y2 A2.d.3 TM 7.3 7 Ordering numbers T	Put 5 chn in a line. Give each a number card 1–20. They hold up their cards. *Who has the smallest number? Who has the largest? Who has a number between these?* Chn arrange themselves in order. Rpt.	**Y1** • Order numbers 0–20 • Find numbers between 2 others (0–20) **Y2** • Order numbers 0–200 • Find numbers between 2 others (0–200)
Day 5	**Name and recognise the properties of 2D shapes.** Play 'Shape pointing'. Each child places a shape board (Y2 PCM 123) flat. *Show me a **shape** with 5 **sides**.* Chn point to the shape. Rpt this including different properties of shapes, eg **straight** sides, **curved** sides, number of **corners**, names of shapes.		**All** Show 101–200 grid. Ask a child to point to 164. *Which numbers are larger/smaller?* Pairs say a number between 164 and 175. *We can find all the in-between numbers by looking at numbers that are below 175 but above 164.* Rpt to find numbers between 135 and 153. **Y1** Count along 1–30 number line. Stick 5 number cards in a row on board: 22, 17, 4, 29, 18. *We will put them in order, smallest to largest, by making swaps.* Chn say smallest number. *Which is largest?* Discuss smallest, largest and in-between numbers. Rpt with 5 new numbers.	Y1 1.2 p10 Ordering sets of four amounts of money	Y1 A2.d.4 TM 6.3 6 Ordering numbers T	Y2 A2.d.2 Generating and comparing numbers TA	Y2 A2.d.2 Generating and comparing numbers TA	Write two sets of 5 numbers on board, eg *17, 13, 6, 3, 27* (Y1s) and *123, 99, 311, 157, 724* (Y2s). Pairs write their set in order on their whiteboards from largest to smallest. Check.	**Y1** • Order numbers 0–20 • Find numbers between 2 others (0–20) **Y2** • Order numbers 0–200 • Find numbers between 2 others (0–200)

Vocabulary
first, second, third, … twentieth
1st, 2nd, 3rd, … 20th
ordinal number
last
next
before
after
position
order
compare
larger/greater/more than
smaller/less than
smaller, smallest
larger, largest
lower, higher
hundreds, tens, units
1 less, 1 more
between
subtraction
double
halve, half
shape
side
straight
curved
corner

Resources
number cards 1–100
individual whiteboards
The Quangle Wangle's Hat by Edward Lear
different coloured cubes
playing cards
hat
number fans (one per child)
labels: *first, second, … tenth*
picture of London Marathon
dice
1–20 number lines (one per pair)
counters (one per pair)
large 100-square
washing line
20 pegs
Post-it notes
four 0–100 number lines with multiples of 10 marked
place-value cards (T, U)
Number boards (Y2 PCM 113)
extra set of number cards 1–20
1–20 number track
four 0–100 number lines with 0, 50 and 100 marked
Shape boards (Y2 PCM 123)
large 101–200 grid
1–30 number line
Blu-tack

Year 1 Block A2.c Activities

A2.c.1 A group of up to 8 children

Lay out a line of at least 8 cubes, each one a different colour. Give each child a coloured cube which matches one of the cubes in the line. They hide their cube so that no one else can see it. Ask each child in turn to state where their coloured cube is, for example *My cube is the third cube in the line.* The other children say what colour their cube must be. Repeat using different shapes.
Adult support may be useful in running this activity.

at least eight cubes of different colours

A2.c.2 A group of 4 children

Shuffle the cards and deal ten each. Children lay out their cards in random order. Allocate each child a suit, for example one is collecting hearts, the second clubs, and so on. Children take turns to play. They may swap any card in their row for any card in another child's row. To do this, they must identify the card they want by position, for example *I want to swap this card for the fifth card in your row.* Children keep taking turns to identify and swap cards until each child has a row with only their suit.
Adult support may be useful in running this activity.

deck of playing cards with the face cards removed

Year 1 Block A2.d Activities

6.1 6 Ordering numbers

A2.d.2 A group of 6 or more children

Start with cards 1, 5, 10, 15 and 20 on the correct pegs, and shuffle the cards, placing 2, 9, 11 and 19 near the top. *What is the smallest number on our line? The largest? Which numbers are in between?* Turn over a card, for example 2. *Where shall we hang this?*
Repeat until you have placed about half the cards, encouraging children to count on or back where necessary, and to use vocabulary such as 'before', 'after' and 'between'. Count up and check that the numbers on the cards are in order.
Continue placing all the cards on the line. *How can we check them?* Write 'before 10' on a Post-it note and stick it to the bottom of the 9 card. Repeat, writing 'after 8' and 'between 8 and 10' on Post-its and sticking to the 9 card. Choose other numbers on the line and ask children to help you write similar facts on Post-its to stick on the cards.
Adult support is needed to run this activity.

washing line with 20 pegs regularly spaced on it; 1–20 number cards; Post-it notes

6.3 6 Ordering numbers

A2.d.4 A group of 6 or more children

Start with cards 10, 20 and 30 on the correct pegs, and shuffle the cards, placing 11, 19, 21 and 29 near the top. *What is the smallest number on our line? The largest? Which numbers are in between?* Turn over a card, for example 11. *Where shall we hang this?*
Repeat until you have placed about half the cards, encouraging children to count on or back where necessary, and to use vocabulary such as 'before', 'after' and 'between.' Count up and check that the numbers on the cards are in order.
Continue placing all the cards on the line. *How can we check them?* Write 'before 20' on a Post-it note and stick it to the bottom of the 19 card. Repeat, writing 'after 18' and 'between 18 and 20' on Post-its and sticking to the 19 card. Choose other numbers on the line and ask children to help you write similar facts on Post-its to stick on the cards.
Adult support is needed to run this activity.

washing line with 20 pegs regularly spaced on it; 10–30 number cards; Post-it notes

A2.d.5 A group of 3 children

Place one set of cards in a pile face down, and spread out the other set face up. Two children each take a card from the pile face down. The third child is the 'between' player who collects the cards between these two numbers from those spread out face up. They all check using the number track. Return the 'between' cards. Children continue, taking turns to be the 'between' player, reshuffling the pile of cards if necessary.
Adult support may be useful in running this activity.

two sets of 1–20 number cards; 1–20 number track

Year 2 Block A2.c Activities

A2.c.1 A group of up to 8 children

Sit children in a circle and show them a shuffled pack of playing cards. Make sure they know what each suit is called. Place 10 cards face up in a line. Give each child three cards: they must hold them so that no one else can see them. Tell children you are looking at, for example, the fifth card in the line and that they must look at their hand of three cards to see if they have a card in the same suit. If they do, they lay it down face up. Continue playing by identifying another card in the line by its ordinal number and mentioning its suit, its number or colour. The winner is the first child to lay down all three of their cards. Play again, beginning with a new line of 10 cards.
Adult support is needed to run this activity.

playing cards

A2.c.3 Pairs of children

Pairs lay out a line of 20 playing cards. Each child takes turns to name a card, and their partner says its position, for example *three of hearts; sixth.* They then record this in a table with two columns headed 'Card' and 'Position'.
Childen keep playing until every card is recorded.
Adult support may be useful in running this activity with several pairs of children.

20 playing cards

Year 2 Block A2.d Activities

7.1 7 Ordering numbers

A2.d.1 A group of 6 or more children working in pairs

Children point to the multiples of 10 as they count in 10s up and down a 0–100 number line. *How do you know where to mark 45 on this line?* Agree that it fits in between 40 and 50 because it is greater than 40 but less than 50. *Is it closer to 40 or to 50, or in the middle?* Pairs mark it on their number line. Repeat for 41 and 49, asking which numbers they are near, then for the numbers between 41 and 49. Continue asking children to place numbers around the 'landmark' tens. Encourage them to talk about where they are placing their numbers using vocabulary such as closer to, greater than, less than, in between, near.
Adult support is needed to run this activity.

large 0-100 number line marked with multiples of 10 only for each pair

A2.d.2 Pairs of children

Pairs use only the digits 1, 9 and 0 to write different numbers less than 100. Each digit may not appear more than once in a number. Challenge them to demonstrate that they have found all the possibilities and write them in order, leaving wide gaps. They then find numbers in between each pair. There is one pair where this is not possible!

7.3 7 Ordering numbers

A2.d.3 A group of 6 or more children working in pairs

Discuss where to place 25 on a large 0–100 number line marked with 0, 50 and 100 only. *Is it nearer 0 or 50, or in the middle?* Pairs mark it on their number line. Repeat for 75, then discuss and mark 30, 40, 35. Continue asking children to place numbers on their number lines, building up the 'landmark' tens and using midpoints. Encourage them to talk about where they are placing their numbers using vocabulary such as closer to, greater than, less than, in between, near, half way.
Adult support is needed to run this activity.

large 0–100 number line marked with 0, 50 and 100 only for each pair

Maths Weekly Plan: Year 1 and 2

Block B2.a: Rehearse addition and subtraction facts for pairs that total up to 7 or 10
Block B2.b: Y1 Know addition facts for pairs that total up to 8; Y2 Add three 1-digit numbers

	Mental oral starter	Objectives	Main teaching	Activities: Group 1 Y1	Activities: Group 2 Y1	Activities: Group 3 Y2	Activities: Group 4 Y2	Plenary	Outcomes
Day 1	**Recognise and order months of the year.** Recite the sequence of **months** together. Shuffle month cards and peg on washing line at random. *We are going to put the months in order by making swaps*. Child can swap any two cards. Choose another child to do the same. Recite sequence again.	**Y1** • Begin to recognise that addition can be done in any order • Know by heart addition facts for pairs of numbers that total up to 7 • Relate number bonds to an understanding of addition, including use of +, −, = **Y2** • Rehearse addition and subtraction facts for pairs of numbers that total up to 10	**All** Show arrays of dots for numbers 1–6 on dominoes. Point to each and ask: ***How many***? Show 4. *What number goes with this to **make** 6? 4 and 2 make 6.* Rehearse **addition pairs**. Show 4+2 domino. *How many dots?* Cover the 2 dots. *How many now?* 6 **take away** 2 is 4. Rpt for 5+1. **Y1** Place 2 large dice on top of each other so that the hidden numbers on the touching faces **add** to 7. *The 2 hidden numbers add to 7. What could they be?* Write *7=_+_* on board. Write three possible sentences. Show the hidden faces. Rpt for other pairs to 7. **[ITR Y1 B2.a]**	Y1 B2.a.1 Using fingers to find pairs which total 5 T	Y1 1.2 p12 Completing additions totalling 6 and 7	Y2 2.2 p13 Adding two numbers to make 10	Y2 B2.a.2 Using dominoes and investigating ways of making 10 TA	Choose a child to throw a 1–6 dice. Write the score, eg 5. Children work out what number adds to the dice score to make 8, eg 3. They show this amount using fingers. *Who is the quickest?*	**Y1** • Practise adding two numbers totalling up to 7 • Use fingers to help solve simple additions **Y2** • Relate addition to subtraction • Add two numbers to make 10
Day 2	**Compare 1- and 2-digit numbers.** Play 'Stand up'. Give a number card 1–50 to each child. *Stand up if your number is **more than** 12.* Chn holding these cards stand up and show to everyone. Check numbers. Repeat activity using different vocabulary. Repeat activity using numbers 1–20 for Y1s.		**All** Show 0–10 number line. A child chooses a number card 1–10, eg 5. *What number adds to this to make 10?* Write *10=5+_*. Chn use fingers to find answer. Rpt for all the numbers, writing **number sentences** on board. Chant bonds to 10 together, folding down fingers to check. **Y2** Write numbers 0–12 on board. *Let's play a domino game, finding the **sum** of the dots on the touching ends.* Stick 1st domino on board. Child places 2nd at end of 1st. Say touching numbers. Chn say total. Write matching addition pair. Chant addition pairs for each **total** 0–12.	Y1 B2.a.3 7.1 7 Addition facts TA	Y1 B2.a.4 Finding ways of making 7p	Y2 B2.a.1 Playing Pelmanism, finding bonds to 10 T	Y2 2.2 p14 Adding pairs of numbers to make totals up to 10	Use two or more sets of dominoes. Remove ones with less than 4 dots or more than 9. Give each child a domino. Throw dice. If chn have the domino number that adds to the dice number to make 10, they get a cube. Rpt.	**Y1** • Practise adding two numbers totalling up to 7 • Use fingers to begin to learn bonds to 10 **Y2** • Use fingers to learn by heart bonds to 10 • Practise adding two small numbers
Day 3	**Add near doubles by doubling and adjusting.** Write *3+4* on board. Chn write total on whiteboards and show their answers. Hold up a tower of 3 cubes and a tower of 4 cubes. Demonstrate by removing a cube from the taller tower that 7 is **double** 3 and 1 more. Repeat.	**Y1** • Know by heart addition and subtraction facts for pairs of numbers that total up to 8 • Relate addition facts for pairs of numbers to an understanding of addition, including use of +, −, = and missing numbers	**All** Write a large *8* on board. *We are looking for pairs that make 8.* Write *8−1=_*. *8 less 1 is 7.* Write *7+1=_*. *7 and **1 more** is?* *8.* Repeat to generate 8−2=6, 6+2=8. *Let's play 'Snap'!* Use sets of number cards 0–8, looking for pairs that total 8. Play teacher against children! **Y2** Use number cards 1–20. Stick 4 and 6 on board. A child adds them: *10*. A child sticks a 3rd card beside 4 and 6. Add the 3rd number by **counting on** together from 10. Write total. Repeat, starting with 3 and 7 and adding a 3rd card. Continue. Chant the number bonds to 10.	Y1 1.2 p14 Finding addition pairs to make 8	Y1 B2.b.3 Creating towers of 8 bricks to find addition pairs that total 8 TA	Y2 2.2 p15 Adding three numbers, looking for 10s	Y2 B2.b.2 Adding three numbers using cards T	Using two sets of number cards 0–9, make several additions on the board. Ask Y1s to add two numbers with totals of 8 or less. Ask Y2s to add three numbers where two of them total 10.	**Y1** • Add two numbers totalling 8 • Learn bonds to 8 **Y2** • Add three numbers by finding bonds to 10 and counting on

	Mental oral starter	Objectives	Main teaching	Activities: Group 1 (Y1)	Activities: Group 2 (Y1)	Activities: Group 3 (Y2)	Activities: Group 4 (Y2)	Plenary	Outcomes
Day 4	**Subtract a 1-digit number from a 'teens' number, crossing 10.** Pairs each place a 0–20 number line in front of them. Write a **subtraction** on the board, eg *13−6=*. Pairs place a counter on the number lines to match the answer. Check their answers. Rpt for other subtractions.	*(Continued)* • Begin to use patterns of similar calculations (e.g. 10−0=10, 10−1=9, 10−2=8, …) **Y2** • Begin to add three 1-digit numbers mentally	**All** Draw 10-space track on board. Write a 3-number addition in each space, eg *6+4+7* (pair adds to 10). Make 2 teams. Stick 2 counters on start. Team A spins coin. If heads, they move counter 2 spaces. If tails, 1 space. They add their 3 numbers. Rpt, teams taking turns. **Y1** Show tray with 8 objects. Remove 1 object. Chn say missing object. *How many objects did we start with?* Write *8*. *How many have been taken?* Write *−1*. *How many left?* Discourage counting. Complete subtraction. Rpt for *8−2=6*. Arrange objects in relevant **patterns**, eg 4+4, 5+3.	Y1 B2.b.2 Colouring grids to partition 8 in different ways	Y1 B2.b.5 Using known number facts to complete additions	Y2 B2.b.3 Practising adding three numbers TA	Y2 2.2 p16 Practising adding three numbers	Draw 5×4 grid. Write column headings: *5, 6, 7, 8*. Below each heading, write addition pairs that total that number. Be systematic, eg *1+4, 2+3; 1+5, 2+4; 1+6, 2+5; 1+7, 2+6*. Complete the table together.	**Y1** • Add two numbers totalling up to 8 • Rehearse bonds to 10 **Y2** • Know bonds to 10 • Add three numbers by finding bonds to 10 and counting on
Day 5	**Recall addition pairs to 10.** Play 'Card pointing'. Pairs each place number cards 1–10 in order in front of them. Say a number, eg *8*. Pairs point to its partner to 10, eg 2. Repeat for different partners to 10. Extend by increasing the pace.		**All** Draw 10-space track on board. In each space, write missing-number sentence about number 8, eg *3+_=8, 8−_=6*. Make 2 teams. Stick 2 counters on start. Team A spins coin. If heads, move 2 spaces. If tails, 1 space. They say missing number. Rpt, teams taking turns. **Y2** Put 10 pegs on hanger. Partition in different ways to match bonds to 10. Push all the pegs to one end. Add 4 more pegs. Show that this is 10 and 4 more, making 14. Repeat, making 10 from 3 and 7, and then adding 6 more pegs. *6 and 10 is 16. We do not need to count on!*	Y1 B2.b.4 Playing 'Snap', looking for pairs that total 8 TA	Y1 1.2 p16 Completing an addition grid	Y2 B2.b.4 Generating additions of three 1-digit numbers, and finding totals T	Y2 B2.b.4 Generating additions of three 1-digit numbers, and finding totals T	Children work in threes. They each roll a dice once, and write the three numbers as an addition on whiteboards. They each write the numbers in a different order. *Do you all get the same total?*	**Y1** • Practise adding two 1-digit numbers • Learn bonds to 5, 6, 7, 8 and 10 **Y2** • Practise adding three numbers, looking for bonds to 10

Vocabulary
how many?
add, addition
addition pair
addition fact
make
sum
total
subtract, subtraction
subtraction fact
take away
number sentence
number pair
1 more
count on
pattern
month
more than, less than
double

Resources
month cards January–December
up to 20 pegs
washing line
at least two sets of dominoes
two large dice numbered 1–6
A3 paper
number cards 1–50
0–10 number line
Blu-tack
1p, 2p and 5p coins
playing cards
individual whiteboards
linking cubes in two colours
small Post-it notes
0–20 number lines (one per pair)
counters (one per pair)
tray
about four sheets of 2×4 grids drawn on squared paper
number cards 0–10 (one set per pair)
coat hanger
about 10 small dice numbered 1–6

Blocks B2.a and B2.b

Year 1 Block B2.a Activities

B2.a.1 A group of up to 8 children working in pairs

First rehearse the six additions of pairs of numbers making five, writing these on the flip chart: *0 + 5 = 5, 1 + 4 = 5, 2 + 3 = 5, 3 + 2 = 5, 4 + 1 = 5, 5 + 0 = 5*. Children now work in pairs and draw round each other's hands on A3 paper. They do this three times each, to give themselves six hands per pair. They now colour each hand using two colours, so that each set of five fingers matches one of the additions on the flip chart. For example, for the second addition above, children might colour one finger red and four fingers green.

Adult support may be useful in running this activity.

A3 paper

7.1 7 Addition facts

B2.a.3 A group of 6 or more children working in pairs

Show children a domino with a total of 6 spots. Write the corresponding number sentence on the board. *If I turn it round, what number sentence could I write now?* Ask children to work in pairs to find other dominoes with a total of 6 spots. They compare their findings with another pair.

Ask: *What's the biggest number of spots we could have on the left-hand side?* Agree that this is 6 and ask the children to place this domino at the top of their group of dominoes. Write *6 + 0 = 6* on the board. *What is the next biggest number we could have on the left?* Ask children to put this domino underneath the 6 + 0 one. Continue finding and recording number facts up to 3 + 3. For 2 + 4 = 6, suggest that they put their dominoes together with those of another pair, so that they have enough dominoes to continue the pattern. Continue finding pairs to make 6 and recording them on the board.

Discuss the patterns in the first and second numbers in the number sentences. Stress that ordering them like this ensures that we don't miss any.

Adult support is needed to run this activity.

set of dominoes per pair

B2.a.4 A group of 2 or 3 children

First rehearse the additions of pairs of numbers that make 7. Then each group explores how many ways of making 7p they can find using coins. Encourage them to show that they have them all.

Adult support may be useful in running this activity.

1p, 2p and 5p coins

Year 1 Block B2.b Activities

B2.b.2 A group of up to 8 children

First rehearse the additions of pairs of numbers that make 8. Children use two colours and try to find as many different ways of colouring their grids as they can. They may experiment with lots of different patterns. Collect up their grids as they do them, and categorise them under the headings of each addition. For example, a grid with 3 blue squares and 5 yellow is categorised under 3 + 5 = 8. Try to find at least one coloured grid to match each addition.

Adult support may be useful in running this activity.

set of 2 × 4 grids drawn on squared paper per child

B2.b.3 Pairs of children

First rehearse the additions of pairs of numbers that make 8. Children use linking cubes and build 2 × 2 × 2 cubes in two colours to match each addition. They explore how many different cubes they can make. For example, the cubes matching 1 + 7 = 8 might consist of one blue and seven yellow cubes. Try to find coloured cube arrangements that match each addition.

Adult support may be useful in running this activity.

linking cubes in two colours

B2.b.4 Groups of 5 or 6 children

Play 'Eight and Snap!'. Deal out all the cards. Children take turns to put a card face up in front of them, each forming a pile of cards face up. Before playing, a child must look around the other cards on the tops of all the piles. If the card they then play adds to make 8 when put with one of the other cards, they can say 'Snap!'. The owner of the matching card can also say 'Snap!'. The one who says it first takes both piles and adds them to their hand. When a child runs out of cards, they can pick up their pile and play it again. The winner is the person with the most cards when they decide to stop, or when one or two children have run completely out of cards!

Adult support may be useful in running this activity.

0–8 number cards, three sets per group

B2.b.5 Pairs of children

Children select a pair of cards from their sets of number cards that total 8, for example a 5 and a 3. They put these together and then choose another card to add. Each child then writes the addition, and they agree what the total is, for example *5 + 3 + 5 = 13*. Children then choose a different pair that total 8 and find a different third card. They write a new addition. They repeat this till they have included all five pairs that total eight (0 + 8, 1 + 7, 2 + 6, 3 + 5, 4 + 4) in their additions.

Adult support may be useful in running this activity.

two sets of 0–10 number cards

Year 2 Block B2.a Activities

B2.a.1 Groups of 4 children

Spread out four shuffled sets of 0–10 number cards face down to play Pelmanism. Children take turns to reveal two cards. They take and keep the pair of cards if the numbers add to 10. If not, they turn them back over and leave them in their places. Continue playing until all the cards have been taken.
Adult support may be useful in running this activity for several groups.

four sets of 0–10 number cards (or playing cards with the king and jack removed and queen = 0)

B2.a.2 A group of 8 children working in pairs

Pairs find as many different ways as they can of using two dominoes to make 10 and record them in a table; for example under the heading 2 + 8 = 10, they might record dominoes 1/1, 2/6; 0/2, 2/6; 1/1, 3/5; and so on.
Tell them that there are 35 ways altogether. Challenge pairs to collaborate with other pairs to find them all.
Adult support may be useful in running this activity.

dominoes for each pair

Year 2 Block B2.b Activities

B2.b.2 Groups of 4 children

Place a pack of four shuffled sets of 0–10 number cards face down in a pile. Children take turns to take three cards each without showing the others. They each add the cards in their hand, write the total on a Post-it and place it in view of the other children. When they have all done this, children lay down their cards, check each other's totals and record their own addition. The child with the total nearest to 10 takes a 10p coin. They return the cards to the bottom of the pile and each takes three more cards from the top to play another round.
Adult support may be useful in running this activity.

four sets of 0–10 number cards (or playing cards with the king and jack removed and queen = 0); small Post-it notes

B2.b.3 Pairs of children

Children select from a set of digit cards a pair of cards that totals 10, for example 7 and 3. They put these together and then choose another card to add. Each child then writes the addition and they agree the total, for example *7 + 3 + 5 = 15*. They repeat the activity until they have used all six pairs that total 10 (0 + 10, 1 + 9, 2 + 8, 3 + 7, 4 + 6, 5 + 5).
Adult support may be useful in running this activity with several pairs of children.

0–9 digit cards per pair

B2.b.4 Groups of 3 children

Place a shuffled set of 1–9 digit cards face down in a pile. Children take turns to pick up the top card until they have three cards each. They each find and record their total, for example *3 + 5 + 9 = 17*, then check each other's totals. If in doubt, use a calculator. The child whose total lies in between the largest and smallest totals collects a counter. Collect up the cards and play again. The winner is the child who collects the most counters.

0–9 digit cards per group of 3; counters

Maths Weekly Plan: Year 1 and 2

Block B2.c: Y1 Describe position; Y2 Recognise right angles
Block B2.d: Y1 Describe direction/movement; Y2 Recognise clockwise/anticlockwise turns;

	Mental oral starter	Objectives	Main teaching	Activities: Group 1 Y1	Activities: Group 2 Y1	Activities: Group 3 Y2	Activities: Group 4 Y2	Plenary	Outcomes
Day 1	**Order a set of numbers up to 20.** Shuffle number cards 1–20. Ask 5 chn to take a card each. Blu-tack the cards in a line on the board. *Which number is **smallest**?* Chn write it on their whiteboards. On *Show me*, chn reveal number. Rpt for **next smallest**, and so on. Rpt with a new set of numbers.	**Y1** • Describe position: above, below, beside, left, right **Y2** • Recognise whole, half and quarter turns • Know that a right angle is a measure of a quarter turn • Recognise right angles in simple shapes	**All** Show 100-square. Point to numbers 1–30 as chn say them. Point to number in 2nd row, eg 17. Ask questions about position, eg *Which number is **above**/**below** it?* Rpt for eg 13. Choose a number, eg 9. Chn make statements about it, eg *9 is to the **right** of 8.* **[ITR Y1 B2.c]** **Y2** Set analogue clock to 12. Rotate minute hand to 3. *The long hand has made a **quarter turn**.* Rotate to 6, …9, …12. Show **half turn**. Show that 1 half turn is 2 quarter turns; 1 **whole turn** is 2 half turns or 4 quarter turns. Show quarter turns: *1 **right angle,** 2 right angles, …*	Y1 B2.c.1 Placing counters on a grid according to position TA	Y1 1.2 p18 Identifying numbers on a grid by their position	Y2 B2.c.1 Creating right-angle measurers from card strips T	Y2 2.2 p19 Identifying right angles in shapes	Show a large 100-square. Explain that you will be using numbers 1–30 only. Play 'I am thinking of a number'. Give clues to a mystery number, eg *It is to the **left** of 15, and below 2.* Chn make guesses.	**Y1** • Describe position using above, below, left, right **Y2** • Identify right angles as quarter turns • Make several quarter turns
Day 2	**Say a number which comes between two other numbers.** Each child writes a number between 5 and 19 on their whiteboard. Shuffle a set of number cards 1–20 and place them face down. 2 chn take a card each, and show the class. Chn who have a number in **between** the card numbers get a cube.		**All** Give each child a sheet of paper. Model folding it in half. Children copy this. *The folded edge can be used to test for **straight lines**.* Demonstrate using it to test the edge of the table. Model folding the paper in half again. Children copy this. *The folded corner can be used to test for **square corners**.* Model using it to test the corner of a book. *Square corners are called right angles.* Children test items in the classroom to find right angles. Show that some angles are **less than** a right angle, and some are **more than** a right angle. Show **right-angled turns** on an analogue clock. **[ITR Y2 B2.c]**	Y1 1.2 p17 Identifying shapes on a grid by their position	Y1 B2.c.2 Finding combinations of 9-counter arrangements on a 3 × 3 grid T	Y2 B2.c.2 Sorting shapes with right angles	Y2 B2.c.3 Drawing shapes with right angles TA	On the board, draw a shape with 1 right angle, eg right-angled triangle. Ask a child to point to right angle. Test it using right-angle tester. Highlight in different colour. Continue like this, drawing shapes with 2 or 3 right angles.	**Y1** • Find positions on a grid according to descriptions • Begin to identify right angles **Y2** • Identify right angles • Identify right angles in shapes
Day 3	**Position 2-digit numbers on a number line.** On the board, draw a 20-point number line with marks for 10s and 5s clearly shown. Label 0 and 100. Use pencil to point to a position on line. Chn write matching number on their whiteboards. On *Show me*, chn reveal answers.	**Y1** • Describe direction and movement: forwards, backwards, up, down, left, right • Make whole turns, half turns and quarter turns • Talk about things that turn	**All** Hold 2 triangles behind your back, 1 with right-angle, 1 without. A child chooses a hand. Show the triangle. *Does it have a right angle?* Show the other. *Any right angles?* Draw 2 shapes on board, 1 with right angle, 1 without. *Which one has a right angle?* Rpt. **Y1** Lay out large 0–20 number track. Ask a child to stand on 0, then walk slowly to 20. Chn say the numbers as child steps on them. Rpt with a child walking back from 20 to 0. Ask a child to stand on 7. *She will walk **forwards** 3 spaces. What number will she end on?* Rpt.	Y1 B2.d.1 Listening to and acting on a series of instructions T	Y1 B2.c.3 Colouring squares on a grid according to position	Y2 B2.c.4 Creating right-angle prints using crayon TA	Y2 B2.c.6 Using a card right angle to draw shapes with a given number of right angles	Select an object in the room, eg a table. Describe the **position** of something else in relation to the table, eg *The bin is below the table.* Ask chn to make their own statements about the position of objects relative to the table.	**Y1** • Understand and use the vocabulary of direction: forwards, backwards, up, down, left and right **Y2** • Identify right angles • Draw right angles in shapes

	Mental oral starter	Objectives	Main teaching	Group 1 Y1	Group 2 Y1	Group 3 Y2	Group 4 Y2	Plenary	Outcomes
Day 4	**Subtract a multiple of 10 from a multiple of 10.** Pairs each write four multiples of 10 between 0 and 100 on their whiteboards. Write a **subtraction** of a multiple of 10 from a multiple of 10, eg *70–30*. Chn find answer. If they have the answer written, they cross it out. First pair to cross off all numbers wins.	*(Continued)* **Y2** • Recognise whole, half and quarter turns • Know that a right angle is a measure of a quarter turn • Recognise right angles in simple shapes • Give instructions for moving along a route in straight lines and round corners • Recognise clockwise and anticlockwise turns	**All** Draw 5x5 grid on board. Insert letters of alphabet in sequence, A–Y. Highlight one of the letters, eg Q. *Start at Q and move **up** 3 spaces. Which letter do you land on?* Chn say letter. Give similar one-step instructions. Continue giving instructions. **[ITR Y1 B2.d]** **Y2** Show **clockwise/anticlockwise** turns on clock. Turn minute hand from 12 to 3. *What **direction** did it turn? What **angle** did it turn through?* Turn anticlockwise to 9. Rpt questions. *If we turn clockwise through 2 right angles from 9, what number will it point to?* **[ITR Y2 B2.d]**	Y1 1.2 p19 Finding a route along a track T	Y1 B2.d.3 Completing a sequence of instructions for a programmable toy TA	Y2 2.2 p20 Identifying clockwise and anticlockwise turns	Y2 B2.d.3 Following instructions to draw routes T	Children stand in a space and raise one arm straight up in the air. *Imagine your arm is a hand of a clock. It is pointing to 12.* Give turning instructions, eg *Turn your arm anticlockwise through 3 right angles.*	**Y1** • Follow directions • Use directions to describe locations on a grid **Y2** • Understand and use the terms clockwise and anticlockwise
Day 5	**Recall addition and subtraction facts for numbers up to 10.** Play 'Fan-tastic'. Write 10 **additions** and subtractions on board. Target for Y1s and Y2s. Point to one. Chn work out the answer and show using number fans. They check using fingers. Rpt for each calculation. Extend by saying calculations.		**All** Chn each stand in a space. They make turns together as you give instructions, eg *Turn clockwise through 1 right angle; turn anticlockwise through 2 right angles.* Give **movement** instructions, eg *Walk 2 paces **towards** me.* Rpt with different instructions. **Y2** Chn stay in large space. Clarify forward and **backward** movements. Clarify left and right directions by asking chn to hold out their right arm. Introduce **sideways** movements. Finally introduce a sequence of movements. Discuss **opposite directions**.	Y1 B2.d.4 Drawing a route according to instructions T	Y1 1.2 p20 Finding a route and identifying positions on a grid	Y2 B2.d.2 Using clocks to identify turns TA	Y2 2.2 p21 Identifying clockwise and anticlockwise turns	Draw 8x8 grid. Use Blu-Tack to stick a plastic/ card object in any square. Describe movement, eg *Move **upwards** 3 spaces.* Choose a child to move the object. Rpt.	**Y1** • Draw a route according to directions **Y2** • Understand and use the terms clockwise and anticlockwise • Recognise and identify right angles

Vocabulary
position
above
below
beside
right
left
whole turn
half turn
quarter turn
right-angled turn
right angle
less/more than a right angle
angle
straight line
square corner
direction
opposite direction
movement
forwards
backwards
sideways
up, upwards
down, downwards
towards
clockwise
anticlockwise
order
smallest, next smallest
largest
between
subtraction
addition

Resources
number cards 1–20
Blu-tack
individual whiteboards
large 100-square
analogue clock with moveable hands
about four large blank 3 × 3 grids
large coloured counters
small coloured counters
a long strip of card about 1·5 cm wide
split-pin paper fasteners
cubes
sheets of paper
about 10 card right angles
variety of plastic/card shapes, including irregular hexagons or pentagons with right angles
two plastic/card triangles, one with a right angle and one without
large 0–20 number track to lay on the floor
access to large space such as hall or playground
about 12 blank 4 × 4 grids
coloured felt-tipped pens
wax crayons
programmable toy
squared paper
number fans (one per child)
about five clock-faces with moveable hands for children to use

Year 1 Block B2.c Activities

B2.c.1 A group of up to 8 children working in pairs

Stick a large red counter in one of the spaces on the grid on the board. Ask pairs to place a matching counter in that space on their grid. Check that they are all correct. Place a large blue counter in another space and ask children to match it. Ask one pair to describe where their blue counter is in relation to the red, for example *It is up one square and one square to the right.* Check whether they are correct on the board. Place a third coloured counter on the grid for children to match with a counter. Ask a pair to describe the position of this counter in relation to one of the other counters, and check. Then move one of the counters, describing the move, for example *We will move red along one and down two.* Children do the same with their counter, describing the move. Keep going like this.
Adult support may be useful in running this activity.

large 3 × 3 blank grid per pair and one on the board; large coloured counters; pile of coloured counters per pair; Blu-tack

B2.c.2 Pairs of children

Ask each pair to place three red, three blue and three yellow counters on their grid so that there is a red, a blue and a yellow counter in each row and in each column. They work together to do this, giving positional instructions: *Try putting a blue counter two to the right of that yellow,* and so on. How many different ways of arranging the counters are there so that there is always one of each colour in each row and each column?

Adult support may be useful in running this activity.

3 × 3 blank grid per pair; coloured counters in three colours per pair

B2.c.3 A group of up to 12 children working in pairs

Children listen as you give instructions as to how to colour their grid, for example *Colour the top square in the left corner red. Move one to the right and down two, and colour that square green, …* When children have coloured six or seven squares according to your instructions, compare them and check that they are all the same. Then give each child a new grid, and ask each pair to work together, giving each other instructions to help them colour a new pattern on their grid. Their instructions must be clear and relate to the last square coloured, for example *Move one to the left and up three.*
Adult support may be useful in running this activity.

two 4 × 4 grids per child; coloured felt-tipped pens

Year 1 Block B2.d Activities

B2.d.1 A group of up to 8 children

Take a group of children into the hall or playground. Explain that you are going to give each other instructions to proceed forwards or backwards, left or right. Choose one child at a time to come out to the front and face the remaining children. This child gives instructions to the remaining children, for example *Walk three steps forwards. Turn left. Take four steps backwards. Turn left again. Jump five times on the spot.* Choose each child in turn to give instructions.
Adult support may be useful in running this activity.

access to hall or playground

B2.d.3 A group of up to 12 children working in pairs

Ask pairs of children to write a short program. Provide cards which they can adapt or select. For example *_ steps forward; _ steps backward; _ steps left; _ steps right; 1 whole turn;* $\frac{1}{2}$ *turn;* $\frac{1}{4}$ *turn.*
Children use these cards and adapt the numbers and repeat instructions to create an 8- or 10-line program.
Each pair in turn has a go at entering their program on the toy. If there is no programmable toy, children could deliver their program as a sequence of instructions for an adult to follow.
Adult support may be useful in running this activity.

programmable toy or turtle

B2.d.4 A group of up to 8 children

Explain that you are going to give a series of instructions and that children are going to draw a route on their grid. Give simple instructions: *Everyone start in the top left square. Draw a line three squares along. Now go down one square. Then go right three squares, …*
After three or four instructions, children compare their routes.
Adult support may be useful in running this activity.

4 × 4 grid per child; felt-tipped pens

Year 2 Block B2.c Activities

B2.c.1 A group of up to 8 children

Show children how to construct an angle-maker. Cut two roughly equal lengths from a long strip of card and colour one red and one blue. Place one strip on top of the other and use a split pin to fasten them close to one end. Demonstrate how to rotate the strips to make different angles. When they each have an angle measurer, children place it so that the red strip is vertical and the blue strip runs horizontally. Check that everyone has done this. Children can then use the inside edges of their strips as 'rulers' and draw a right angle on their page. Practise doing this.
Adult support is needed to run this activity.

a long strip of card about 1·5 cm wide; split pin paper fasteners

B2.c.2 Pairs of children

Give each child a card right angle. Pairs use their right angles to sort a variety of 2D shapes into two piles, those with a right angle and those without. They draw round all the shapes that have at least one right angle. Remind children to count the sides to help them name each shape.
Adult support may be useful in running this activity with several pairs.

card right angle for each child; variety of card or plastic 2D shapes for each pair including irregular hexagons or pentagons with right angles

B2.c.3 Pairs of children

Give each child a card right angle. The card should be thick enough for children to draw along its sides and produce straight lines. Children use their card to draw a right angle. They then use a ruler to draw some more straight lines incorporating their right angle into a shape with straight sides (a polygon), for example a rectangle, a triangle, a hexagon. Pairs compare their shapes, count the sides and agree their names. Repeat the activity, drawing as many shapes as possible that contain at least one right angle.

card right angle for each child

B2.c.4 A group of up to 8 children

Provide each child with a card right angle. Children use their card to produce a right angle by crayoning over the edges of the two sides of the card and making a print. Encourage them to keep the crayon lines short and very close together at right angles to the card so that there will be straight edges to their crayoning when they lift the card and reveal a perfect right angle! Children repeat this using several different colours.
Adult support may be useful in running this activity.

card right angle for each child; wax crayons

B2.c.6 Pairs of children

Children use a card right angle to draw shapes with only one right angle. Then they draw shapes with only two right angles, then only three right angles… Children cut out the shapes for display.

card right angle (as in B2.c.2) for each child

Year 2 Block B2.d Activities

B2.d.2 Pairs of children

Give each child a clock-face with moveable hands. Children set the hands to an o'clock time, for example 4 o'clock, and write down the time, for example *4:00*. Ask them to imagine turning the big hand through four clockwise right-angle turns. They discuss in pairs what time the clock will then say and write down their guess. Children then turn the big hand through four right angles in a clockwise direction and see if they were correct. Repeat this activity starting at different times and then turning the big hand through four right-angle turns in an anticlockwise direction.
Adult support may be useful in running this activity.

clock-face for each child

B2.d.3 A group of 4, 6 or 8 children

Give each child a piece of squared paper and a bright felt-tipped pen. Explain to children that you are going to give them a series of instructions for drawing a route on squared paper. Give simple instructions using the words: up, down, along, turn, clockwise, anticlockwise. Children must draw what they hear you say, for example *Draw a line up the page along four squares. Stop, turn clockwise through one right angle and draw a short line along three squares. Stop, turn clockwise through one right angle and draw a line along six squares. Then turn clockwise again through one right angle and draw a line seven squares long.* Pairs compare drawings. Repeat the activity, making the instructions more complicated.
Adult support is needed to run this activity.

squared paper; felt-tipped pens

Maths Weekly Plan: Year 1 and 2

Block C2.a: Estimate, measure and compare weights
Block C2.b: Y1 Measure weights; Y2 Read the time to the hour and half hour

	Mental oral starter	Objectives	Main teaching	Activities: Group 1 Y1	Activities: Group 2 Y1	Activities: Group 3 Y2	Activities: Group 4 Y2	Plenary	Outcomes
Day 1	**Recognise and say ordinal numbers.** Play 'Birdsong'. Divide class into three groups, eg robins, blackbirds, sparrows. Choose a group to start 'singing' the **ordinal** numbers: ***First*, *second*, *third*, …** After a few counts, 2nd group takes over, then 3rd, until they reach ***twentieth***. Rpt, starting with a different group.	**Y1** • Compare two or more weights by direct comparison **Y2** • Estimate, measure and compare weights using standard units: kilograms, grams • Begin to recognise the relationship between grams and kilograms • Begin to read simple weighing scales to the nearest labelled division	**All** Seat chn in circle. Hold up a **heavy** object, eg a hardback book. *This is heavy.* Hold up a **light** object. *This is not heavy. It is light.* Show chn **bucket balance**. *We can use this to find out which of the two objects is* ***heavier***. Demonstrate. *The bucket with the heavier object goes* ***down***. Choose another pair of objects to demonstrate. Pass the heavy book around. *Let's see* ***how many*** *bricks* ***balance*** *the book.* Count the bricks. Write: *The book* ***weighs*** *14 bricks*. Rpt for different objects. **Compare weights**. *Which weighs most? Which is* ***heaviest***?	Y1 C2.a.1 Comparing two objects by weight (T)	Y1 1.2 p21 Comparing two objects by weight	Y2 C2.a.1 Estimating and weighing objects (TA)	Y2 2.2 p23 Reading scales to say weights	Investigate how many bricks have a total weight of 1 kg. Take **estimates**. Place a 1 kg weight in one bucket of a balance. Count bricks as you add them. Compare results with children's estimates.	**Y1** • Compare objects by weight • Use correct vocabulary, for example heavier, lighter, balance, weigh **Y2** • Estimate and weigh objects
Day 2	**Order a set of 2-digit numbers.** Play 'Swapping'. Ask six chn to stand in a line facing the class. Shuffle number cards 1–50. Give one card to each of the six chn. Challenge the rest of the chn to rearrange the six chn into **order**, **smallest** to **largest**, by making swaps. Rpt for another set of six chn.		**All** Seat chn in circle. Put three objects in the centre. *We will compare their weights.* Pass objects round for chn to estimate which they think is the heaviest/**lightest**. Weigh the objects, showing how the bucket goes down with the heaviest. Rpt for three other objects. **Y2** Write ***kilogram, kg*** and ***gram, g***. *These are shorthand.* Chn feel 1 kg and 100 g weights. *Which is* ***lighter****/heavier?* Put 100 g weights in bucket until they balance 1 kg. Count: *100 g, 200 g, … 1 kg. 10 × 100 g = 1 kg.* Weigh different objects, counting 100 g weights as you add them.	Y1 1.2 p21 Comparing two objects by weight	Y1 C2.a.3 Ordering a small set of objects by weight (TA)	Y2 C2.a.2 Estimating and measuring weights of objects, then placing in weight order (T)	Y2 C2.a.2 Estimating and measuring weights of objects, then placing in weight order (T)	Count together in units of 100 g up to 1 kg: *one hundred grams, two hundred grams, … one kilogram.* Emphasise that 10 hundreds equal 1 thousand, and that 1 kg = 1000 g.	**Y1** • Order objects according to weight **Y2** • Order objects according to weight • Measure weight in kilograms and grams
Day 3	**Find totals of sets of coins.** Place several of each type of **coin** (1p, 2p, 5p, 10p) in a bag. Ask a child to take a coin. Other chn hold up the matching number of fingers. Rpt. All chn who have 1p coins stand together. *How much* ***altogether***? Chn show with their fingers. Rpt for 2p, 5p.		**All** *What happens if two objects weigh the* ***same***? *The buckets stay level.* Find the weight of a packet of biscuits, using linking cubes as the unit. Chn estimate first. After **measuring**, write a label and put it next to the biscuits, eg *15 cubes*. Rpt for other objects. **Y2** Hold up **weighing scales**. Draw large version of **reading scale** on board. Discuss how to read the labelled and unlabelled **divisions**. Put 1 kg weight on scales. Check reading. Add 100 g weights until you reach 2 kg. Show bag of sugar. *How heavy?* Measure together.	Y1 C2.b.1 Weighing shoes using pens as units (TA)	Y1 1.2 p22 Weighing classroom objects using cubes as units	Y2 C2.a.4 Finding sets of three objects with a combined weight of 1 kg (T)	Y2 53 Reading different types of scale	Challenge chn to suggest two objects that weigh the same, eg two identical books. Check by weighing them using a bucket balance.	**Y1** • Estimate and weigh objects using non-standard units **Y2** • Read a set of scales • Estimate and weigh objects using standard units

	Mental oral starter	Objectives	Main teaching	Activities: Group 1 (Y1)	Activities: Group 2 (Y1)	Activities: Group 3 (Y2)	Activities: Group 4 (Y2)	Plenary	Outcomes
Day 4	**Recognise half-way numbers, for example between 60 and 70.** Play 'Half-way'. Write two multiples of 10 on the board. Chn decide what number is **half-way between** them, and show it using their fans. Start with numbers that are 20 apart. Progress to 40 apart, then 10 apart, then 30 apart.	**Y1** • Measure weights using uniform non-standard units (whole and half) • Estimate then measure weights, recording estimates **Y2** • Read the time to the hour and half hour on analogue and 12-hour digital clocks	**Y2** Rehearse reading the **time** on an **analogue clock**. Emphasise the positions of **long** (**hour**) **hand** and **short** (**minute**) **hand**. Set clock to a **half-past** time. Show **digital** clock. Set it to 2 **o'clock**. Write *02:00* on board. Emphasise meaning of **digits**. Set to 02:30. *The 30 shows that it is half past.* Child rotates hands of analogue clock to show matching time. Continue advancing both analogue and digital clocks in half hour intervals. Set the clocks to various half-past times and match to events during the day. **[ITR Y2 C2.b]**	Y1 1.2 p22 Weighing classroom objects using cubes as units	Y1 C2.b.2 Ordering a small set of potatoes by weighing them using crayons as units TA	Y2 2.2 p24 Matching analogue and digital times	Y2 C2.b.2 Working out time intervals T	Choose a child to set an analogue clock to show a half-past time. Chn write the matching digital time on their whiteboards. Check answers. Rpt for different half-past times.	**Y1** • Estimate and weigh objects using non-standard units • Order objects according to weight **Y2** • Tell the time to the hour and half hour on analogue and digital clocks
Day 5	**Read analogue clocks (half past).** Play 'Clock pointing'. Each child places a Clock board (Y2 PCM 117) in front of them. *Show me half past one.* Chn point to the matching clock. Repeat several times, varying instructions.		**All** Rehearse o'clock and half-past times on analogue clock. Set to 4:00. Slowly advance to 4:30, then 5:00. Then turn from 5:00 to 5:15. Use intersecting card circles to model quarter turns. *What time is it?* (**nearly** half/quarter past…). *Now it's time for some weighing!* **Y1** A child counts 20 cubes into one side of a bucket balance. *Let's find objects **heavier than** 20 cubes.* Chn choose objects and weigh them to check. Extend to looking for objects that are **almost exactly** the same weight as 20 cubes. Then find objects **lighter than** 20 cubes.	Y1 C2.b.3 Weighing and ordering a large set of objects T	Y1 C2.b.3 Weighing and ordering a large set of objects T	Y2 C2.b.1 Guessing times, setting analogue clock to match, then comparing to digital clock TA	Y2 2.2 p25 Telling analogue and digital times	Play 'Guess the weight'. Choose an object. Choose a unit. Chn write an estimate of the object's weight in the given unit. They then measure it using a bucket balance. Whose estimate is the **closest**?	**Y1** • Estimate and weigh objects using non-standard units • Order objects according to weight **Y2** • Tell the time to the hour and half hour on analogue and digital clocks

Vocabulary
heavy, heavier (than), heaviest
light, lighter (than), lightest
the same
bucket balance
up, down
how many?
how heavy?
balance
weigh
weight
estimate
close, closest
kilogram, kg
gram, g
measure
weighing scales
reading scale
divisions
time
clock
analogue
digital, digits
long (hour) hand
short (minute) hand
o'clock
half past
nearly
almost exactly
about
ordinal
first, second, third, … twentieth
order
smallest
largest
coin
pence
amount
total
altogether
half-way between

Resources
bucket balance
plastic bricks
variety of fruit and vegetables
about four 1 kg weights
a shoe and things to fill it with, e.g. interlocking cubes, rice, beads, plastic 10 g weights
number cards 1–50
ten 100 g weights
about 16 slippers, shoes or boots
items of food for weighing, e.g. packets of biscuits, tins, jam
linking cubes
1p, 2p, 5p and 10p coins
bag
weighing scales
bag of sugar
large felt-tipped pens
number fans (one per child)
analogue clock with moveable hands
digital clock
crayons
about 12 potatoes of different weights
small coloured stickers
clock-face stamp
individual whiteboards
Clock boards (Y2 PCM 117)
intersecting card circles
about 12 small toys
labels
about four analogue clock-faces for children to use

Year 1 Block C2.a Activities

C2.a.1 A group of up to 8 children

Pass round the fruits and/or vegetables. Children feel each one. Ask them to decide which is the heaviest and which is the lightest. They should discuss this, and try to agree. Record some suggestions with names. Put the object the children think is lightest on the balances. Try every other object against it. *Do the others all make their side go down? If so, this object is the lightest!* Repeat this, now trying the object the children think is heaviest. If time, repeat to find the next heaviest.

Adult support may be useful in running this activity.

bucket balance; a variety of fruit and vegetables, for example apples, pears, potatoes, carrots, etc.

C2.a.3 A group of 8 children working in pairs

Explain that children need to place their set of shoes in an estimated order lightest to heaviest, for example the slipper with the red bobble is lightest, the green shoe is next lightest, etc. Ask each pair to weigh their shoes: they choose the shoe they believe to be heaviest and weigh all the others against this. Were they correct? Now repeat with the next heaviest, and so on. How does the real order compare with their estimated order?

Adult support may be useful in running this activity.

bucket balance per pair; selection of at least four different slippers, shoes, boots, etc. per pair

Year 1 Block C2.b Activities

C2.b.1 A group of up to 9 children in groups of 3

Tell the groups they are going to weigh each child's shoe. In turn, they remove a shoe and weigh it, using the pens. They record their results. Come back together as a large group, and discuss the weights of their shoes. *Which shoe is the heaviest of all? Do we have to weigh it to find out? No, we can look at our weights – the number of pens it weighs. It weighs more pens than any other.* Repeat for the lightest shoe of all.

Adult support may be useful in running this activity.

bucket balance and lots of fat felt-tipped pens per group of three

C2.b.2 A group of up to 9 children in groups of 3

Give each group four potatoes. Their task is to place them in order of weight, heaviest to lightest. They weigh each potato using crayons. Discuss whether it takes an exact number of crayons to balance each potato. *For some potatoes, we may need to use a half crayon to get an exact balance.* Write each weight in crayons on a sticker to label the potato, for example *12 $\frac{1}{2}$ crayons*. Come back together as a large group, and discuss the weights of their potatoes. *Which potato is the heaviest of all? Do we have to weigh it to find out? No, we can look at our weights – the number of crayons it weighs. It weighs more crayons than any other.* Repeat for the lightest potato of all.

Adult support may be useful in running this activity.

bucket balance; lots of crayons; four potatoes of different weights per group; small coloured stickers

C2.b.3 A whole class investigation, working in pairs or 3s

With the whole class watching, pin or stick a name label to each toy, for example 'pterodactyl', 'brown teddy', 'fluffy dog', etc. Then pass around the toys for each group to weigh using their cubes. Warn children that they need to think of a way of recording what each object weighs. Explain that every group should place the objects in order from heaviest to lightest. The challenge is for children to record the weights in some way so that they can order the toys. Allow 20 minutes or so for weighing, then take feedback as a class. Try to agree which toy is the heaviest, then which is the next heaviest, and so on. Study how each group chose to approach this task, especially the recording of results.

Adult support is needed to run this activity.

bucket balance and lots of cubes per two or three children; about 12 small toys, for example beanie babies, plastic dinosaurs, small dolls, teddies, etc.; labels

Year 2 Block C2.a Activities

C2.a.1 A group of up to 8 children

Show children a shoe full of interlocking cubes. Pass it round, then pass round a kilogram weight. *Do you think the shoe is less heavy or more heavy (heavier) than the kilogram weight?* Allow each child to feel both, then to decide and record their opinion. Place the shoe and the weight one on each side of the balances. Discuss which is heavier. Tip out the cubes and repeat the exercise filling the shoe with rice, sand, beads, weights…

Adult support is needed to run this activity.

1 kg weight; a shoe and things to fill it with, for example interlocking cubes, rice, sand, beads, plastic 10 g weights

C2.a.2 A whole class investigation with children working in pairs

Organise a collection of a wide variety of food for weighing, for example packets of biscuits, tins, butter, tubs of margarine, sugar, jam, yogurts, potatoes, apples. Children work in pairs or threes with a bucket-balance and interlocking cubes to help order the foods from lightest to heaviest. Talk about how to estimate before measuring and recording the weight of each food item: agree and draw up a suitable whole-class chart positioned so that each group can come and record the weights of their items. As they weigh, encourage children to use any weights printed on packets to compare their set of food items, for example *This butter weighs 250 grams and this sugar weighs 500 g, so the sugar weighs more*. Some children may be able to use the given weights to predict the weight in cubes, for example *This yogurt weighs 100 g or 42 cubes. So the margarine weighing 200 g will need double the number of cubes – 84.*

Finally bring the class together and arrange all the items of foods in order of weight. Discuss the results. *Is the largest item the heaviest? Is the smallest the lightest? What types of food are heavy/light for their size?*

Adult support is needed to run this activity.

bucket-balance; interlocking cubes and items of food for each group

C2.a.4 Groups of 3 children

Children use a balance and a kilogram weight to find three objects that together weigh 1 kg. To make weighing easier, suggest that they tape or tie the three objects together. Repeat for a different set of three objects.

Adult support may be useful in running this activity.

bucket-balance and 1 kg weight for each group

Year 2 Block C2.b Activities

C2.b.1 A group of up to 8 children working in pairs

Give each pair an analogue clock-face. Set a time on the digital clock and do not show children. Give them a clue to guess your time, for example *My time is half way between seven o'clock and eight o'clock*. Each pair discusses the time and agrees how to set it on their analogue clock-face. Show children the digital clock. *Does this digital time match the time on your clock-face?* Together tell the time, using both analogue and digital. Discuss what children might be doing at that time in the day. Repeat the process for a different digital time.

Adult support is needed to run this activity.

large digital clock; analogue clock-faces for each pair

C2.b.2 Pairs of children

Each child uses digital notation to write a time. They use a clock stamp to print a clock-face next to their time. They look at their partner's digital time and draw/write its matching analogue clock time on the clock-face. Challenge each child to work out how long it is from the earlier time to the later and then check the answer with their partner's. Repeat this six times.

clock-face stamp

Maths Weekly Plan: Year 1 and 2

Block C2.c: Y1 Read time on an analogue clock; Y2 Create and interpret block graphs
Block C2.d: Organise and interpret information in simple tables and pictograms

	Mental oral starter	Objectives	Main teaching	Activities: Group 1 Y1	Group 2 Y1	Group 3 Y2	Group 4 Y2	Plenary	Outcomes
Day 1	**Add a 1-digit number to a 'teens' number not crossing 20.** Chn place their number line in front of them. Say an **addition**. Chn place a counter on their number line to show their total. Check answers. Rpt for different additions.	**Y1** • Read the time to the hour on analogue clocks **Y2** • Sort, organise and interpret information in a block graph	**All** Show **analogue clock**. Demo that it has 2 hands: a **long hand** and **short hand**. Set to 1 **o'clock**. *The short hand points at 1; the long hand points at 12.* Say time together. Rpt for 2 o'clock. Set clock to other o'clock times. Chn say time. Stress need to check hand positions. **Y2** Write **title** *Cube colours*. Draw rectangular **grid**. **Label horizontal axis** *Colour*. Headings: *blue, red, green, yellow*. Label **vertical axis** *Number*. Headings: *1, 2, 3, … 10*. Chn choose cube from bag and shade square on grid to build a **graph**. *What does this* ***block graph*** *tell us?*	Y1 C2.c.1 Matching daily events to o'clock times TA	Y1 1.2 p24 Matching o'clock times to real events	Y2 C2.c.1 Drawing a block graph of letters in names T	Y2 2.2 p27 Creating block graphs	Divide the class into two teams, giving teams 6 number cards from a set of 1–12. Do not look at the cards yourself. Set an o'clock time. The team with the matching card collects a cube.	**Y1** • Tell the time to the hour on analogue clocks • Identify different times of day **Y2** • Draw a simple block graph • Interpret a simple block graph
Day 2	**Find a number in between two other numbers less than 20.** Chn choose a number between 5 and 19. Place number cards 1–20 face down. Two chn each take a card. Show to class. Point at both numbers on number line. Chn choose a number that comes in between these two numbers.		**All** Write title *Class bedtimes*. Draw grid. Horizontal axis: *Bedtimes*. Headings: *7, 7:30, 8, 8:30*. Vertical axis: *Number of children*. Headings: *1, 2, 3, … We're making a block graph to show what time we go to bed.* Colour a square for each child's bedtime. Interpret graph. **Y1** Chant o'clock times. *What time do you wake up?* Ask child to set analogue clock to 7 o'clock. Show this to the class. *Is the long hand pointing at 12? Is the short hand pointing at 7?* Rpt for different times. Discuss times when chn will be asleep. **[ITR Y1 C2.c]**	Y1 1.2 p23 Drawing o'clock times on analogue clocks	Y1 C2.c.4 Setting clock times for start and finish of TV programmes T	Y2 C2.c.2 Drawing a block graph of domino totals TA	Y2 p9 Interpreting block graphs	Each child chooses a coloured cube. They make a human block graph by lining up in 4 **columns**, 1 for each colour. Ensure **rows** are clearly distinct. *We have made a block graph.* Ask questions to interpret the graph.	**Y1** • Tell the time to nearest hour • Identify o'clock times of daily events, e.g. lunch, bedtime **Y2** • Draw a simple block graph • Interpret a simple block graph
Day 3	**Recall doubles of numbers 1–20.** Play 'Ping-pong'. Say a number up to 20. (Y1s 1–10, Y2s 10–20). Chn respond with the number's **double**. Start slowly and gradually increase the pace. Occasionally say *Ping* to which their response is *Pong*.	**Y1** • Organise information in simple lists, tables, pictograms or block graphs • Interpret information from simple lists, tables, pictograms or block graphs	**All** Place 4 different types of **2D shapes** in a box, eg **squares**, **triangles**, **circles** and **rectangles**. *There are four shape names in the box.* Choose four chn to be team captains, one team for each shape type. Ask a child to select a shape from the box. *What shape is it?* The child gives it to the captain of the team collecting that type of shape. Continue. Draw a **table** and ask the captains to write their total number of shapes in it. Ask questions based on the table.	Y1 C2.d.1 Completing a 3-column grid TA	Y1 1.2 p26 Completing a table of card numbers and suits	Y2 2.2 p26 Creating block graphs	Y2 C2.c.3 Drawing a block graph of favourite films T	Create a table to show the number of children in each maths group, or some other class grouping. Ask questions about the table.	**Y1** • Show information in a table • Interpret a simple table **Y2** • Interpret a table • Draw and interpret a block graph

	Mental oral starter	Objectives	Main teaching	Activities: Group 1 (Y1)	Activities: Group 2 (Y1)	Activities: Group 3 (Y2)	Activities: Group 4 (Y2)	Plenary	Outcomes
Day 4	**Recall addition facts for numbers up to 20.** Play 'Thumbs up, thumbs down'. Write 10 or more additions on the board, some correct, and some incorrect. Point to one. Chn have to decide if it is right or wrong. Say: *Thumbs out!* Chn show thumbs up if correct, thumbs down if not.	*(Continued)* • Sort and organise information using objects or pictures **Y2** • Sort, organise and interpret information in a pictogram	**All** Transform the results from Day 3's table of shapes into a graph. Use a grid and ask chn how and where to label it. *Write shape names along the bottom with number of each shape up the left-hand side.* Colour in one square for each shape, using a different colour for each type of shape to make it easy to read. Explain how it shows the same information as the table but in a different way – it is easier/quicker to read. Interpret the graph.	Y1 C2.d.3 Making a table and block graph of favourite pets T	Y1 C2.d.3 Making a table and block graph of favourite pets T	Y2 2.2 p28 Completing pictograms	Y2 C2.d.1 Creating a pictogram of favourite wild animals TA	Invite chn to choose their favourite TV programme from a choice of five. Draw a table to show the **results**. Discuss the information available from the table.	**Y1** • Draw and interpret simple tables • Draw and interpret simple block graphs **Y2** • Draw and interpret pictograms • Draw and interpret simple block graphs
Day 5	**Add 11, 21, 31 to a 2-digit number.** Draw 4 × 4 grid on board. Ask chn to copy on their whiteboards. Write *+11* on board. Write a number in a square, eg *46*. Chn perform the addition, eg 46 + 11, and write answer in matching square on their boards, eg *57*. Continue until grid is full. Check answers.		**All** Write five drink flavours in a column on the board. *Which do you like best? We will draw a picture (a graph) to show the results.* Write title *Our favourite drinks*. Draw picture of a glass. Explain that the glass picture represents 1 vote. Complete the graph. *This graph is called a* ***pictogram*** *(or* ***pictograph****).* Write the word on the board. Interpret the graph.	Y1 1.2 p25 Completing a table of bird colours	Y1 C2.d.4 Making a table of domino scores TA	Y2 C2.d.1 Creating a pictogram of favourite wild animals T	Y2 p58 Interpreting a pictogram of favourite wild animals	Draw a pictograph showing favourite colours, using a circle as the picture. Ask the chn to say different things they can 'read' from the graph.	**Y1** • Draw and interpret simple tables • Draw and interpret simple block graphs **Y2** • Draw and interpret pictographs • Draw and interpret simple block graphs

Vocabulary
addition
analogue clock
long hand
short hand
o'clock
title
grid
label
horizontal axis
vertical axis
graph
block graph
columns
rows
double
2D shapes
square
triangle
circle
rectangle
table
results
pictograph
pictogram

Resources
individual number lines
counters
analogue clocks
different coloured cubes
bag
sheet with 6 space track with blank clock face in each space
cards with first name of each child in class
sheet with large squares
number cards 0–20
clock face with movable hands
2 sets of dominoes
2D shapes (squares, triangles, circles and rectangles)
box
Favourite pet block graph template (Y1 PCM 128)
individual whiteboards
Post-it notes

Year 1 Block C2.c Activities

C2.c.1 A group of up to 8 children

Talk to children about their day. *What do you do first thing in the morning? What time is this?* Show 7 o'clock and then 8 o'clock on the large clock face. Look at the position of the hands. Ask each child to draw the clock hands to represent either 7 or 8 o'clock on the first space on their track. This is when they get up! Repeat this to fill in the times of five other events through the day.

Adult support may be useful in running this activity.

large clock face with movable hands; sheet with a six-space track and a blank clock face in each space per child

C2.c.4 A group of up to 8 children working in pairs

Tell children that we are going to work out the times when some TV programmes start and finish. Ask a child to name a favourite programme. Ask when it is on TV (afternoon, morning, evening). Establish a rough o'clock time and ask each pair to show you that time on their clock face. Ask if the programme is short, long or very long. If long, say that we need to know the time one hour later – this is when it finishes if it lasts an hour. If it is very long, say we need to know the time two hours later. If short, say we need to know the time half an hour later. In each case, demonstrate the clock hands moving through that time – one hour, two hours or half an hour. Children imitate you on their clock face. They write the name of the programme or draw a quick picture, and write the starting and finishing times. Repeat for different programmes.

Adult support may be useful in running this activity.

clock face with movable hands per pair

Year 1 Block C2.d Activities

C2.d.1 A group of 3 or 4 children

Children draw a three-column grid and write the headings 'straight', 'curved' and 'straight and curved'. They take a number card, one at a time, and decide if the number is constructed from straight lines, curved lines or both. They write the number in the matching column. Discuss what the table shows. Extend to include numbers 11–20.

Adult support may be useful in running this activity.

0–9 number cards

C2.d.3 A group of up to 8 children

Children discuss which three pets they would like to own, or already own. They must choose only three favourite pets each. Explain that we are going to produce a table of favourite pets. Write the heading and draw a table with column heads drawn from the children's discussions: dogs, cats, fish, hamsters, etc. Tell children they can now vote for just one animal! Take each animal in turn and ask who wants to vote for it. Count and record the number of votes for each column. Explain that children are going to draw a graph to show the results. Provide children with a template to create this block graph (Y1 PCM 128). They transfer the information from the table to their graphs, colouring the appropriate number of blocks in each column.

Discuss the graph. *What does it show?*

Adult support may be useful in running this activity.

Favourite pets block graph template (Y1 PCM 128)

C2.d.4 A group of up to 8 children working in pairs

Give each pair six or seven dominoes. Explain that we are going to produce a table of domino scores. Each pair adds up the dots on each of their dominoes, writes the total on a Post-it note and sticks it on the domino. Write the heading and draw a table with column heads: 1, 2, 3, 4, …, 12. Tell children to check the scores on their dominoes. Take each number in turn. *Who has a domino which has this score?* Count and record the number in each column on the table. Discuss the results. *Which scores were most common? Which were more rare?*

Adult support may be useful in running this activity.

dominoes; Post-it notes

Year 2 Block C2.c Activities

C2.c.1 A group of up to 8 children

Give each child four or five cards from a set of class first-name cards, including their own name. Explain that you are going to draw a block graph of the letters in the class's names together. Draw two axes on squared paper, label the horizontal axis letters and the vertical axis number. Write the heading: *The letters in our names*. Write the vowels along the bottom of the graph: *a e i o u*. Take each one in turn and ask children to put up their hands if they have that letter in their name. Record by shading in blocks on the graph. Involve selected children in this process. Then add the letters: c, d, h, m, r, s, t, y, and any others that appear to be common. Discuss the results of your graph. *Which letters are very common? Which letters are rare?*
Adult support is needed to run this activity.

cards with the first name of each child in the class; paper with large squares

C2.c.2 A group of up to 8 children

Give out all the dominoes from one or two sets so that children have at least four each. Explain that you are going to draw a block graph of the sum of the dots on dominoes together. Draw two axes on squared paper and label the horizontal axis sum and the vertical axis number. Write the heading: *The sum of the dots on dominoes.*
Write along the bottom of the graph: *0 1 2 3 … 12*. Take each number in turn. Ask children to add the dots on their dominoes to see if they have any with a total of that number of dots. Record how many by shading in blocks on the graph. Involve selected children in this process. Repeat for each total. Discuss the results of your graph. *Which totals are very common? Which are rare?*
Adult support is needed to run this activity.

two sets of dominoes; paper with large squares

C2.c.3 A group of up to 8 children

Ask each child to write the names of four films that they really like. Explain that you are going to draw a block graph of your favourite films together. Draw two axes on squared paper and label the horizontal axis *films* and the vertical axis *number*. Write a heading: *Our favourite films*. Quickly discuss and agree a list of the most commonly written films and write them along the bottom of the graph. Tell children they can now only vote for two films. Take each one in turn and ask children if they wish to give it a vote. Count the votes and record the number by shading in the blocks on the graph. Involve selected children in this process. Discuss the results of your graph. *Which films are very popular? Which are less popular?*
Adult support is needed to run this activity.

paper with large squares

Year 2 Block C2.d Activities

C2.d.1 A group of up to 8 children

Ask each child to write the names of four wild animals that they really like/are interested in. Explain that you are going to draw a pictograph of the class's favourite wild animals. Draw two axes on the squared paper and label the horizontal axis *wild animals* and the vertical axis *number*. Write a heading: *Our favourite wild animals*. Agree a picture or symbol to use and suggest that it should represent two animals. Draw the key. Quickly discuss and agree a list of about ten of the most commonly written animals and write them along the bottom of the graph. Tell children they can now only vote for three animals. Take each one in turn and ask children if they wish to vote for it. Count the votes and record the number by drawing pictures in the spaces on the graph. Discuss the results of your graph. *Which animals are very popular? Which are more rarely liked?*
Adult support is needed to run this activity.

paper with large squares

Maths Weekly Plan: Year 1 and 2

Block D2.a: Use the names of common 3D shapes
Block D2.b: Sort 3D shapes and describe their features

	Mental oral starter	Objectives	Main teaching	Activities: Group 1 Y1	Activities: Group 2 Y1	Activities: Group 3 Y2	Activities: Group 4 Y2	Plenary	Outcomes
Day 1	**Say how many 10s in a multiple of 10.** Write 5 multiples of 10 on board as amounts of money. *How many* ***10p coins*** *would I need to make each amount?* Go through amounts, **counting in 10s** by dropping 10p coins into a mug.	**Y1** • Begin to relate solid shapes to pictures of them • Begin to use the names of common 3D shapes: cube, cuboid, cylinder, sphere, cone, pyramid **Y2** • Relate solid shapes to pictures of them • Use the names of common 2D shapes, including: cube, cuboid, cylinder, sphere, cone	**All** Hold up **cuboid**. *What is this shape called?* Discuss **properties**. Hold up a label: *Cuboid*. Rpt for **cube, pyramid** and **sphere**. Stick four labelled card houses on a wall behind a table so that shapes can be placed on the table. *This is Solid Shape Street and four families live here: the Cube family, the Pyramid family, …* Look at the different shapes in the 'street'. Hold up a pyramid with a **square base**. *It has a flat, square bottom (base) and pointed top.* Rpt with **triangular**- and **pentagon**-based pyramids. *All pyramids have pointed top, but they can have different bases.* Ask chn to place pyramids in the correct 'home'.	Y1 D2.a.1 Identifying 3D shapes by name T	Y1 1.2 p28 Matching shapes to shape names	Y2 D2.a.1 Identifying 3D shapes in a cloth bag TA	Y2 2.2 p30 Identifying 3D shapes	Look around for cube- and cuboid-shaped objects in the classroom and add them to the families on Solid Shape Street. Search for **cylinders**.	**Y1** • Begin to know names of common 3D shapes **Y2** • Recognise common 3D shapes and know their names • Begin to identify bases of pyramids
Day 2	**Recognise odd and even numbers.** Play 'Stand up'. Give each child one number card 10–100. *Stand up if your number is an* ***odd*** *number.* Chn holding odd numbers stand up and show their cards. Check their numbers. Rpt activity using different instructions. Use 100-square to help.		**All** Hold up a **cone**. *This is a cone.* Discuss its properties. Rpt for cylinder. Hide **3D shapes** behind a screen. Slowly lift one shape up. When it is half revealed, chn decide what shape it is and label it. Child places shape in its correct family home. Continue for all shapes. **Y2** Describe a cone. *It has 1* ***flat***, ***circular face***, *and 1* ***curved*** *face. It has a flat base and a pointed top.* Discuss difference between cone and pyramid. Rpt for cylinder. Use paper to make a cylinder to show that the curved face, when opened out, makes a **rectangle**.	Y1 1.2 p27 Matching shapes to shape names	Y1 D2.a.2 Identifying and making 3D shapes TA	Y2 2.2 p29 Identifying shape names	Y2 D2.a.2 Identifying faces of 3D shapes T	Use a 'sloping board' test to see which shapes will roll down a slope. Before testing each shape, ask chn to **predict** whether or not it will roll, and give a reason.	**Y1** • Identify common 3D shapes and know their names **Y2** • Identify 3D shapes • Differentiate between curved and flat faces
Day 3	**Find 1 less, 2 less or 3 less than a number less than 20.** Pairs draw a 2 × 2 grid on whiteboards. They write a number between 1 and 20 in each square. Place number cards 5–21 face down. Choose a card. Chn **count back** 1, 2 or 3 from card number, and cross it off if they have the answer on their grid.	**Y1** • Describe features of familiar 3D shapes: number, shapes and types of faces	**All** Hold up a cube. *Look at its faces. Are they flat or curved?* Do the same for a cone and a sphere. Sit chn in circle. Place two hoops on the floor so that they overlap. Show chn a box full of 3D shapes. They take turns to choose a shape and place it in a hoop according to whether it has a curved or flat face. *It may have both, and then it goes in the middle!* Emphasise that solid shapes have flat or curved faces, or both.	Y1 D2.b.1 TM 8.1 8 Printing shapes T	Y1 1.2 p29 Identifying square faces	Y2 D2.b.4 Sorting 3D shapes TA	Y2 D2.b.4 Sorting 3D shapes TA	Hold up a pair of shapes. Discuss what is different about them and what is the same. Rpt for different pairs of shapes.	**Y1** • Count faces of common 3D shapes • Sort 3D shapes **Y2** • Count faces of common 3D shapes • Sort 3D shapes

	Mental oral starter	Objectives	Main teaching	Activities: Group 1 Y1	Activities: Group 2 Y1	Activities: Group 3 Y2	Activities: Group 4 Y2	Plenary	Outcomes
Day 4	**Recall names and properties of 2D shapes.** Give each child a 2D shape. Describe one of the shapes, eg *It has 4* ***sides****, it has 4* ***corners****, it is blue.* Chn holding a shape matching the description hold it up for everyone to see. Rpt several times.	*(Continued)* **Y2** • Sort 3D shapes and describe their features: number of faces and corners	**All** Place hoop in centre of circle of chn. Label the hoop *Square face*. *Put all shapes that have a square face inside the hoop.* Start music, pass box of shapes around. When music stops, child takes shape and places it in correct place. Name/discuss properties of all shapes. **Y2** Child finds cube from set of 3D shapes. *How many corners? How many faces?* Rpt for cuboid. Explain that cuboids/cubes have same number of faces and corners. Chn find different pyramids. Show different number of corners on base. *Cylinders/spheres have no corners.*	Y1 D2.b.4 Identifying 3D shapes by properties TA	Y1 1.2 p30 Identifying flat and curved faces T	Y2 2.2 p31 Identifying properties of 3D shapes	Y2 D2.b.2 TM 8.1 8 Printing shapes T	Write names of all 3D shapes on board and choose chn to read the names, and match them to actual shapes. Discuss the 4 Cs (the 4 shapes that begin with the letter C: cube, cuboid, cylinder, cone).	**Y1** • Identify shape of faces on 3D shapes • Sort and name common 3D shapes **Y2** • Name common 3D shapes according to properties: faces and corners
Day 5	**Count in 3s.** Play 'Birdsong'. Arrange class into three groups. Choose a start number, eg 3. Choose a group to start 'singing' or counting forwards in 3s. After two counts, a different group takes over, and so on. Rpt counting back and forwards, extending beyond 30.		**All** Child finds cube. *How many faces? What shape are the faces?* Put label next to it: *Square*. Child finds cuboid. Discuss shape of faces. Put label next to it: *Rectangle*. Rpt for other shapes. Place all shapes on table. *Find a shape that has a triangular face.* Rpt activity. **Y1** Put 3D shapes in a cloth bag and choose a child to come and pick one. They keep the shape hidden from the class, then describe it so the class can guess which shape they have. Encourage them to count the faces, say the shape of the faces, and so on.	Y1 2.2 p29 Identifying square faces	Y1 D2.b.2 Identifying 3D shapes by properties T	Y2 D2.b.3 Describing 3D shapes in terms of numbers of faces, edges, corners TA	Y2 p12 Identifying properties of 3D shapes	Play 'I am thinking of a shape'. Describe a shape without naming it, eg *It has 6 corners and 6 faces. 2 of the faces are square and 4 are rectangles.* Chn work out the mystery shape. Rpt.	**Y1** • Identify common 3D shapes according to properties: number of faces **Y2** • Name common 3D shapes according to properties: faces and corners

Vocabulary
properties
cuboid
cube
cone
pyramid
sphere
square
rectangle
pentagon
circle
base
triangular
3D shapes
flat face
curved face
sides
corners
predict
10p coins
counting in 10s
odd
count back
counting forward

Resources
10p coins
mug
3D shapes: cuboid, cube, cone, sphere, cylinder, prism, pyramids: square-based, triangular-based, pentagon-based
cloth bag
box
number cards 5–100
100-square
wooden plank or board to make a slope
2 hoops
counters
squared paper 20 cm × 20 cm
paper clip
pencil
labels: square face; rectangle face; triangle face; pentagon face; hexagon face (Y2 PCM 120)
CD player
property cards: flat faces; curved faces; more than 2 corners

Year 1 Block D2.a Activities

D2.a.1 A group of up to 8 children working in pairs

Line up the 3D shapes. Go along the shapes and name and hold up each one. Each pair holds up a matching shape. Take your set of shapes and place them in a cloth bag. Choose a child to come and secretly remove one shape from the bag. They say the name of the shape, e.g. *pyramid*. The pairs hold up the shape they believe is that shape. The child shows the shape taken from the bag. Does it match those shown by each pair? Repeat the activity.
Adult support may be useful in running this activity.

3D shapes: pyramid, cone, cube, cuboid, cylinder, sphere per pair; cloth bag

D2.a.2 Groups of 2 or 3 children

Groups study each shape carefully and choose one of them to make. Support children in folding and sticking the net to make their chosen shape. Each child makes the shape carefully and compares it with their solid shape. Is it the same?
Adult support may be useful in running this activity.

3D shapes: pyramid, cone, cube, cuboid, cylinder; net for making shapes per child

Year 1 Block D2.b Activities

8.1 8 Printing Shapes

D2.b.1 A group of 6 or more children

Make a spinner: divide the paper into quarters and draw a shape in each quarter: equilateral triangle, square, rectangle and circle. Hold a pencil point down in the centre and spin the paper clip around it.
Give each child a 3D shape. Spin the paper clip. If it lands on a shape that forms one of the faces of their shape, they should say the name of their shape. If correct they receive a counter. If they can say a sentence such as *My cube has six square faces* or *My pyramid has some triangle faces,* they receive a bonus counter. The child with most counters after ten spins is the winner. Ask them to choose a different 3D shape and to play the game again. *Is it easier to win counters with a cube or a different shape?*
Adult support is needed to run this activity.

one 3D shape per child: pyramid (square or triangular base), cone, cube, cuboid (square or rectangular faces), cylinder, sphere; counters; square paper (20 cm × 20 cm); pencil; paper clip

D2.b.2 A group of up to 8 children working in pairs

Give each child a different shape. Each child in turn describes their shape in terms of the numbers of curved faces, flat faces and corners. Each pair records these on their table.
Adult support may be useful in running this activity.

one 3D shape per child: pyramid, cone, cube, cuboid, cylinder, sphere; table drawn on the board and one copy per pair: the table has four columns headed 'Shape name', 'Curved faces', 'Flat face' and 'Corners'

D2.b.4 A group of 6 to 9 children working in pairs or 3s

Give each small group one property card. Hold up a shape, e.g. a cone. Children from each group must argue to have that shape. For example, the group with 'flat faces' can point out that a cone has a flat face. The group with 'curved faces' can point out that a cone has a curved face. The group with 'more than 2 corners' cannot, however, argue that they should have it! Give each group which has a good argument one of that type of shape. Then show a new shape. Continue until each group has at least three shapes. Discuss the shapes that are in more than one group.
Adult support may be useful in running this activity.

property cards: 'flat faces', 'curved faces', 'more than 2 corners', one per pair; 3D shapes

Year 2 Block D2.a Activities

D2.a.1 A group of up to 8 children working in pairs

Place a set of 3D shapes in view. Give each pair of children a matching set of shapes. Without showing children, place one shape in a cloth bag. Choose a child to feel the shape through the bag. They describe what they feel, for example *It has corners. It has curved faces.* The rest of the children decide which one of their shapes matches the shape they think is in the bag and place it next to the bag. Check to see if they are correct.

Adult support is needed to run this activity.

cloth bag; set of 3D shapes and a matching set for each pair

D2.a.2 A group of 8 children working in pairs

Give each group a set of 3D shapes. Children begin by drawing a square. Then they look at each 3D shape and decide if it has any faces that are square. If it does, they write the name of the 3D shape beside the square.

Children then draw a different 2D shape and find the 3D shapes that have any faces of that shape.

Adult support may be useful in running this activity.

set of 3D shapes

Year 2 Block D2.b Activities

8.1 8 Printing Shapes

D2.b.2 A group of 6 or more children

Secretly hide one of the 3D shapes in a cloth bag and play twenty questions. Children ask you questions about the shape in the bag to which you must only answer 'yes' or 'no'. Encourage them to use correct vocabulary and ask questions about the shape's properties, for example *Does it have any square faces?* Pairs now take turns to choose one of their shapes to describe to the rest of the group. They should think of three sentences to describe the shape they have chosen clearly enough for the rest of the group to guess which shape it is.

Adult support is needed to run this activity.

3D shapes for each pair: cylinder, cone, cube, cuboid, square-based pyramid, triangular-based pyramid; cloth bag

D2.b.3 A group of up to 8 children

Draw a table with the headings 'Shape name'; 'Faces'; 'Edges'; and 'Corners' on the board for children to copy, or provide copies.

Give each child a different 3D shape. Each child in turn describes their shape in terms of the numbers of faces, edges and corners. All children record these on their chart.

Adult support is needed to run this activity.

3D shapes

D2.b.4 A group of up to 8 children

Place two hoops on the table so they overlap. Choose a face label (Y2 PCM 120) to put above each hoop. Place the 3D shapes in the bag. Children take turns to pick a shape from the bag and place it in the correct position inside or outside the hoops. When all the shapes have been placed, repeat the activity with a different choice of labels.

Adult support is needed to run this activity.

3D shapes with flat faces: cubes, cuboids, pyramids, prisms; face labels: square face, rectangle face, triangle face, pentagon face, hexagon face (Y2 PCM 120); two hoops; cloth bag

Maths Weekly Plan: Year 1 and 2

Block D2.c: Y1 Add by counting on; Y2 Add/subtract 9/11 by adding/subtracting 10
Block D2.d: Add or subtract multiples of 10 by counting on or back in 10s

	Mental oral starter	Objectives	Main teaching	Activities: Group 1 Y1	Activities: Group 2 Y1	Activities: Group 3 Y2	Activities: Group 4 Y2	Plenary	Outcomes
Day 1	**Say the position of one thing in relation to another.** Draw a picture of a large table on the board. Draw a cat **on** it and a mouse **under** it. Draw a dog **beside** and a bird flying **over** it. *Draw the creature that is on the table.* Continue to ask similar questions.	**Y1** • Add by counting on, not bridging a multiple of 10 other than 10 or 20 **Y2** • Add and subtract 9 and 11 by adding and subtracting 10 • Begin to add and subtract 19 and 21 by adding and subtracting 20	**All** Show chn Pobble, a jar of marbles and a 1–30 number line. Write *15. Pobble's jar has 15 marbles.* Write *+4. How many marbles now?* Point at 15 on line. *Hold 15 in our heads*. Hold up 4 fingers and count on. Write *19* and read together. Rpt for 14+6 and 13+4. **[ITR Y1 D2.c]** **Y2** Read *The Owl and the Pussycat*. Draw purse. Write *36p* on it. *We'll give them 9p.* Write *36p+9p=*. Pick chn to be Cat and Owl. Give them three 10p and six 1p coins. *9p is nearly 10p*. Write *36p+10p=*. ***Count on** 10. 46p. **Take** 1p **away**. 45p.* Rpt for 62p+9p and 38p+19p.	Y1 D2.c.1 TM 9.1 9 Counting on and back TA	Y1 1.2 p32 Counting on using a number track	Y2 D2.d.1 9.1 9 Addition and subtraction T	Y2 2.2 p35 Subtracting 9 by subtracting 10 and adjusting	Write *13+4=*. Ask Y1s how they might solve this. *What method is best?* Child models counting on using fingers. Write *24+9=*. Ask Y2s how to solve this. *Is it best to use the same method as Y1s? Why not? Add 10 then take away 1.*	**Y1** • Add on 1-digit numbers by counting on using fingers **Y2** • Add 9 by adding 10 and subtracting 1 • Subtract 9 by subtracting 10 and adding 1
Day 2	**Recognise and say ordinal numbers.** Point at 1 on 1–20 number line. *This is the **first** number*. Point at 2. *This is the **second** number*. Continue up to **twentieth**. Point at the numbers randomly, chn say the position of each one. Arrange the chn in two queues. Chn say their position.		**All** Use 1–30 number line. Hang pictures of Wolf at each multiple of 10. Count along line discussing 'Wolf' numbers. Write *18+6=*. Point to 18 on line and point to +6. *Hold up 6 fingers*. *Count on 6.* Move Pobble along line to 24. Rpt for 14+9, Y2s +10 and –1, Y1s count on 9. **Y1** Write *16+7=*. Place Pobble on number 16 on the number line. Point at +7. *This is how many more jumps Pobble takes.* Count on from 16. Complete the **addition**. Rpt for 18+5 and 17+6.	Y1 1.2 p31 Counting on with pictures	Y1 D2.c.2 Counting on using money T	Y2 D2.d.3 Subtracting 9 by using a 100-square and subtracting 10 then adding 1 TA	Y2 D2.d.3 Subtracting 9 by using a 100-square and subtracting 10 then adding 1 TA	Place large 1–20 number track across the floor. Write *17+5=* on board. Ask a child to stand on 17 on the number track. They are a 'human counter'! Ask chn to count on 5 from 17. Point out the 'Wolf' number.	**Y1** • Add on 1-digit numbers by counting on using fingers/ number tracks **Y2** • Add or subtract 9 or 11 by adding or subtracting 10 and adjusting
Day 3	**Name and recognise the properties of 3D shapes.** Play 'Stand up'. Give each child a **3D shape**. Give instructions involving names and **properties** of 3D shapes. *Stand up if your shape is a **cuboid***. Check shapes. Rpt using different objects.		**All** Give a child (Owl) 75p in 10ps and 1ps. Give another (Cat) one 1p. Write *75p–9p=*. *Owl gives Cat 9p. How much does he have left?* Find 75 on 100-square. ***Count back** 10.* Move finger 1 row up. *We count back 10 then give back 1.* Y1s count back 10 on 100-square. **[ITR Y2 D2.d]** **Y2** Write *44p+11p=*, *62p–9p=*, *27p+9p=*, *82p–11p=*. Stress adding/**subtracting** 10p coins and then **adjusting**. Pairs choose a calculation. They look at amount they are adding/subtracting and think about **nearest 10**. Have they given or taken too much? *Give or take 1p to make it right.*	Y1 D2.c.4 Counting on to reach 10 or 20 TA	Y1 1.2 p33 Counting on using a number track	Y2 2.2 p35 Subtracting 9 by subtracting 10 and adjusting	Y2 D2.d.5 9.3 9 Addition and subtraction T	Write 6 calculations on board, some involving adding 10 (Y1s), and some adding or subtracting 9 (Y2s). Three of the answers should be incorrect. Chn work in pairs to establish which are incorrect.	**Y1** • Count on using number tracks and fingers • Count back 10 on 100-square **Y2** • Add or subtract 9 or 11 by adding or subtracting 10 and adjusting

	Mental oral starter	Objectives	Main teaching	Activities: Group 1 Y1	Activities: Group 2 Y1	Activities: Group 3 Y2	Activities: Group 4 Y2	Plenary	Outcomes
Day 4	**Say the number 10, 20, 30 more than a number.** Class gets into 2 teams. Child from team A chooses a number card 1–70 and shows it to team B. Team B say number that is **10 more** (Y1s) or **20/30 more** (Y2s). If correct they keep the card. Child from team B chooses a card for team A and so on.	**Y1** • Add two multiples of 10 by counting on in 10s **Y2** • Subtract a multiple of 10 from a 2-digit number by counting back in 10s	**All** Draw or stick pictures of wolves on multiple-of-10 number cards. Stick these on the board. *These are Wolf numbers.* Point at 40. *How many 10s in this Wolf number?* Show four 10p coins to demo. *How many 10s in 80?* Count using 10p coins. Rpt to find how many 10s in 60.	Y1 D2.d.1 Making amounts of money using 10p coins then adding them (TA)	Y1 D2.d.1 Making amounts of money using 10p coins then adding them (T)	Y2 D2.c.1 Using a 100-square to count back in 10s (T)	Y2 1.2 p34 Subtracting 10s	Chn write a multiple of 10 40–100 on their whiteboards. Write *40* on board. Throw a dice, eg 3. Chn add that number of 10s (eg 30) to 40 by counting on in 10s. Chn with that number written cross it off. Rpt.	**Y1** • Add multiples of 10 by counting on in 10s • Recognise multiples of 10 **Y2** • Add and subtract multiples of 10 by counting on and back in 10s
			Y2 Point to number in top row of 100-square. Use Bisky Bat to **count on in 10s**. Write *167*. Cover 1, say *67*. Uncover and say *167*. Write *67−30=*. *To subtract 30 we count back 3 tens.* Model this. Write *167−30=*. *What might the answer be?* Rpt for 73−40 and 173−40. **[ITR Y2 D2.c]**						
Day 5	**Estimate lengths in non-standard units and centimeters.** Hold up an object longer than 30 cm. Y1s: *How many crayons long is this?* Write **estimates**. Y2s: *How many cm long do you think this is?* Hold up a 30 cm ruler to help them compare. Whose estimate is closest? Rpt for different objects.		**All** Show chn a teddy bear. Label it *84p*. *The shop has* ***reduced*** *the price by 30p. What is the new price? We can subtract 30p by counting back three 10s.* Relate to removing 10p coins from an amount. Complete subtraction by handing out 10p coins while counting back. Rpt.	Y1 1.2 p34 Identifying number of 10p coins in an amount	Y1 D2.d.3 Exploring the combinations when adding 10p and 20p coins (T)	Y2 1.2 p32 Counting back in 10s	Y2 D2.c.2 Subtracting multiples of 10 using 100-square (T)	Write 2 amounts, eg *20p* and *72p*. Throw a dice, eg 4. Y1s add that number of 10ps to the multiple of 10: *20p+40p=60p*. Y2s subtract that number of 10ps from the higher number: *72p−40p=32p*. Rpt.	**Y1** • Add multiples of 10 by counting on in 10s • Recognise multiples of 10 **Y2** • Add and subtract multiples of 10 by counting on and back in 10s
			Y1 Use the Wolf-number number line from Day 4. Count in 10s in unison. Write *30+40=*. Place Bisky Bat on 40. *We can count on in 10s. We can count on three 10s.* Move Bisky Bat while counting on. Complete addition. Read together. Rpt for 60+20 and 50+40.						

Vocabulary
count on
count back
count in 10s
addition
adding
10, 20, 30 more
multiple of 10
take away
subtracting
adjusting
nearest
reduced
3D shape
shape properties
cuboid
estimates
first, second… twentieth

Resources
Pobble
Bisky Bat
Wolf
jar of marbles
1–30 number line
0–100 number line
1p, 2p, 5p, 10p and 20p coins
card with arrow on it
100-bead string
number cards 1–100
large 100-square
counters
large 1–20 number track
small 1–10 or 1–20 number tracks
3D shapes
multiples of 10 number cards
2 purses
Post-it notes
dice
ruler
teddy bear

Blocks D2.c and D2.d

Year 1 Block D2.c Activities

9.1 9 Counting on and back

D2.c.1 A group of 6 or more children

Seat the children in a circle. Hold the arrow so that it points forwards (clockwise round the circle). Children count forwards round the circle, starting at 10. When they reach 19, turn the arrow so that it points backwards (anticlockwise) and ask them to count backwards round the circle. Turn the arrow round again when they reach 7 so that they count forwards. Repeat, giving plenty of practice in counting forwards and backwards through 10.

Hold up the arrow so that it points forwards. Say a number, for example *thirteen*, and ask children to shout out the next number. Hold the arrow so that it points backwards. *Which number comes before thirteen?* Repeat for other numbers, including 10 and 20.

Adult support is needed to run this activity.

a card with an arrow on it

D1.c.2 Pairs of children

One child takes a number card, for example 18; the other throws the dice, for example 4. Children record this as a money addition: *18p + 4p =*. The first child makes the amount on the number card with coins, and the second child adds the dice amount in 1ps, counting on as they do so: *Eighteen, nineteen, twenty, twenty-one, twenty-two.* They record the answer to their addition: *18p + 4p = 22p*, and check the amount. Then repeat, swapping roles, until they have generated seven additions.

Adult support may be useful in running this activity.

8–18 number cards; 1p, 2p, 5p and 10p coins; dice

D2.c.4 Pairs of children

Give each pair a starting number. They use their number track to work out how many they add to that number to reach 10 or 20. They may use their fingers, for example putting 17 in their head and counting on, holding up one finger for each number spoken. They write the addition, for example *17 + 3 = 20*. Copy the additions onto the board and read them together. Repeat the activity, starting with numbers with different units.

Adult support may be useful in running this activity.

1–10 or 1–20 number track per pair (allocate appropriately)

Year 1 Block D2.d Activities

D2.d.1 Pairs of children

Each child puts a number of 10p coins in a purse, between 10p and 60p. They then label their purse with the amount using a Post-it note. The pair then work out how much is in the two purses together. They add the amounts on the two Post-its by counting in 10s from the larger to the smaller. They write an addition, for example *60p + 30p = 90p*, and then tip out the coins in both purses and count in 10s to find the total. Does it match their addition? Replace the coins and start again.

Adult support may be useful in running this activity.

two purses; 10p coins; Post-it notes

D2.d.3 A group of up to 8 children working in pairs

Ask each pair to make amounts of money using equal numbers of 20p and 10p coins. They note an addition for each amount, for example *10p + 10p + 20p + 20p = 60p*. When each pair have made several, look at the amounts they have made. Discuss whether they can make any amount (as long as it is a multiple of 10). Are there any amounts that cannot be made?

Adult support may be useful in running this activity.

10p and 20p coins per pair

Year 2 Block D2.c Activities

D2.c.1 A group of up to 8 children

Each child places a counter on a number in the bottom half of a large 100-square. They write the number on which they have placed their counter on their whiteboard, for example *56*. Ask children to write – 30 = after their number to make, for example, *56 – 30 =* .
Explain how to subtract 30 by moving the counter three spaces up the grid. Stress that subtracting means counting back in 10s and this means moving up the grid. Support children as they do this and write the answer to complete their subtraction. Repeat the process at least six times, subtracting a tens number up to 50 so that children become confident in using a 100-square to subtract tens.
Adult support is needed to run this activity.

large 100-square

D2.c.2 Pairs of children

Place a shuffled set of 50–100 number cards in a pile next to a shuffled set of 10–40 multiple of 10 cards. Give each pair a 100-square. Pairs take a card from each pile and place them to make and record a subtraction, for example take 67 and 40 and write *67 – 40 =*.
Encourage children to use a 100-square to help them count back (i.e. up the grid) and support them as appropriate in doing this. Pairs agree and record their answer. They replace the cards on the bottom of the appropriate piles and take another card from each pile to perform another subtraction. Children should complete at least six subtractions in this way.
Adult support may be useful in running this activity with several pairs of children.

50–100 number cards; 10–40 multiple of 10 cards; 100-square

Year 2 Block D2.d Activities

9.1 9 Addition and subtraction

D2.d.1 A group of 6 or more children

Pull five beads to the left-hand end of the string as children see it. Slide a group of 10 beads across to join them. *How many beads are there now?*
Continue sliding groups of 10 beads across and counting in 10s until you reach 35. Slide another 10 beads across. *There were 35 beads at this end and then I slid another 10 beads across, so how many beads are there now? But I meant to slide 11, so what shall I do?*
Agree that you can slide 1 more bead across to make 46 beads. Keep adding another 11 until you reach 79 beads, encouraging children to predict each answer.
Reverse the activity to subtract 11 repeatedly, beginning by showing how you can move 10 back to leave 69, and then 1 more to leave 68.
Adult support is needed to run this activity.

100-bead string

D2.d.3 A group of up to 8 children

Each child places a counter on a number anywhere below the top row of a large 100-square.
Write – 9 on the board. Show children how to use the 100-square to subtract 9. Subtract 10 by moving a counter one space up the grid and then along one to add back the one too many subtracted.
Replace the counter in its original position and ask children to move their counters in the same way to subtract 9.
Practising the movement 'up and along' may help them to get the hang of it.

Each child then records their subtraction, for example *34 – 9 = 25*.
Repeat this until everyone has completed six subtractions.
Adult support may be useful in running this activity.

large 100-square; counters

9.3 9 Addition and subtraction

D2.d.5 A group of 6 or more children

Circle 45 on the number line. *What is 45 add 20? How did you work it out?* Draw a jump from 45 to 65 on the number line. *What if we only wanted to add 19, not 20? Would the answer be bigger or smaller?* Ask a child to circle the answer on the number line and write a number sentence. *What if we'd meant to add on 21 not 20? Would the answer be bigger or smaller?* Write the number sentence. Ask pairs to write groups of three number sentences, first adding 20 to a 2-digit number and then using the answer to write number sentences adding 19 and 21, for example

45 + 20 = 65
45 + 19 = 64
45 + 21 = 66

Adult support is needed to run this activity.

0–100 number line

Maths Weekly Plan: Year 1 and 2

Block E2.a: Y1 Count on/back in 10s; Y2 Count on in 2s/5s/10s, recognise odd/even numbers
Block E2.b: Y1 Count on/back in 1s/10s; Y2 Understand multiplication as 'lots of'

	Mental oral starter	Objectives	Main teaching	Activities: Group 1 Y1	Activities: Group 2 Y1	Activities: Group 3 Y2	Activities: Group 4 Y2	Plenary	Outcomes
Day 1	**Recall addition pairs for numbers up to 7.** Play 'Ping-pong'. Start with pairs to 5. Say number less than 5. Chn must reply with the number that is its partner to 5. Start slowly, then gradually increase pace. Extend to include number pairs to 6 and 7.	**Y1** • Count on and back in 10s from any number up to 100 **Y2** • Count in 2s, 5s or 10s up to 100 • Begin to recognise odd and even numbers up to 100	**All** Read *One Pink Sari* by Ann Marie Linden. Discuss what the poem does. *It **counts forward** in ones!* Recite *Ten fat sausages*. *This poem **counts backwards***. Practise counting forwards and backwards in 1s from different numbers. Place Bisky Bat on 0 on a 100-square. **Count on in 10s**, writing the **multiples of 10** on the board. Place Bisky on 2. Count in 10s to 92. Then place Bisky on 98, and count back to 8. Count back in 10s from 95. Hold up 1 hand. *5 fingers.* Hold up 2 hands. *10 fingers.* **Count in 5s**, pointing out that the numbers always end in 5 or 0.	Y1 E2.a.1 Counting in 10s using number cards 1–100 (T)	Y1 E2.a.1 Counting in 10s using number cards 1–100 (T)	Y2 E2.a.1 (TM) 10.1 10 Counting in 2s, 5s and 10s (TA)	Y2 2.2 p38 Counting in 10s, 5s and 2s	Lay out number cards in a line: 10, 20, 30, … 100. Ask chn to shut their eyes. *I am going to remove one card.* Take away 60. Chn say which card has gone. Rpt, choosing a child to remove another card.	**Y1** • Count on and back in 10s from any number up to 100 **Y2** • Count in multiples of 2, 5 and 10 from a given number up to 100
Day 2	**Count to 100; recognise numbers to 100.** Give a selection of chn some number cards between 1 and 100. Count from 1 up to 100. Match the units to fingers. Every time you reach a number held by a child, they stand up. At the end, count back from 20 to 1, ending with *Blast off!*		**All** Show chn a purse. Ask them to shut their eyes while you put three 2p coins in the purse. *I've put 6p in here. Which coins did I use?* Discuss combinations. *I'm going to add 10p coins one at a time.* Chn count in 10s. *How much now?* Check. Rpt starting with 9p. **[ITR Y1 E2.a]** **Y2** Cover **even numbers** on 100-square with Post-it notes. Count in 1s to 30, saying **odd numbers** in a whisper and even numbers loudly. **Count in 2s**, uncovering each number as you say it. Ask chn to come and write even numbers to 20 on the board, counting in 2s as they go.	Y1 1.2 p37 Counting on in 10s	Y1 E2.a.3 Counting in 10s past 100 (TA)	Y2 E2.a.3 Identifying even and odd numbers (T)	Y2 p15 Writing the next odd or even number after 2- and 3-digit numbers	Use six number cards 1–100, and six multiple-of-10 cards. Muddle all the cards up and display them. Pairs write the numbers in **order** from **smallest** to **largest**. Ask Y2s to sort the cards into odd and even numbers.	**Y1** • Count on/back in 10s from any number up to 100 • Count on in 10s beyond 100 **Y2** • Recognise even and odd numbers • Count in 2s
Day 3	**Recall addition pairs to 10 and 20.** Play 'Ping-pong'. Start with pairs to 10. Say a number. Chn say its partner to 10. Start slowly then gradually increase the pace. Extend to pairs to 20.	**Y1** • Say the number that is 1 or 10 more or less than a given number • Count on and back in 1s or 10s from any number up to 100	**All** Put six 2p coins in a purse. *How much money is in here?* Write 6 × 2 =. *6 lots of 2 are…? Count in 2s to find out how much.* Hold up 6 fingers to match 6 coins. Count in 2s, folding down 1 finger for each number spoken. Write *12p* to complete sentence. Rpt for 9 × 2 = and 8 × 2 =. **Y1** Recite 'Five little monkeys' (see below). Rpt for 4, 3, 2 and 1 monkeys. Discuss how it counts backwards. Write *8*. *What is 1 less than 8?* Pairs discuss. Support by whispering the counting back chant. Write *7* before the 8. Rpt for 18, 28 and 38. Encourage **pattern making**.	Y1 E2.b.2 Making number tracks (T)	Y1 1.2 p41 Identifying the number 10 more and 10 less	Y2 2.2 p38 Counting in 10s, 5s and 2s	Y2 E2.b.1 (TM) 10.3 10 Counting in 2s, 5s and 10s (TA)	Use another nursery rhyme that counts back in 1s, eg 'Five little ducks went swimming one day'. *If we started with 15 ducks, **how many** would there be in the next verse?* Rpt starting with 25 ducks.	**Y1** • Say 1 more/less than a given number • Say 10 more/less than a given number **Y2** • Count in 2s, 5s, 10s • Count in multiples to solve multiplications

	Mental oral starter	Objectives	Main teaching	Activities: Group 1 (Y1)	Activities: Group 2 (Y1)	Activities: Group 3 (Y2)	Activities: Group 4 (Y2)	Plenary	Outcomes
Day 4	**Recognise the value of each digit in a 2-digit number.** Play 'Detective maths'. Pairs have 100-squares in front of them. Give clues for chn to solve, eg *Find the number with six tens and four units.* Pairs place a counter on matching number. Rpt for different clues, eg *10 less than 85*; *half-way between 60 and 70.*	*(Continued)* **Y2** • Introduce multiplication as 'lots of' • Introduce the × sign	**All** Recite 'Ten fat peas' together (see below). Draw 4 pea pods. *How many peas in each pod?* (10) *How many peas in 4 pods?* Count in 10s to find out. Draw 3 pods and 4 peas. Write *34*. Draw another pod. Chn count on 10. Continue up to 4 more pods. **[ITR Y1 E2.b]** **Y2** Recite 'Five jam tarts' (see below). Rpt, changing last line to *Start with two…* Draw 1 packet of 5 jam tarts. Draw another packet below the first. *How many tarts in 2 packets?* Write *2×5=*. Hold up 2 fingers to match packets. Count in 5s. Rpt for 3 packets. **[ITR Y2 E2.b]**	Y1 1.2 p40 Identifying the number 1 more and 1 less	Y1 E2.b.1 Making number crosses TA	Y2 2.2 p41 Completing ×2 multiplication facts	Y2 E2.b.3 Writing the 2, 5 and10 times tables T	Give pairs of chn a small handful of 2p coins. They count in 2s to establish how much they have. They write a matching **multiplication**. Check. Rpt, giving Y1s 10p coins and Y2s 5p coins.	**Y1** • Say 10 more/ less than a given number • Count on in 10s and 1s **Y2** • Count in 2s, 5s, 10s • Count in multiples to solve multiplications
Day 5	**Recall simple multiplication facts.** Write multiplication fact on board (×10 for Y1s, ×2, ×5, ×10 for Y2s). Read together. Chn write answer on whiteboards. On *Show me*, they reveal them. Check. Rpt for different × facts. Encourage Y1s to check by counting in 10s, Y2s by counting in 2s, 5s, or 10s.		**All** Read *The Owl and the Pussycat*. Show £5 note. Draw 6 £5 notes. *How many fives?* Write *6×5=*. Hold up 6 fingers. Count in 5s, folding down 1 finger for each number spoken. Draw 4 £10 notes. Write *4×10=* and hold up 4 fingers. Complete sentence. Rpt for 8 £2 coins. **Y1** Show 1–50 grid. Use Bisky Bat to count up and down in 10s from different 1-digit numbers. *Bisky is on 26. Find the number that is 10 more*. Show Pobble. *Pobble counts in 1s*. Rpt, finding 10 more or 1 more. *Pobble moves* ***across*** *the grid and Bisky moves* ***up and down***.	Y1 E2.b.3 Exploring number patterns on a 100-square T	Y1 E2.b.3 Exploring number patterns on a 100-square T	Y2 E2.b.2 Making towers of 5 and 10 TA	Y2 E2.b.4 Making towers of 5 and writing matching multiplication sentences	Give each pair a 100-square. Write a number on the board, eg *68. What is the number that is 10 more?* Chn find the number on their 100-squares and move their finger down one space, eg 78.	**Y1** • Say 1 or 10 more/less than a given number • Find number patterns on a 100-square **Y2** • Complete ×2, ×5, ×10 facts • Use multiplication sign

Vocabulary
count forward, backward
multiples of 10
count in 1s, 2s, 5s, 10s
even numbers
odd numbers
order
smallest
largest
pattern making
how many?
half way between
multiplication
across
up and down

Resources
One Pink Sari by Ann Marie Linden
Bisky Bat
Pobble
100-square
number cards 1–100
2p, 5p, 10p and £2 coins
£5 note
tin
purse
Post-it notes
long strips of paper
coloured felt pens
individual whiteboards
empty number tracks (10 spaces)
blank number crosses
The Owl and the Pussycat by Edward Lear
1–50 grid
calculators
individual 3×3 grid taken from 100-square
interlocking cubes

Rhymes

Five little monkeys were jumping on the bed
One fell off and bumped her head.
Mummy called the doctor and the doctor said,
'No more jumping on that bed!'

Ten fat peas in a pea-pod pressed
One grew, two grew, and so did all the rest.
They grew and they grew and they did not stop
Until one day, the pod went POP!

Five jam tarts in each packet all yummy
Greedy gorilla with a hungry tummy
Lots of packets in gorilla's pot
Start with one and scoff the lot!

Year 1 Block E2.a Activities

E2.a.1 Groups of 3 children

Spread out the 10–100 cards face up. Shuffle the 1–9 cards and put them in a pile face down. Children take it in turns to take a card from the pile. They read their card numbers, for example *three, six* and *one*. They then each count in tens from their card number and find all the number cards to lay out the matching sequence. For example, the child who said *three* finds 13, 23, 33, … 93 and lays them out in order. When all three children have completed their sequence, they count along them together in unison. They then take another card each from the pile, and repeat the process. Repeat again so that they each have three sequences. Look at the cards left spread out on the table. What numbers are these?
Adult support may be useful in running this activity.

1–100 number cards

E2.a.3 A group of up to 8 children working in pairs

Each pair chooses a 1-digit number on the 100-square, for example 6, and counts in 10s, pointing at each number as they say it: *sixteen, twenty-six, thirty-six, forty-six, …* They then continue writing the numbers in the sequence on one of their strips of paper, for example 96, 106, 116, 126, 136, 146, … They go as far as they like, or are able! They start again, choosing a different 1-digit number, and write that sequence on a different strip in a different colour.
Adult support may be useful in running this activity.

100-square; long strips of paper; coloured felt-tipped pens

Year 1 Block E2.b Activities

E2.b.1 A group of up to 12 children

Show the group a number cross: five squares in a cross shape. One child says a number for the middle of the cross (not a multiple of 10), e.g. 36. Everyone writes this in. Explain that the line across the middle is part of a number track. *Before the middle number we write the number one less, and after it we write the number one more.* Help children to write 35 to the left of 36, and 37 to the right. The numbers going down are Bisky Bat's numbers, counting in 10s. Write 46 below 36, saying *thirty-six, forty-six*. Then count back in 10s, *forty-six, thirty-six, twenty-six* and write 26 above 36. (This example is shown on p.41 of Workbook 2.) Once children understand how a number cross works, ask them to generate their own crosses, writing any starting number they choose in the middle.
Adult support may be useful in running this activity.

lots of blank number crosses per child

E2.b.2 A group of up to 8 children

Each child chooses one row on the 100-square, and makes a number line from it on their empty track, e.g. 21, 22, 23, … 30 or 91, 92, 93, …. 100. Compare the number lines. What is the same/different?
Adult support may be useful in running this activity.

empty track with 10 spaces per child; 100-square

E2.b.3 A whole-class investigation, working in pairs

Children explore patterns on their number grids. Match the difficulty of the patterns to ability levels. Encourage children to use calculators and explore patterns rather than do hard sums! They might find patterns in:

- the numbers down each column
- the numbers along the leading diagonal (top left to bottom right)
- the numbers along the other diagonal (bottom left to top right)
- adding the numbers in their first row, then adding the numbers in their second row, then adding those in their third row (use calculators); compare answers with other groups
- how much larger the number in the bottom right-hand space is than the number in the top left-hand space; compare answers
- how much larger the number in the bottom left-hand space is than the number in the top right-hand space; compare answers
- adding the numbers in the top left-hand corner and the bottom right-hand corner and finding half (use calculators). Repeat with the two numbers in the other corners.
- finding the total by adding all nine numbers on the grid. Some groups can divide this by the number in the middle of the grid.

Adult support is needed to run this activity.

100-square; calculators; individual 3 × 3 grid taken from the 100-square per child, matching grids to abilities

Year 2 Block E2.a Activities

10.1 10 Counting in 2s, 5s and 10s

E2.a.1 A group of 6 or more children

Drop ten 10p coins into the tin one by one, asking children to count the amount with you:
ten, twenty, thirty… one hundred. What is 100 pence?
Take out the coins.
Drop three 10p coins into the tin: *ten, twenty, thirty*.
Drop in one more coin. *How much money is in the tin now?*
Drop in three more coins: *fifty, sixty, seventy*. *What comes next?*
Drop in another 10p coin. *How much is in the tin now?*
Repeat the activity using 5p coins.
Adult support is needed to run this activity.

ten 5p and ten 10p coins; a tin

E2.a.3 Groups of 3 children

Make sure children understand how to tell if a number is even or odd by looking at the **last** digit. List the options for the last digit on the board under the headings 'even' and 'odd': 2, 4, 6, 8 or 0 for even numbers; 1, 3, 5, 7, 9 for odd numbers. Give a set of 1–40 number cards to each group to spread out face down. Children take turns to touch a card, guess whether it is even or odd and turn it over to see if they are correct.
Help children to tell if the number is even or odd by focusing their attention on the last digit. They keep the card if their guess is correct. If not, they turn the card face down and leave it in its place. They should collect their cards in two piles: even and odd. Continue until all the cards have been taken and then find who has the most even numbers and who has the most odd numbers.
Play again.
Adult support may be useful to run this activity with one or two groups of children.

1–40 number cards for each group

Year 2 Block E2.b Activities

10.3 10 Counting in 2s, 5s and 10s

E2.b.1 A group of 6 or more children

Explain that you are going to drop some 10p coins into a tin. Ask children not to count but to secretly raise a finger each time a coin is dropped. Drop four 10p coins one by one. *How much money is in the tin?*
Then children shut their eyes as you drop five 10p coins into the tin.
Repeat with 2p and 5p coins. When counting in 2s, also start with 1p in the tin so that the children count odd numbers.
Ask children to spot the missing number as you count five coins into the tin: *ten, twenty, forty, fifty, sixty*. Repeat with different amounts and with 2p and 5p coins.

one 1p coin; ten each of 2p, 5p, and 10p coins; a tin

E2.b.2 A group of up to 6 children

Explain that you will count in steps of 5. Children make various towers of 5 cubes. Ask each to take a number of towers, count in 5s to find the total number of cubes and write a matching multiplication sentence; e.g. in 4 towers, count 5, 10, 15, 20 and write $4 \times 5 = 20$. Actively discourage counting in 1s. Continue until each child has written several multiplications.
Repeat with towers of 10.
Adult support may be useful in running this activity.

interlocking cubes

E2.b.3 Groups of 3 children

Children write out the 2, 5 and 10 times-tables in standard form (one each). Together they consider each table in turn and create rhymes to help them learn it, for example
1 × 5 = 5 alive!
2 × 5 = 10 again
3 × 5 = 15 bean …
Children should attempt to do this for at least two tables. Their work can be displayed to help everyone learn their tables.
Adult support may be useful in running this activity.

E2.b.4 A group of up to 8 children

Children each take some interlocking cubes and build a few towers of five cubes. Each tower should be a different colour. They lay these side by side to make an array.
They copy this into their books by drawing round a matching rectangle of three rows of five squares. They then write the matching multiplication:
$3 \times 5 = 15$. Encourage children not to count in 1s but to count in 5s to work out the total. They compare their rectangle with other children's rectangles and talk about which multiplication facts they have written. Repeat this activity with towers of two, then 10 cubes.
Adult support may be useful in running this activity.

interlocking cubes

Maths Weekly Plan: Year 1 and 2

Block E2.c: Y1 Subtract 1-digit numbers; Y2 Multiply by adding repeatedly
Block E2.d: Y1 Subtract by counting back; Y2 Divide by grouping

	Mental oral starter	Objectives	Main teaching	Activities: Group 1 (Y1)	Activities: Group 2 (Y1)	Activities: Group 3 (Y2)	Activities: Group 4 (Y2)	Plenary	Outcomes
Day 1	**Double numbers up to 60.** In pairs chn write two even numbers between 2 and 12 (inclusive) on whiteboards. Throw a dice, eg 6. Ask chn to double this number and write the answer, eg 12. *Has anyone got that number on their board?* If they have, they cross it out. Rpt.	**Y1** • Begin to subtract a 1-digit number from a 2-digit number by counting back, not crossing 10 **Y2** • Introduce multiplication as repeated addition or as describing an array • Record multiplication facts using × and = in number sentences	**All** Recite 'Each little monster' together (see below). Draw 1 monster with 4 legs. Write *4* below. ***How many** legs on 2 monsters?* Write $4+4$. Draw 2nd monster. Count 8 legs. Complete addition: $4+4=8$. *2 **lots of** 4 are 8.* Write $2\times4=8$ below $4+4=8$. Rpt with 3rd monster. **[ITR Y2 E2.c]** **Y1** **Count back** along a number line from 20. Rpt starting from different numbers. Show chn 'jumping back' frog. *Frog jumps back along the line.* Write $18-5=$. *We must count back 5. Hold up 5 fingers*. Use frog to count back from 18. Complete **subtraction**. Rpt for 19–6 and 16–5.	Y1 E2.c.2 Counting back using pegs T	Y1 1.2 p44 Counting back using pegs	Y2 E2.c.1 Using cubes to generate 'sets of' TA	Y2 2.2 p44 Counting sets of tins, matching to multiplications	Stick six 10p coins on the board. Chn **count in 10s** to work out **how much** money. They write the total on their whiteboards and show you. Rehearse how to work out six 10s (*ten*, *twenty*, *thirty*, *forty*, *fifty*, *sixty*).	**Y1** • Count back from a given number • Use – sign **Y2** • Solve multiplication by grouping and repeated addition
Day 2	**Know the numbers that pair to make 4, 5, 6 or 10.** Write a large *4* on board. Throw a beanbag to a child and say 3. They must throw it back saying the number that goes with 3 to make 4. Rpt for the other pairs to 4. Move on to pairs that make 5, 6 and 10.		**All** Write $17-4=$ on board. Count 10 blue pegs and 7 yellow pegs onto coat hanger. Point at $17-4$. *We need to **take away** 4 pegs. We must count back 4. Hold up 4 fingers*. Slide the yellow pegs away one at a time. Write *13* to complete the subtraction. Rpt for other subtractions. **Y2** Read 'Some aliens came to Earth' (see below). *How many hands do the aliens have?* Draw 5 aliens with 3 hands. Write $3+3+3+3+3$. *We **count in 3s**. How many 3s?* Write $5\times3=$. Count in 3s, whispering *1, 2* and saying *3*, etc. *To find answer either do five 3s or add 3 five times.*	Y1 1.2 p43 Counting back using a number line	Y1 E2.c.3 TM 10.3 10 Addition and subtraction TA	Y2 E2.c.2 Drawing sets of rectangles to represent multiplications T	Y2 E2.c.2 Drawing sets of rectangles to represent multiplications T	Play 'What is the **take away**?' Give an answer, eg *13*. Chn have to invent different subtractions that have this answer. Record different suggestions on the board. Rpt.	**Y1** • Solve subtractions by counting back • Write subtraction sentences **Y2** • Recognise that multiplication is repeated addition • Solve multiplications by counting in multiples
Day 3	**Count back in 10s, 5s and 2s.** Play 'Team counting'. Divide class into 2 teams to count back in 5s. Say starting number, eg *75*. Point to one team who say the next number, eg *70*. Teams alternate saying next number. Rpt, counting back in 5s, 10s and 2s. Teams take turns to start.	**Y1** • Subtract by counting back to a multiple of 10	**All** Show chn a 10p coin then show purse. *I have 60p in the purse in 10p coins.* Write *60p* on board. *How many 10p coins are there in the purse?* Write $\_\times10p=60p$. Discuss how to find out by counting in 10s. Hold up 1 finger for each **multiple**. Rpt this process with 40p in 5p coins. **Y1** Write $40p-4p=$ on board. *How can we find the answer?* Remind children about counting back to solve subtractions. Use 'jumping back' frog on number line to demonstrate. Complete the subtraction: *36p*. Rpt for other subtractions. **[ITR Y2 E2.d]**	Y1 E2.c.1 TM 10.2 10 Addition and subtraction T	Y1 1.2 p45 Counting back using number lines	Y2 2.2 p43 Counting sets of 4 legs on monsters	Y2 E2.d.2 Using number cards to make missing number multiplications TA	Choose child to place frog at a number on a number line and silently jump back along it, stopping at another number. Challenge chn to state the subtraction. Record and rpt.	**Y1** • Count back to solve a subtraction • Count in 10s **Y2** • Solve multiplications by counting in multiples

	Mental oral starter	Objectives	Main teaching	Activities Group 1 Y1	Group 2 Y1	Group 3 Y2	Group 4 Y2	Plenary	Outcomes
Day 4	**Recognise and order the months of the year.** Recite the sequence of **months** together, starting at January. Shuffle month cards and peg them on a washing line at random. *We need to put these in order.* Ask pairs to swap two cards at a time until the cards are in order. Recite sequence again. Rpt.	*(Continued)* **Y2** • Begin to understand division as grouping • Introduce division as the inverse of multiplication • Understand that division sometimes leaves a remainder • Introduce the ÷ sign	**All** Count back along number line in 1s from 30. Rpt starting from different numbers. Write *14 – 4 =* on board. Place frog on 14. *We need to count back 4.* Complete the subtraction, using fingers to help. Rpt for 17 – 7 or 19 – 9. Extend by doing 26 – 6 and 24 – 4. **[ITR Y1 E2.d]** **Y2** Show tower of 4 cubes, and bag with cubes in. *There are 20 cubes in the bag. How many towers of 4?* Write *_ × 4 = 20*. Chn **count in 4s**. Open bag and make 5 towers. Complete multiplication. *We can also write it as 20 ÷ 4 =. How many 4s make 20?* Rpt for 18 cubes in towers of 3.	Y1 E2.d.1 Counting back using coins	Y1 1.2 p47 Counting back to a multiple of 10	Y2 E2.d.1 Using coins to make missing number multiplications	Y2 2.2 p46 Dividing as the inverse of multiplying	Challenge chn to say some subtractions that have an answer of 10. Record different suggestions on board. Extend to answers of 20.	**Y1** • Subtract by counting back to a multiple of 10 • Count back, bridging 10 **Y2** • Solve division by grouping • Understand divison is the inverse of multiplication
Day 5	**Name and recognise the properties of 3D shapes.** Play 'Stand up'. Give a **3D shape** to each child. Give instructions involving names and **properties**, eg *Stand up if your shape is a cuboid.* Check shapes. Rpt using different instructions.		**All/Y2** *How many 5p coins make 15p? How can we work it out?* ***Count in 5s.*** Remind chn that to solve **multiplications** they should count in the number, eg 2s, 3s, 4s, 5s, 10s, … Chn count three 5s: *5p, 10p, 15p*. Write *3 × 5p = 15p*. **Y1** Show teddy. *Teddy has saved some money.* Show 18p in 10p and 1p coins. *Teddy has to give his mum 8p. How much will he have left?* Write *18p – 8p =*. Model counting back using fingers. Check by using 1p coins. Write *10p* as answer. Rpt for 25p–5p. Chn **predict** answer.	Y1 1.2 p46 Counting back to a multiple of 10	Y1 E2.d.2 Counting back, bridging 10	Y2 2.2 p46 Solving divisions by circling sets	Y2 E2.d.4 Investigating division as grouping with remainders	Have bag with 3 towers of 10 cubes. *I have 30 cubes in towers. All towers are the same size.* Ask pairs to guess how many towers and how many cubes in a tower. Take suggestions and match these to multiplications.	**Y1** • Subtract by counting back to a multiple of 10 • Count back, bridging 10 **Y2** • Understand divison is the inverse of multiplication • Divide with remainders

Vocabulary
how many?
how much?
lots of
count back
count forward
subtraction
take away
addition
multiplication
multiple
division
number pairs
count in 10s, 3s, 4s, 5s
predict
addition
missing number
months
3D shapes
shape properties

Resources
number fans
'jumping back' frog
clothes hanger
10 blue pegs
7 yellow pegs
other coloured pegs
place-value cards (T,U)
interlocking cubes
10p coins
1p coins
individual whiteboards
beanbag
100-bead string
0–100 number line
purse
number cards 4–99
real 2p, 5p and 10p coins
3D shapes
teddy bear

Rhymes

Each little monster with four fat legs,
Two little monsters, steady on their pegs!
Three little monsters jumping and free,
Four little monsters sitting in a tree,
Five little monsters, happy not sad,
Six little monsters being very bad!

Some aliens came to Earth one day,
All very excited and wanting to play.
The children shouted, 'Hip hip hooray!
With three hands you can certainly stay'.

Year 1 Block E2.c Activities

10.2 10 Addition and subtraction

E2.c.1 A group of 6 or more children

Pull 24 beads to the left of the string. Slide 3 beads across singly, counting on from 24. *24 and 3 more is?* On the number line draw three hops from 24 to 27, and write 24 + 3 = 27. Repeat, adding small numbers to numbers <50 without bridging ten until all are confident.

Pull 24 beads to one side of the string. Slide 3 of these across singly, counting back from 24. *24 take away 3 leaves what?* On the number line draw three hops back from 24 to 21 and write 24 – 3 = 21. Repeat, subtracting small numbers from numbers <50 without bridging ten until all are confident.

Adult support is needed to run this activity.

100-bead string; 0–100 number line

E2.c.2 A group of up to 8 children

Write a suitable subtraction, e.g. 14 – 2 = , and read as a group. Place ten blue pegs and some yellow pegs (e.g. 4) on the hanger. Match this to the place-value cards 10 + 4. Point at the subtraction. *How many do we take away? Two*. Point at the four yellow pegs: *We take away two.* Do this, counting back from 4 to 2. We still have the ten blue pegs. Show using the place-value cards that the 10 stays the same. Complete the subtraction.

Ask pairs to do a subtraction using their hanger and place-value cards, and record. Repeat several times.

Adult support may be useful in running this activity.

hangers with ten blue pegs and other coloured pegs per pair; tens and units place-value cards per pair

10.3 10 Addition and subtraction

E2.c.3 A group of 6 or more children

Pull 35 beads to the left of the string. Slide 7 more beads across singly, counting on from 35. *35 and 7 more is?* On the number line draw 7 hops from 35 to 42 and write 35 + 7 = 2. *What tens number did we count through?* Slide 7 beads to join 35 again, this time starting with a group of 5. *What is 40 add 2? Can you do that without counting?* Repeat, adding small numbers to numbers <50, bridging ten until all are confident. Pull 35 beads to one side of the string. Slide 6 of these across singly, counting back from 35. *35 take away 6 leaves what?* On the number line draw 6 hops back from 35 to 29 and write 35 – 6 = 29. *What tens number did we count through?* Slide 35 beads to one end of the string. *How many do I take away to get to 30? And how many more do I take away?* Repeat, subtracting small numbers from numbers <50, bridging ten until all are confident.

Adult support is needed to run this activity.

100-bead string; 0–100 number line

Year 1 Block E2.d Activities

E2.d.1 A group of up to 8 children

Place a pile of coins where all the children can reach them. Give each child a 2-digit number card. Ask them all to match their cards to coins. Go round the group taking each child in turn. Ask them how much they have, for example *Twenty-four pence*. Record this amount and generate a subtraction to remove the units: *24p – 4p =* . Ask that child to remove the 1p coins. *How much is left?* Record the answer: *24p – 4p = 20p.* Continue round the group, generating subtractions in the same way.

Adult support may be useful in running this activity.

2-digit number cards; 10p and 1p coins

E2.d.2 Pairs of children

Place a pile of 2-digit cards where all the children can reach them. Each pair takes a card. They generate the subtraction to remove the units, for example *36 – 6 = 30*. They record this. They then discuss what the answer will be if they take off one more than this, i.e. 36 – 7 = . They discuss what counting back one from the multiple of 10 gives them: *Thirty, twenty-nine.* They record the answer, for example *36 – 7 = 29*. Each pair generates five pairs of subtractions, the first removing the units to give an answer of a multiple of 10, the second taking away one more.

Adult support may be useful in running this activity.

2-digit number cards

Year 2 Block E2.c Activities

E2.c.1 A group of up to 8 children

Ask children to make towers of 4 interlocking cubes. Place six towers on the table. *How many lots of four have we got?* (6) Write $6 \times 4 =$ on the board, and say this together as: *six sets of four is?* Encourage children to count in 4s to work out the answer. They each do this individually and write the total. Repeat this for other sets of four, for example $8 \times 4 =$ and $5 \times 4 =$ and $7 \times 4 =$.
If you have time, move on to write multiplications for sets of three or sets of five.
Adult support is needed to run this activity.

interlocking cubes

E2.c.2 A group of up to 8 children

On the board draw four squares in a row, end to end. This is a 'rod'.
Ask children to use different colours to draw three of these, one above the other with no gaps. Then ask them to write a matching multiplication: $3 \times 4 =$.
Count together in 4s as children point to each rod from the bottom one upwards: *four, eight, twelve*. They complete the multiplication. Pairs now work together to draw some rods of four squares long to generate their own multiplication.
They should repeat this until they have at least six drawings in all, each with matching multiplications. Children may draw rods of lengths other than four, but remind them that within any one drawing (multiplication) the rods must all be of the same length.
Adult support is needed to run this activity.

squared paper

Year 2 Block E2.d Activities

E2.d.1 A group of up to 8 children

Pairs take a handful of one type of each coin, for example six 2p coins. Ask each pair to count their coins, and write a matching multiplication, for example $6 \times 2p =$. Read each multiplication as, for example, *Six lots of two are?* Then each child counts, for example in 2s, to work out the total. They write the answer to complete the multiplication and check it before replacing the coins.
Now ask children to close their eyes and meanwhile put five 5p coins in a purse. Show the purse and explain there are some 5p coins in it that make 30p.
Write $\_ \times 5p = 30p$ on the board and read this as: *How many 5ps make thirty pence?* Encourage children to count on their fingers to find out how many 5ps: *five, ten, fifteen… thirty… Six 5ps*. Write 6 in the space for the missing number and read the multiplication together. *Six lots of 5p make 30p*. Repeat for 16p in 2p coins and then for other sets of 2p, 5p and 10p coins. *How many lots of 2p make 16p?*
Adult support is needed to run this activity.

real 2p, 5p and 10p coins in separate piles; opaque purse

E2.d.2 A group of 4, 6 or 8 children working in pairs

Pile a shuffled set of 4–40 multiple of 4 cards face down. Each pair takes a card and writes a missing number multiplication; e.g. for card 20, write $\_ \times 4 = 20$. They find the missing number by taking 20 cubes and using them all to make groups of 4 cubes. *How many towers can you make?* Children replace their card at the bottom of the pile and take another card to repeat the activity at least four times. You may wish them to use 3–30 multiple of 3 cards or 5–50 multiple of 5 cards, building towers of 3 or 5 respectively.
Adult support may be useful in running this activity.

interlocking cubes; 4–40 multiple of 4 cards

E2.d.4 Pairs of children

Pile the shuffled number cards face down. One child turns over the top card. Both take cubes to match the card number. They each divide the number by 4, following these steps:

- Write the division, for example $33 \div 4 =$.
- Make towers of 4 cubes using their set of cubes.
- Find out how many towers they have, and how many are left over.
- Complete the division, for example $33 \div 4 = 8$ *with 1 left over.*

Pairs complete five divisions. They may then invent some more divisions using divisors other than 4.

21–39 number cards (odd numbers only); cubes

Maths Weekly Plan: Year 1 and 2

Block A3.a: Y1 Count by grouping in 5s or 10s; Y2 Partition numbers into H, T, U
Block A3.b: Y1 Add multiples of 10 to 2-digit numbers; Y2 Begin to round to nearest 10

	Mental oral starter	Objectives	Main teaching	Activities Group 1 Y1	Activities Group 2 Y1	Activities Group 3 Y2	Activities Group 4 Y2	Plenary	Outcomes
Day 1	**Count on/back in 10s to/from a 2-digit number.** Play 'Birdsong'. Put chn into 3 groups of birds. Choose a start number, eg 97, and a group to start **counting back** in 10s. After a few counts, a different group takes over the count, and so on. Rpt, **counting on** and back in 10s from different numbers.	**Y1** • Count a number of objects by grouping 5s or 10s **Y2** • Read and write numbers up to 100 in words • Begin to partition 3-digit numbers into H, T and U • Begin to read and write numbers up to 1000 in figures	**All** Read *The Three Little Pigs*. **Count in 10s** from 0 to 100. Show jar of 1p coins. *This is Mr Wolf's savings!* **Estimate total**. Ask chn to **group** the coins in 10s, then count in 10s. Take about half of the coins away. *How much left?* Group in 5s and count. **[ITR Y1 A3.a]** **Y2** Show picture of a crowd. ***How many** people? **More than** 100? More than 200? More than 1000?* Write *461*. Cover 4. Read *61*. Uncover 4. Read *461*. 1st child says 100s, 2nd says 10s, 3rd says units. Give them matching p-v cards. Point to the cards as you read them. Rpt for 739.	Y1 A3.a.1 Counting in 10s, grouping in 10s TA	Y1 1.3 p3 Grouping in 5s and counting	Y2 A3.a.1 TM 11.1 11 Making amounts T	Y2 2.3 p3 Partitioning into H, T and U	Invite chn to estimate how many people are in the class today. Count them, grouping in 5s.	**Y1** • Estimate a number of objects • Count objects by grouping in 5s or 10s **Y2** • Partition into H, T and U • Read 3-digit numbers in words and write in figures
Day 2	**Subtract 10 from a 'teens' number.** Play 'Quick on the draw'. Say a **'teens' number**, eg *16*. Chn must **subtract** 10 from this number and hold up fingers, eg 6, as quickly as possible. Rpt for different numbers 10–20. If necessary, model answers on first two rows of 100-square.		**All** As a class, count in 10s from 0 to 100. Then **count in 1s** from 0 to 100, waving every time you say a multiple of 10. Make three number lines using number cards: 100–900 (multiple-of-100 cards), 10–90 (multiple-of-10 cards), and 1–9 (digit cards). Count along each line. Ask one child to say a multiple of 100 and take the matching card. Ask a 2nd child to do the same for a multiple of 10, and a 3rd to do the same for a **1-digit number**. Write the three numbers as an **addition**. *What is the total?* Rpt for several more additions. **[ITR Y2 A3.a]**	Y1 1.3 p2 Grouping in 10s and counting	Y1 A3.a.3 Investigating how many 0s in numbers 1 to 100, how many 1s, how many 2s, and so on T	Y2 2.3 p2 Partitioning into T and U	Y2 A3.a.2 Making 4-digit numbers, ordering them, then writing in-between numbers TA	Ask chn to each write a **3-digit number** on their whiteboards. Say a number of **hundreds**. Chn stand up if their number has the given number of hundreds. Rpt for **tens** and **units**. Rpt several times.	**Y1** • Estimate a number of objects • Count objects by grouping into 5s or 10s **Y2** • Begin to understand place value • Partition into H, T and U
Day 3	**Count in 4s.** On the board, write a sequence counting in 4s with missing numbers, eg _ _ *12* _ *20* _ _ *32*. Chn work in pairs to write the sequence on their whiteboards, then fill in the missing numbers. Discuss the sequence, then chant the numbers together.	**Y1** • Say the number that is 10 more or less than a given number • Begin to add a multiple of 10 to a 2-digit number by counting on in 10s	**All** Draw cheque for £361. Read amount in **words** then **figures**. Write *one hundred and sixty-three*. Chn read it, and write in figures. *361 and 163 have same **digits**. Are they the same?* Write 163 as an addition: *100+60+3*. Rpt for 361. *Look at the 100s digit to see which is **larger***. **Y1** Show Bisky Bat. *He counts in 10s*. Put Bisky on 16 on 100-square. Count on in 10s to 96. Put Bisky on 38. *What number will Bisky say next?* Move Bisky down 1 space: 48. Put Bisky on 63. *What number did Bisky say before 63?* Move Bisky up 1 space: 53. Rpt several times.	Y1 A3.b.1 Counting on in 10s using a 100-square T	Y1 1.3 p5 Adding several 10s	Y2 A3.a.4 Making 3-digit numbers and writing the number 1 more TA	Y2 p19 Partitioning into H, T and U	Ask a few Y1 chn to give examples from their activities where they found the number **10 more** or **10 less**. They say the number and the rest of the class must say the number 10 more or 10 less.	**Y1** • Count on in 10s on a 100-square • Add multiples of 10 by counting on in 10s **Y2** • Partition numbers into H, T and U • Write 3-digit numbers in figures

Maths Weekly Plan: Year 1 and 2

Block A3.c: Y1 Partition into T and U; Y2 Add by bridging a multiple of 10
Block A3.d: Y1 Order numbers; Y2 Find the difference between two numbers

	Mental oral starter	Objectives	Main teaching	Activities: Group 1 Y1	Activities: Group 2 Y1	Activities: Group 3 Y2	Activities: Group 4 Y2	Plenary	Outcomes
Day 1	**Count on 1, 2, 3 or 4 more from any number up to 100.** Pairs each write a 1- or 2-digit number on whiteboards. Use a dice marked 1, 2, 3, 4, 1, 2. Throw the dice. Pairs **count on** the number thrown and write answer on whiteboards. Rpt several times.	**Y1** • Begin to partition 2-digit numbers into T and U **Y2** • Add a 1-digit number to a 2-digit number, crossing a multiple of 10 (rehearse) • Begin to add by bridging a multiple of 10 (36+8=36+4+4)	**All** Show Midgard the dragon. *Midgard likes to fly, but also to rest!* Write 36+8=. Draw 30–50 number line. Put Midgard on 36. *He rests on numbers ending in 0. What is the next number like this? 40. How far to 40? 4.* ***How many more*** *must he fly? 4. 36+8=44.* Rpt for 45+7 and 28+5. **Y1** Show a teddy bear. *Bear has 17p!* Show Blue Baboon. *He collects 10s.* Child counts out 17 1p coins. When they reach 10, make Baboon jump up. Exchange ten 1p coins for a 10p coin. *One 10p coin and seven 1p coins.* Write *17p=10p+7p*. Rpt for 26p, 32p, 23p, or 33p.	Y1 A3.c.2 Making 2-digit numbers with coins (T)	Y1 1.3 p8 Writing 2-digit numbers as tens and units	Y2 A3.c.1 Adding by counting on (TA)	Y2 2.3 p9 Bridging 10 to add	Play 'Bingo'. Pairs each write four 2-digit numbers on their whiteboards. Show a number card 0–9 and say the number. If chn can **add** that number to one of their 2-digit numbers to make a **multiple of 10**, they cross it out. Rpt.	**Y1** • Partition into T and U • Know the value of each digit in a 2-digit number **Y2** • Add by counting on, bridging 10 • Recognise multiples of 10 • Rehearse number bonds to 10
Day 2	**Add three numbers, total up to 12.** Three chn roll a dice each. Write the three numbers as an addition, with **largest** number **first** and **smallest last**, eg *5+2+1*. Chn write answers on whiteboards. Ask a child to model jumps along a number line. Rpt. Encourage Y2s to look for bonds to 10.		**All** Count on together from 1 to 50, pointing to numbers on 100-square as you count. Emphasise that there are 10 numbers in each row. Highlight 14. *Baboon says there is one 10 in 14, and there are four 1s.* Write *14=10+4* on the board. Rpt for other **'teens' numbers**. **Y2** Show Midgard and a 100-square. Write *26+8=*. *Where should Midgard start?* Put him on 26. *What is the* ***next*** *number he can rest on? 30. How far to 30?* Count on 4 from 26 to 30. Point at +8. Count on past 30 to 34. Complete the addition. Rpt for 37+5 and 46+6. **[ITR Y2 A3.c]**	Y1 1.3 p7 Matching 2-digit numbers to 10p and 1p coins	Y1 A3.c.3 TM 11.3 11 Place value	Y2 2.3 p8 Adding by bridging 10 (TA)	Y2 A3.c.3 TM 12.3 12 Number puzzle (T)	Play 'I am thinking of a number'. Give clues to a mystery number, eg *It is ten and six; it is two* ***tens*** *and seven* ***ones****; it is eight more than twenty.*	**Y1** • Know the value of each digit in a 2-digit number • Make 2-digit numbers **Y2** • Add by counting on, bridging 10 • Recognise multiples of 10 • Rehearse number bonds to 10
Day 3	**Estimate and count a set of objects by grouping in 10s.** Spread out a large handful of 1p coins. Chn **estimate total** number of coins. They place their counter on matching number on 100-square. A child counts out the coins, giving any set of 10 to another child to hold. Rpt for different numbers of 1p coins.		**All** Count round counting hoop from 1 to 10. Point at a mark. *What number is this?* Count round again. *Baboon is happy because we counted a whole turn, which is 10!* Model counting round, then continuing to 13. *One 10 and 3 more.* Write *13=10+3*. Extend to 25. **[ITR Y1 A3.c]** **Y2** Write *38p. Midgard has saved 38p. His mum gives him another 5p. How much does he have?* Write *38+5=*. Show 38 on 100-square. *What is the next number ending in 0? How many more 1ps would give Midgard 40p? 2.* Give him 3 more. Complete the addition. Rpt for 58p+7p.	Y1 A3.c.1 Saying 2-digit numbers and making them using coins and place-value cards (TA)	Y1 72 Using place-value cards to write 3-digit numbers	Y2 A3.c.2 Adding by counting on (T)	Y2 p21 Adding by counting on	Count the number of chn in the class by **grouping** them into 10s and seeing how many are **left over**. Write the matching addition, eg *32=30+2*.	**Y1** • Say and write 2-digit numbers • Make 2-digit numbers from tens and units **Y2** • Add by counting on, bridging multiples of 10 • Know number bonds to 10

Year 2 Block A3.a Activities

11.1 11 Making amounts

A3.a.1 A group of 6 or more children

Show children a £1 coin. *How much money do I have?* Add two 10p coins to the £1 coin. *How much money now? I need £1·25. How much more should I take?* Remind children how to write £1·25.

Show children two £1 coins and two 1p coins. *How much money do I have? If I wanted £2·22, what would I need to do?* Remind children how to write £2·22. Repeat the activity, showing only two types of coin at once and asking what other coins are needed to make an amount needing all three types of coin. Adult support is needed to run this activity.

£1, 10p and 1p coins

A3.a.2 A group of 4, 6 or 8 children working in pairs

Place thousands, hundreds, tens and units place-value cards in separate shuffled piles face down. Pairs take a card from the top of each pile and arrange them to make a 4-digit number. They repeat this to make a second number, then take turns to say the numbers round the group. They record their numbers with a gap between them, smaller first, then fill the gap with an in-between number. They check each other's ordered sequence of three numbers. Children repeat the process until they have used all the cards. They shuffle the cards and start again.

place-value cards (Th, H, T, U)

A3.a.4 Pairs of children

Place hundreds, tens and units place-value cards in separate shuffled piles face down. Children take a card from the top of each pile and arrange them to make a 3-digit number. They both say this number out loud, write the number one larger on a Post-it and stick the Post-it on the cards. Repeat the process until they have used all the cards.

small Post-it notes; place-value cards (H, T, U)

Year 2 Block A3.b Activities

A3.b.2 A group of up to 8 children

Remove the multiples of 10 from a set of 1–100 number cards and give five cards of those remaining to each child. Write a multiple of 10 on the board, for example 30. Ask children if anyone is holding a card with a number that rounds to 30. Look on the number line and point out the numbers that do round to 30. If any child is holding one of them, they hand in their card. Write a new multiple of 10 and continue like this to see who gets rid of all their cards first. Play again. Adult support is needed to run this activity.

large 0–100 number line; 1–100 number cards

A3.b.5 A group of 2, 3, or 4 children

Place a shuffled set of 5–100 cards face down in a pile. Take turns to reveal a card and round the number to the nearest 10. If correct, keep the card. If incorrect, return the card to the bottom of the pile. Check each other's rounding, using a 100-square if necessary. See who collects the most cards.

5–100 number cards; 100-square

Year 1 Block A3.a Activities

A3.a.1 A group of up to 8 children working in pairs

Give each child a multiple of 10 card. *You are holding a 'wolf' number!* Spread out the remaining cards face down. Count in 10s from 0 to 100, with each child saying the number on their card. When you reach a missing 'ten', turn over one of the cards that is face down. If that is the missing multiple, continue the count. If not, turn that card back over and start the count again from 0. Continue like this until you reach 100.

Lay all the cards in order where children can see them. Show a bag of cubes or beads. Ask each pair to estimate the number of cubes in the bag. They should talk about it and feel the bag, comparing with the multiples of 10 in the line, for example *Are there more than 20? More than 30? …* Record one estimate that each pair has agreed.

Count the cubes, showing the children how to group in 10s. *Whose estimate was closest?* Repeat.

Adult support may be useful in running this activity.

multiple of 10 cards; bag of 30–100 cubes or beads

A3.a.3 Pairs of children

Give each pair a book. Without opening it they discuss how many pages there might be, and then look to check. Ask the pairs to work out how many page numbers have a '0' in them. They should think about this and record their answer. Then challenge each pair to work out how many pages have a '1' in them.

This is much harder! They can then work out if the same number of pages have a '2' in them.

Adult support may be useful in running this activity.

a book with numbered pages, up to about 80, per pair

Year 1 Block A3.b Activities

A3.b.1 A group of up to 8 children

Ask each child to choose a starting number not larger than 60. They place their counter on that number on their 100-square, for example 56. *Everyone should add 30 to their number.* Write *+ 30* on the board. Support any children who need it, encouraging every child to move their counter three spaces down the grid, counting in 10s as they do so. Check round each child to see that they have done this correctly. Ask each child to record their addition on their whiteboard, for example *56 + 30 = 86*.

Repeat, asking children to start on a new number.

Adult support may be useful in running this activity.

100-square; counters and individual whiteboard per child

A3.b.2 Pairs of children

Shuffle the cards and place them in a pile face down. One child takes a card from the pile. The second child throws the dice. They must add that number of 10s to the card number, for example if the card is 24, and the dice throw is 4, they add 40 to 24. Children can use the 100-square to help them, identifying their number and counting down the grid. Ask children to record the addition: *24 + 40 = 64*. Repeat this at least six times, recording each addition.

Adult support may be useful in running this activity.

100-square; dice; 10–60 number cards

A3.b.3 A group of 3 or 4 children

Each child takes a card. They take turns to throw the dice. With each throw they subtract that many multiples of 10 from their number and record the answer.

For example, a child starts with card 104, and throws a 3. They subtract 30 and write 74. Continue throwing and subtracting until one child reaches a 1-digit number. If the dice throw is too large for them to subtract it, they miss a turn. For example, if they have 24 and throw 3, they cannot subtract 30. It may take some time to reach a 1-digit number! The first child to reach a 1-digit number is the winner, and play stops.

Start again, each taking a new card.

Adult support may be useful in running this activity.

100–110 number cards; dice

	Mental oral starter	Objectives	Main teaching	Activities: Group 1 (Y1)	Activities: Group 2 (Y1)	Activities: Group 3 (Y2)	Activities: Group 4 (Y2)	Plenary	Outcomes
Day 4	**Read the time to the hour on an analogue clock.** Play 'Clock pointing'. Pairs use clock boards (Y1 PCM 116). Give an instruction, eg *Show me 2* ***o'clock***. Pairs point at the matching clock. Rpt many times. Extend to saying: *Look at the clocks in the first row. What is the time on the second clock?*	*(Continued)* **Y2** • Begin to round numbers less than 100 to the nearest 10	**All** Show p-v cards 70 and 4. *Write the* ***2-digit number***. Write *74*. *Turkey wants to give Owl £74, but the bank only gives £10 notes. How* ***close*** *to £74 can we get?* Show 74 on number line. *More than 70,* ***less than*** *80. Is it* ***closer*** *to 70 or to 80? 70 is the* ***nearest 10***. Rpt for 38. **Y1** Show mug with 10ps and 1ps in it. *This is Bisky's savings mug.* Count the 10ps first then the 1ps. Write *45p*. Show three more 10p coins. Write *45p + 30p =*. *How much will Bisky have now?* Say *45*, then count on in 10s. Complete the number sentence. Rpt.	Y1 1.3 p4 Writing the numbers 10 more and 10 less	Y1 A3.b.3 Subtracting multiples of 10	Y2 A3.b.2 Using a number line to round numbers	Y2 2.3 p6 Rounding 2-digit numbers to nearest 10	Chn each write a 2-digit number on their whiteboards. Say a multiple of 10, eg *40*. Chn stand up if their number **rounds** to 40. Check they are correct. Rpt for another multiple of 10.	**Y1** • Count on/back in 10s from any 2-digit number • Count on and back in 10s on a 100-square **Y2** • Round numbers to nearest 10 using a number line
Day 5	**Say a number 20/30 more/less than a 2-digit number.** Pairs place 100-squares in front of them. Give an instruction, eg *Show me 20 more than 62*. Pairs place a counter on the number 20 more. Check. Use a large 100-square to model if necessary. Rpt many times for 20/30 more/less.		**All** 5 chn each build a tower of 10 cubes. Add 3 loose cubes. *How many in total?* Count the 10s, then the 1s: 53. *If we added 3 more towers of 10, what would be the total?* Count on in 10s from 53 on 100-square. Write *83* to complete sentence. Rpt for 45 + 20. **[ITR Y1 A3.b]** **Y2** Write *83p*. *This is the price of a packet of biscuits. We are going to make the price a multiple of 10 so we can pay with 10p coins. 83 must be rounded to the nearest 10.* Look on 100-square: *Is 83* ***nearer*** *to 80 or 90? Nearer to 80p.* Rpt for eg 38p. **[ITR Y2 A3.b]**	Y1 A3.b.2 Adding multiples of 10 to 2-digit numbers	Y1 71 Adding 30p to the price of different items, some crossing £1	Y2 2.3 p6 Rounding 2-digit numbers to nearest 10	Y2 A3.b.5 Playing a card game rounding 2-digit numbers to nearest 10	On the board, write: *46 + 20 = 66, 23 + 40 = 62, 74 + 20 = 94. One of these is not correct. You're going to be the teacher and mark the sums!* Pairs identify the incorrect sum and write the correct answer.	**Y1** • Add a multiple of 10 to a 2-digit number • Add a multiple of 10 by counting on in 10s on a 100-square **Y2** • Round 2-digit numbers to the nearest 10

Vocabulary
count on, count back
count in 1s, 5s, 10s, 100s
estimate
total
group in 5s, 10s
how many?
more than
less than
1-, 2-, 3-digit number
add, addition
hundreds
tens
units
words
figures
larger
smallest
10 more, 10 less
close, closer, closest
near, nearer, nearest
round, round up
nearest 10
exact
half-way
'teens' number
subtract
o'clock

Resources
a version of *The Three Little Pigs*
transparent jar
about 35 1p coins
photo of a crowd of several hundred people
place-value cards (Th, H, T, U)
multiple-of-10 cards 0–100
cloth bag
up to 100 linking cubes
up to nine £1 coins
up to nine 10p coins
large 100-square
multiple-of-100 cards 100–900
number cards 1–110
three or four books with up to 80 numbered pages
individual whiteboards
picture of Bisky Bat
small 100-squares (one per pair)
counters (one per pair)
small Post-it notes
clock boards (Y1 PCM 116)
large 0–100 number line
mug
dice numbered 1–6

	Mental oral starter	Objectives	Main teaching	Activities: Group 1 Y1	Activities: Group 2 Y1	Activities: Group 3 Y2	Activities: Group 4 Y2	Plenary	Outcomes
Day 4	**Halve even numbers to 20.** Play 'Fan-tastic'. Say a **double**, eg *14*. Chn work out which number has 14 as its double and show it on number fans (7). If necessary, check on a line of number cards 1–20: start at 7 and make 7 jumps until you reach 14. Rpt for different even numbers up to 20.	**Y1** • Order numbers up to at least 30 • Say a number lying between two numbers up to at least 50 **Y2** • Extend understanding of relationship of subtraction to difference • Find the difference between two numbers by counting on	**All** Write *28, 34. Which is* ***larger****? What is the* ***difference between*** *them?* Show 20–40 number line. *Midgard will fly along the line to find out.* Put him on 28. *What number will he rest on? How many to 30? 2. How many more to 34? 4. What is the difference? 6.* Rpt for 47 and 52. **Y1** Put 1–30 number track on the floor. Count along from 1 to 30. Two chn each put one toy on a number. *Which number is* ***smaller****?* Chn say a number **in between** these two. Chn put toys on three different numbers. *Which number is in between the largest and smallest?*	Y1 1.3 p9 Finding in-between numbers	Y1 A3.d.5 Ordering number cards smallest to largest T	Y2 A3.d.1 TM 12.1 12 Number puzzle TA	Y2 2.3 p10 Finding the difference	Each pair writes a 2-digit number. On board write: *22, 32, 42, 52, 62, 72, 82, 92.* Pairs choose the next number after theirs (ie if they wrote 36, they would choose 42) and count on to find the difference.	**Y1** • Order numbers up to 30 • Say the largest of two or three numbers **Y2** • Find a difference by counting on • Understand that difference can be seen as subtraction
Day 5	**Subtract a 1-digit number from a 'teens' number crossing 10.** Play 'Quick on the draw'. Write a **subtraction** of a 1-digit number from a 'teens' number, crossing 10, eg *13–7*. Give chn some thinking time. On the command *Go!* chn hold up fingers to match the answer. Rpt for similar subtractions.		**All** Give 4 chn a number card 1–30 each. Ask them to stand at the front. *Let's put the numbers in* ***order****.* Use 100-square to help. *The smallest number will come nearest the beginning of the grid.* Continue until all numbers are in order. Rpt for five numbers. **[ITR Y1 A3.d]** **Y2** Write *42–37*. Put Midgard on 37 on 30–50 number line. Move him on 3 to rest on 40. *Hold up 3 fingers.* Move him on to 42. *Hold up 2 more fingers. 5 fingers in total.* Complete the subtraction: *42–37=5. The difference between 37 and 42 is 5.* Rpt for 65–59. **[ITR Y2 A3.d]**	Y1 A3.d.1 Comparing numbers using a number line TA	Y1 1.3 p9 Finding in-between numbers	Y2 2.3 p10 Finding the difference	Y2 A3.d.2 Finding a small difference T	Write a number on the board, eg *19. This is an in-between number.* Chn have to say two numbers that 19 is in between, eg *14 and 26*. Rpt several times.	**Y1** • Order numbers up to 30 • Say numbers in between two numbers **Y2** • Find a difference by counting on • Understand that difference can be seen as subtraction

Vocabulary
count on
how many more?
add, addition
multiple of 10
'teens' number
next
tens
ones, units
digit
group in 10s
left over
difference between
in between
larger, largest
smaller, smallest
first
last
order
estimate
total
double
subtract, subtraction

Resources
individual whiteboards
dice numbered 1, 2, 3, 4, 1, 2
picture of Midgard the dragon
teddy bear
picture of Blue Baboon
up to thirty-five 1p coins
up to forty 10p coins
list of made-up cake/sweet prices
small 100-squares (one per pair)
number cards 0–50
dice numbered 1–6
1–20 number line
large 100-square
100-bead string
0–100 number line
up to four sets of digit cards 0–9
counters (one per pair)
counting hoop marked with tape at 10 equidistant intervals, with start and half-way marks in a different colour
place-value cards (T and U)
up to four 1–50 number tracks
number fans (one per child)
20–40 number line
1–30 number track
three small toys
1–50 number line
up to four 0–20 number lines
30–50 number line
large 1–30 number line

Blocks A3.c and A3.d

Year 1 Block A3.c Activities

A3.c.1 A group of up to 12 children working in pairs

Say a 2-digit number, for example *fifty-six*. Each pair must make this number, one child using coins and the other using place-value cards. Check each pair's amounts and numbers. Then say a new number, and the children swap roles. Continue playing like this.
Adult support may be useful in running this activity.

tens and units place-value cards; 10p and 1p coins

A3.c.2 A group of up to 8 children

Give each child a pile of 10p and 1p coins. Draw a cake and tell children its price. They must give you the correct money in 10p and 1p coins. Check each child's amount. Continue, discussing the prices of different things as you go. Can children think of other things that cost less than £1?
Adult support may be useful in running this activity.

10p and 1p coins per child; catalogue of cake/sweet prices, or make these up

11.3 11 Place value

A3.c.3 A group of 6 or more children

Pull 23 beads to one end of the string. *How many beads can you see? How many groups of ten? How many ones? How do we write that number?* Repeat with other two-digit numbers.
Slide 40 beads to one end of the string. *I want to make 45. How many more beads do I need? How do you know? How do we write 45?*
Slide 6 beads to the middle of the string. (Make sure they are next to whole groups of 10.) *I want to make 26. How many more beads do I need? Do I need to count them one by one? How do we write 26?*
Repeat with other 2-digit numbers, including teens.
Adult support is needed to run this activity.

100-bead string

Year 1 Block A3.d Activities

A3.d.1 Pairs of children

Shuffle the cards and place them in a pile face down. Children take turns to take a card. They compare their numbers, if necessary looking at the large number line. Who has the larger number? That child takes both cards and places them face up, with a counter on the larger number. They continue to play like this. At the end, the winner is the one with most pairs.
Adult support may be useful in running this activity.

1–30 number cards; counters; large 1–30 number line displayed

A3.d.5 A group of 3 or 4 children

Deal four cards to each child. The children place them in a line, in order, from smallest to largest. They check each other's lines using the number line. They then place all their cards together in one long ordered line. Then collect up the cards, shuffle and deal again to repeat the activity. Extend by dealing five or six cards each.
Adult support may be useful in running this activity.

1–50 number cards; 1–50 number line

Year 2 Block A3.c Activities

A3.c.1 A group of 4, 6 or 8 children working in pairs

Give each pair a 100-square and a different starting number ending with the same units digit, for example 17, 27, 37, 47. Pairs use their 100-square to work out how many to add to their starting number to reach Midgard's next resting number, i.e. the next multiple of 10.

They may prefer to use their fingers by putting, for example, 17 'in their heads', counting on and holding up one finger for each number spoken. They write their addition, for example *27 + 3 = 30, 17 + 3 = 20. Copy these onto the board and discuss* why each pair has added the same number to reach Midgard's resting number. Repeat the activity, starting with numbers with different units.

Adult support is needed to run this activity.

100-square for each pair

A3.c.2 A group of 4, 6 or 8 children working in pairs

Give each pair the same starting number, for example 37. They write the addition that will take them to Midgard's next resting number ending in 0, for example *37 + 3 = 40*. Give each pair a 3–8 digit card. They use a 1–50 number track to add their card number to the starting number, remembering to 'rest' as they cross the multiple of 10. Each pair agrees writes the addition below the first one, for example *37 + 5 = 42*.

Ask pairs how they did the addition. They should show how they rested on the multiple of 10. Repeat, giving a new starting number, for example 28.

Adult support is needed to run this activity.

3–8 digit cards; 1–50 number track for each pair

A3.c.3 A group of 6 or more children working in pairs

Each pair uses a set of 0–9 digit cards to make two 2-digit numbers with a difference of 2. Note that there is only one card for each digit, for example 38 and 40 or 39 and 41 are possible but not 32 and 34. Check that their pairs of numbers have a difference of 2 by circling them on the 0–100 number line and drawing a jump between them.

If children are correct, ask them to record their pairs of numbers in number sentences, for example *41 – 39 = 2*.

What do you notice about your pairs of numbers? Elicit that they cannot have the same tens digit. Challenge children to find as many pairs as they can with a difference of 2.

What is the largest pair of numbers you can make using two digit cards for each number? What do you notice about your pairs of numbers? Are they odd or even?

Elicit that both numbers in each pair are either odd or even because the pattern of odd or even numbers goes up in 2s.

Adult support is needed to run this activity.

0–100 number line; 0–9 digit cards for each pair

Year 2 Block A3.d Activities

12.1 12 Number puzzle

A3.d.1 A group of 6 or more children

Together look for some pairs of numbers with a difference of two on a 0–20 number line. Draw a jump between the two numbers to show the difference and record this in a number sentence, for example *10 – 8 = 2*. Children work in pairs to look for other pairs of numbers with a difference of two, ringing the two numbers and drawing the jump between them. Help them to record the relevant number sentence.

What do you notice about your pairs of numbers? Are they odd or even?

Elicit that both numbers in each pair are either odd or even because the pattern of odd or even numbers goes up in 2s.

0–20 number lines for each pair

A3.d.2 Pairs of children

One child chooses any number on a 100-square, for example 67. Their partner chooses a number in the row above **or** in the row below. The number they choose must not be directly above or directly below, for example 74. The two children write down both numbers, smallest first, for example *67, 74*. They then work out the difference by counting on from the smaller to the larger number. They may either use the 100-square to help or their fingers, putting 67 'in their heads', counting on and holding up one finger for each number spoken. They write the difference: 7. Children repeat this activity, choosing two different numbers, until they have found six differences.

Adult support may be useful in running this activity with several pairs of children.

100-square per pair

Maths Weekly Plan: Year 1 and 2

Block B3.a: Y1 Know addition/subtraction pairs up to 9; Y2 Describe 2D and 3D shapes
Block B3.b: Y1 Know addition/subtraction pairs up to 10; Y2 Recognise halves and quarters

	Mental oral starter	Objectives	Main teaching	Activities: Group 1 Y1	Activities: Group 2 Y1	Activities: Group 3 Y2	Activities: Group 4 Y2	Plenary	Outcomes
Day 1	**Names and properties of common 2D shapes.** Choose 4 shape captains: **squares**, **circles**, **triangles** and **rectangles**. Place 2D shapes in a bag. Child chooses a shape from the bag. They say its name and give it to the appropriate captain. Rpt.	**Y1** • Know by heart addition and subtraction facts for pairs of numbers that total up to 9 • Record addition and subtraction facts for pairs of numbers that total up to 9, using +, – and = in number sentences	**All** Stick 9 'planets' on left side of board. ***How many*** *planets?* Move 1 planet to right side. *How many planets now?* Write and read matching **number sentence**: *8+1=9*. Move a 2nd planet across. Record the matching **addition**: *7+2=9*. Rpt for other pairs to 9. **[ITR Y1 B3.a]** **Y2** Show chn some **2D shapes**. Ask a child to come to the front and describe one, eg *This is a square. It has 4* ***sides****, 4* ***corners*** *and 4* ***right angles***. Rpt for triangle, **hexagon**, **pentagon**, **octagon**.	Y1 B3.a.2 Making 5, 6 and 7 using cubes to form addition pairs TA	Y1 1.3 p12 Making 9 using addition pairs	Y2 B3.a.1 Matching irregular 2D shapes by looking at properties T	Y2 2.3 p13 Identifying properties of 2D shapes	Write the **days** of the **week** along the board and rehearse them. Rub out the first two days. *Two days in the week have gone,* ***how many*** *are* ***left***? Write matching addition: *5+2=7*. Rpt for 3 days gone, 4 days gone.	**Y1** • Begin to learn addition pairs totalling 5, 6, 7, 8 and 9 • Use objects to practise addition **Y2** • Identify properties of 2D shapes
Day 2	**Add near doubles by doubling and adjusting.** Write *4+5* on board. Chn write total on their whiteboards, then show their answers. Hold up a tower of 4 cubes and a tower of 5 cubes. Demonstrate by removing a cube that 4+5 is **double** 4 and 1 more. Rpt for other additions of **near doubles**.	**Y2** • Classify and describe common 2D and 3D shapes • Make models, shapes and patterns and describe their features	**All** Make a pentagon on a pinboard. *How many sides? Corners? Right angles?* Make a 2nd pentagon and compare with the 1st. Secretly make a **quadrilateral**. Describe it in terms of sides, corners, etc. Chn draw it. Compare drawings with pinboard shape. **[ITR Y2 B3.a]** **Y1** Draw table on board with 6 rows and 5 columns. Add column headings: *5, 6, 7, 8, 9*. Give pairs 9 cubes each. Chn show different ways to make 5 using cubes. Write the matching additions in the column: *0+5, 1+4, 2+3*. Rpt for 6, 7, 8 and 9 until the table is complete.	Y1 1.3 p11 Making 7 and 8 using addition pairs	Y1 B3.a.4 Working out all the number bonds to 4, 5, 6, 7, 8, 9 and 10 T	Y2 2.3 p13 Identifying properties of 2D shapes	Y2 B3.a.2 Drawing irregular 2D shapes TA	Give an instruction to draw a shape, eg *Draw a 5-sided shape with two long sides.* Share results and discuss any different shapes that match the same criteria. Rpt.	**Y1** • Rehearse number bonds to 5, 6, 7, 8, 9 **Y2** • Draw 2D shapes • Describe properties of 2D shapes
Day 3	**Add three numbers, looking for pairs that make 10.** Play 'Fan-tastic'. Write about 10 additions of 3 digits on board, each with a pair that makes 10, eg *3+4+7=*. Point to an addition. Ask a child to read it. Chn mentally add the numbers, then show answers on number fans. Rpt.	**Y1** • Know by heart addition and subtraction facts for pairs of numbers that total 10 • Record addition and subtraction facts for pairs of numbers that total 10, using +, – and = in number sentences	**All** Play a game practising **number bonds**. *We'll start by writing all the different ways of making 5.* Say a number, eg *4*. Chn call out its pair to 5 as quickly as possible: *1*. Write the matching addition. Rpt for all bonds to 5, then rpt for 6, 7, 8 and 9. **Y2** Make a **pyramid** from Polydron. Describe it in terms of **faces**, **edges** and **vertices**. *Five 2D shapes have been used to make the* ***3D shape****. The number of 2D shapes we need to make a 3D shape is the same as the number of faces.* Rpt with a triangular **prism** and a **cuboid**.	Y1 B3.a.3 TM 12.1 12 Addition and subtraction facts TA	Y1 1.3 p13 Making 5, 6, 7, 8 and 9 using addition pairs	Y2 B3.a.3 Following instructions to draw 2D shapes T	Y2 B3.a.3 Following instructions to draw 2D shapes T	Give each pair a sheet of paper with a 3×3 array of dots drawn on it. They must draw a line partitioning the set, then write a matching addition, eg *3+6=9*. Discuss different solutions.	**Y1** • Rehearse number bonds to 5, 6, 7, 8, 9 **Y2** • Identify properties of 3D shapes • Identify 2D faces of 3D shapes

	Mental oral starter	Objectives	Main teaching	Activities: Group 1 Y1	Activities: Group 2 Y1	Activities: Group 3 Y2	Activities: Group 4 Y2	Plenary	Outcomes
Day 4	**Count back in 10s from a number up to 100.** Play 'Pass the bear'. Chn sit in a circle. Give a teddy bear to a child and say a start number, eg *53*. The child says the number **10 less**, and passes the bear to the next child. The next child **counts back** another **10**, and so on. Rpt several times with different start numbers.	*(Continued)* **Y2** • Begin to recognise halves and quarters of shapes • Recognise fraction notation • Begin to recognise halves and quarters of small numbers of objects	**All** Fold square of paper in **half**. *Two **equal parts**: halves.* Fold a 2nd square in half and in half again. *Four equal parts: **quarters**.* Show there are 2 halves and 4 quarters in 1 **whole**. Write $\frac{1}{2}$. *This is how we write a half. The 2 shows the number of equal parts.* Rpt for $\frac{1}{4}$. **Y1** Show flexigrid (Y1 PCM 119). *How many rockets?* Chn count, grouping in different ways. Fold a row back so 1 rocket is hidden. *1 rocket has taken off! How many are still on the ground?* Chn count. Write *1+9=10*. Fold a 2nd rocket behind. Rpt for other pairs to 10.	Y1 B3.b.1 Using strips of paper to make bonds to 10 T	Y1 1.3 p15 Completing addition pairs to make 10	Y2 B3.b.1 Finding half of shapes and amounts TA	Y2 2.3 p16 Identifying halves and quarters of amounts	Show a set of cubes. *This is half of my cubes. How many cubes did I start with?* Discuss, choosing children to demonstrate dividing a set of cubes into halves. Rpt for quarters.	**Y1** • Use objects to rehearse bonds to 10 **Y2** • Identify halves and quarters of shapes • Begin to recognise fraction notation
Day 5	**Find the difference between two numbers.** Play 'Quick on the draw'. Say two numbers that have a small **difference**. Give chn some thinking time, then on the command *Go!* they hold up fingers to match the answer as quickly as possible. Rpt for other pairs of numbers.		**All** Each pair makes a tower of 10 cubes, using two different colours. Ask chn to tell you all the number bonds to 10. Write each one on the board as chn say it. Ask each pair to come to the board, show their tower, and point to the matching addition. **[ITR Y1 B3.b]** **Y2** Ask a child to count out 8 cubes. Ask 2 chn to stand at front. *I will give each of them $\frac{1}{2}$ of the cubes. How many will they each get?* **Share** the cubes **equally**: *4 each.* Write $\frac{1}{2}$ *of 8=4*. Rpt to show halves of other quantities. Rpt to show quarters of quantities. **[ITR Y2 B3.b]**	Y1 1.3 p14 Adding two numbers to make 10	Y1 B3.b.3 TM 12.3 12 Addition and subtraction facts TA	Y2 2.3 p15 Identifying quarters of shapes	Y2 B3.b.3 Investigating numbers which can be halved but not quartered T	Chn count the total number of rockets on the flexigrid (Y1 PCM 119). Fold some rockets behind so they are hidden. Ask chn to show on their fingers the number of rockets that are missing. Rpt several times.	**Y1** • Know by heart bonds to 10 • Use bonds to 10 to write matching subtractions **Y2** • Identify halves and quarters of amounts • Recognise fraction notation

Vocabulary
2D shape
circle
triangle
square
rectangle
quadrilateral
pentagon
hexagon
octagon
side
corner
angle, right angle
3D shape
cuboid
pyramid
prism
face
edge
vertex, vertices
how many?
how many left?
number sentence
addition
number bond
number pair
equal parts
share equally
half, halve
quarter
whole
fraction
day
week
Monday, Tuesday, …
double
near double
10 less
count back 10
difference

Resources
2D shapes: circles, triangles, squares, rectangles, pentagons, hexagons, octagons
cloth bag
'planets' cut out of card
Blu-tack
up to 100 linking cubes in two colours
shape cards (Y2 PCM 121)
pinboard
rubber band
individual whiteboards
number fans (one per child)
Polydron
up to four sets of dominoes
sheets of paper with 3×3 array of dots drawn on (one per pair)
teddy bear
square sheets of paper
flexigrid (Y1 PCM 119)
10 strips of paper 10 squares long
felt-tipped pens
squared paper
coloured pencils
coat hanger
five blue pegs
five red pegs
a cloth, e.g. a tea towel
up to four strips of card with 10 dots in a row with a gap between each set of five
number cards 16, 20, 24, 28, 36, 40, 44, 48

Year 1 Block B3.a Activities

B3.a.2 A group of up to 12 children working in pairs

Ask each child in each pair to make a tower of five cubes using two colours. They must make it different from their partner's. Come together and record each different tower of 5 as an addition, for example *1 + 4 = 5* (one blue and four red), etc. Ensure that you have all five possible additions – if not, build towers to match those which are missing.

Repeat this for towers of 6 and then towers of 7.

Adult support may be useful in running this activity.

linking cubes in two colours

12.1 12 Addition and subtraction facts

B3.a.3 A group of 6 or more children working in pairs

Ask pairs to find a domino with a total of 7 spots, trying to find one different from their neighbour's. *What's the biggest number of spots we could have on the left-hand side?* Agree that this is 7 and stick this domino to the top of the board using Blu-tack. Write the number sentence *7 + 0 = 7*. *What's the next biggest number we could have on the left?* Put the 6 + 1 domino underneath the 7 + 0 one. Continue finding and recording number facts. For 4 + 3, agree that we have already used this domino the other way up. Draw it rather than moving the domino and continue the pattern.

Discuss the patterns in the first and second numbers in the number sentences. Stress that ordering them like this ensures that we don't miss any.

Ask children to work in pairs to repeat this process to find all the pairs with a total of 8 spots.

Adult support is needed to run this activity.

set of dominoes per pair; Blu-tack

B3.a.4 A group of up to 10 children working in pairs

Ask children to work in pairs to find out how many different '_ + _ = ' additions there are that total each of 4, 5, 6, 7, 8, 9 and 10. They should record the different addition pairs for each number (for example 0 + 4, 1 + 3, 2 + 2) and then write the total number of addition pairs, for example 3. When they have done this for 4, 5, 6, 7, 8, 9 and 10, can they predict how many there will be for 11?

Adult support may be useful in running this activity.

Year 1 Block B3.b Activities

B3.b.1 A group of up to 8 children working in pairs

Each child colours their paper strip using two colours. Feed back together, and match each child's strip to an addition, counting the number of each colour. For example, a child has coloured alternate squares red and blue, so their strip matches to 5 + 5 = 10. Ask each child to colour another strip, making this one different. Continue until you have strips to match all the possible addition pairs.

Adult support may be useful in running this activity.

strips of paper ten squares long per child; felt-tipped pens in two colours

12.3 12 Addition and subtraction facts

B3.b.3 A group of 6 or more children

Slide 7 pegs to the left of the coat hanger and the remaining 3 to the right. Agree that you could write 7 + 3 = 10. Ask children to close their eyes while you hide the last 3 pegs with the cloth. *Open your eyes. How many pegs have I hidden? What colour are they? What subtraction could I write?* Agree on 10 – 3 = 7.

Remove the cloth. Turn the hanger around so that the 3 pegs are now first. *What addition fact could I write now?* Agree on 3 + 7 = 10. Cover the 7 pegs. *What subtraction fact can I write?* Write 10 – 7 = 3.

Repeat, covering up other numbers of pegs and building up groups of four number facts for different pairs of numbers, for example 6 + 4 = 10; 4 + 6 = 10; 10 – 6 = 4; 10 – 4 = 6.

Ask children to cover up the last dot on their cards. *What subtraction fact could you write?* Help them to record 10 – 1 = 9. Ask them next to cover up the last two dots. *What subtraction fact could you write now?* They continue covering up one more dot and writing as many subtraction facts as they can.

Adult support is needed to run this activity.

coat hanger; ten pegs (five blue and five red); a cloth (for example a tea towel); strip of card with 10 dots arranged in a line in two groups of 5 per pair

Year 2 Block B3.a Activities

B3.a.1 A group of up to 8 children

Sit children in a circle. Place one set of shape cards face up in the middle. Place the other set face down in a pile. Choose a child to take a card from the pile. They keep it hidden and describe the shape on it. Children listen hard to the description and decide which card in front of them matches the description. Discuss what the child has said, come to a decision together and compare the card to the one the child is holding. Repeat the activity, choosing different children to take cards from the second set and describe them.

Adult support is needed to run this activity.

two sets of shape cards made from two copies of Y2 PCM 121 – include hexagons, pentagons and quadrilaterals (square, rectangle and others)

B3.a.2 A group of 2, 3, 4 or 5 children

Children take one shape from a set of regular 2D shapes and count its sides. They each draw an irregular example of the same type of shape, i.e. one with unequal sides and unequal angles. They should each try to draw a really different example of this type of shape. They then take a different regular shape, and repeat the activity. They colour some of their best shapes.

regular 2D shapes

B3.a.3 A group of up to 8 children

Show children your special bag of shapes. Explain that you are going to give them instructions for drawing one of the shapes in your bag. Children must listen hard and try to copy what you say. If they follow the instructions well, the shape will turn out the same. They can talk to their partner and get advice. Start by giving instructions for drawing a square: *Draw a shape that has four sides. All the sides are the same length. It also has four corners, and all the corners are right angles.* When they have all drawn the shape, take the 'square' card out of the cloth bag. Compare their drawings and yours. Repeat this, now giving them instructions to draw an arrow-shaped hexagon.

Adult support is needed to run this activity.

shape cards made from Y2 PCM 121 – include hexagons (regular, arrow-shaped and others), pentagons (regular and others) and quadrilaterals (square, rectangle and others) in a cloth bag; individual whiteboards/paper and appropriate felt-tipped pen

Year 2 Block B3.b Activities

B3.b.1 A group of up to 8 children

Children fold a piece of squared paper in half carefully along a line. They use the lines to draw a shape up to the fold line on one side of it, then the exact same shape on the other side of the line. Stress that it is very important that both shapes cover the same number of squares. Children colour the shapes on both sides of the line. Then they count all the coloured squares and write the total, for example *16*. Underneath they write $\frac{1}{2}$ *of 16 =* and count the squares on one side of the line. They complete their number sentence: $\frac{1}{2}$ *of 16 = 8*. Repeat this activity if there is time.

Adult support may be helpful in running this activity.

squared paper; coloured pencils

B3.b.3 A group of up to 8 children

Give each child one of the number cards. They take a matching number of cubes. Ask children to work out half of their number of cubes and record the answer, for example $\frac{1}{2}$ *of 24 = 12*, and then to work out one quarter of their number of cubes and record the answer, for example $\frac{1}{4}$ *of 24 = 6*. When each child has done this, share their results. *Was it possible to divide all the amounts into half, and then into quarters?* Discuss whether there are numbers it is not possible to divide into halves or into quarters. Ask children to find some numbers that can be divided into halves but **not** into quarters.

Adult support is needed to run this activity.

number cards 16, 20, 24, 28, 36, 40, 44, 48; interlocking cubes

Maths Weekly Plan: Year 1 and 2

Block B3.c: Y1 Add TU + U; Y2 Know pairs of multiples of 10 that total 100
Block B3.d: Y1 Find the difference between two numbers; Y2 Add to the next multiple of 10

	Mental oral starter	Objectives	Main teaching	Activities: Group 1 (Y1)	Activities: Group 2 (Y1)	Activities: Group 3 (Y2)	Activities: Group 4 (Y2)	Plenary	Outcomes
Day 1	**Multiplication facts for the 5 times table.** Pairs each write four **multiples** of 5 on their whiteboards. Shuffle number cards 1–10. Take a card, eg 6. Ask chn to **multiply** it by 5, eg 30. If a pair has the answer on their board, they cross it out. The 1st pair to cross out all their numbers wins.	**Y1** • Add a 1-digit number to a 2-digit number, not crossing a multiple of 10 • Add a 1-digit number to a 2-digit number, crossing a multiple of 10 **Y2** • Know by heart addition and subtraction facts for pairs of numbers that total up to 10 • State the subtraction corresponding to a given addition, and vice versa • Know by heart pairs of multiples of 10 that total 100 • Use patterns of similar calculations	**All** Put 10 pegs on a hanger. Chn count pegs. Move 1 peg across to the other side of the hanger. Point to left side. ***How many** pegs? 9*. Point to right side. *How many pegs? 1. 9 **and** 1 **make** 10.* Ask a child to write $9+1=10$ on the board. Rpt this for all pairs that make 10. **Y1** Draw 1–20 number line. Draw fish at 20. Write $12+5=$. Put picture of shark at 12. *If shark starts on 12 and moves 5, will he reach the fish?* Chn **count on** 5 from 12, using fingers. Move the shark 5 spaces to 17. Complete the **addition**. Rpt for $13+6$ and $14+6$. **[ITR Y1 B3.c]**	Y1 B3.c.2 Counting on using fingers T	Y1 1.3 p17 Adding using a number line and bridging 10	Y2 B3.c.1 Making and rehearsing pairs to 10 TA	Y2 2.3 p19 Making pairs to 10, and pairs of multiples of 10 to 100	Draw a 3×3 grid on the board. Chn do the same on whiteboards. In the first space in your grid, write a number 0–10, eg *6*. Chn write its partner to 10, eg *4*. Continue until the grid is full.	**Y1** • Add by counting on • Use a number line or fingers to aid counting on **Y2** • Know bonds to 10 by heart • Use knowledge of bonds to 10 to solve additions
Day 2	**Recall doubles of numbers 1 to 10.** Play 'Front and back'. Use number cards 1–10 with **doubles** written on the backs. Hold up the $\frac{1}{2}$ card, with 1 facing chn. *What is double one, or one and one?* Turn the card round to reveal the answer. Rpt for each card. Rpt, showing the double and asking chn to say **half**.		**All** Use 1–30 number line with wolves at multiples of 10. Show Pobble. *Pobble is scared of wolves!* Put Pobble on 15. Write $15+7=$. *Pobble is worried he is going to cross a 'wolf' number. Will he have to?* Count on 7 spaces to 22. Complete the **number sentence**. Rpt for $17+8$. **Y2** Show 100-square. Count down the multiples of 10. Point to 50 on 100-square. *What **adds** to 50 to make 100?* Count on in 10s to 100, holding up 1 finger for each number said. *5 fingers, 5 more 10s. That's 50.* Write $50+50=100$. Rpt for all pairs to 100. **[ITR Y2 B3.c]**	Y1 80 Counting on 3 on number tracks	Y1 B3.c.3 TM 13.3 13 Number puzzle TA	Y2 2.3 p17 Making pairs to 10	Y2 B3.c.5 Making pairs of multiples of 5 that total 100 T	Choose chn to show rest of class how they counted on across a 'wolf' number. Each child challenges the class by giving them an example to try. They must know if the answer given is correct!	**Y1** • Add by counting on, crossing a multiple of 10 • Find a difference by counting on **Y2** • Know by heart bonds to 10 • Begin to know pairs of multiples of 10 that total 100
Day 3	**Partition a 2-digit number into 10s and units.** Play 'Stand up'. Give each child a number card 1–99. *Stand up if your number has 3 **tens***. Chn holding these cards stand up and hold their number for all to see. Check their numbers. Rpt many times.		**All** Show 1–50 number grid, with wolves on multiples of 10. Write $35+4=$ on board. Place Pobble on 35. Point at +4. *Pobble is worried! Do you think he will have to cross a 'wolf' number?* Hold up 4 fingers and count on. Complete number sentence. Rpt for $37+6$. **Y2** Write *6p + _ = 10p. What adds to 6p to make 10p?* Demo using fingers. Complete addition. Write *10p − 4p = _*. Show 10 fingers; fold down 4. *10 **take** 4 **leaves** 6*. Complete **subtraction**. Rpt. Use 10p coins to demo 40p+60p=100p and 100p−60p=40p. Rpt for 70p+30p.	Y1 1.3 p16 Adding by counting along a number line	Y1 B3.c.4 Creating TU+U additions and finding answers TA	Y2 B3.c.4 TM 13.1 13 Addition facts T	Y2 p25 Making pairs to 100 and 10 (additions and subtractions)	Write 5 additions with answer 10, eg $4+6=10$. Chn must write a matching subtraction for each addition, eg $10-4=6$. Discuss answers. *Are there always two subtractions which match each addition?*	**Y1** • Add TU + U, crossing a multiple of 10 **Y2** • Know pairs of multiples of 10 that total 100 • Use knowledge of addition to solve subtractions

	Mental oral starter	Objectives	Main teaching	Activities: Group 1 (Y1)	Group 2 (Y1)	Group 3 (Y2)	Group 4 (Y2)	Plenary	Outcomes
Day 4	**Recognise clockwise and anticlockwise turns.** Chn stand in their own space. Remind chn about **clockwise** and **anticlockwise** turns. Give **turning** commands involving direction and size (**right angles**), eg *Turn clockwise through 1 right angle*. Check their turns. Rpt several times.	*(Continued)* **Y2** • Estimate, measure and compare capacities using standard units: litres, millilitres • Read a simple capacity scale to the nearest labelled and unlabelled division	**All** Show litre measure. *This holds 1 litre of water*. Show **half-litre measure**. *This holds half a litre*. Demonstrate that two full levels of the half-litre measure fill the litre measure. Fill the litre measure with water from one full half-litre measure. Mark the water level with a rubber band. Pour the water away. *Now we can use this to measure how much containers will hold in litres and* ***half-litres***. Fill a container with water. Chn estimate capacity in litres. Pour the water into the litre measure, counting half-litres. Empty the measure when full, if necessary. Rpt to measure other containers.	Y1 1.3 p23 Measuring how many small containers fill a larger one TA	Y1 C3.b.3 Ordering and measuring containers, using spoons as a unit T	Y2 2.3 p24 Looking for more and less than a litre	Y2 C3.b.2 Finding the capacity of a watering can TA	Measure the capacity of one container using four or five different units, eg small cups, yoghurt pots, egg-cups, thimbles.	**Y1** • Estimate and measure capacities using non-standard units **Y2** • Estimate and measure capacity in litres and half-litres
Day 5	**Recall addition and subtraction facts for numbers up to 20.** Pairs place 0–20 number lines in front of them. Write an **addition** or subtraction on board, eg *16−5*=. Pairs place a counter on the answer, without jumping the counter along the line. Check answers. Rpt. Vary by saying the fact instead of writing it.		**All** Show 4 containers. Chn **predict** which holds most/least. Find correct order by filling 1 container and pouring into another. Place in order from smallest to largest capacity. Measure capacities using egg-cups of water. Label each container with its capacity in egg-cupfuls. **Y2** *There is another way to measure capacity. We can use* ***millilitres***. Write *millilitres* and *ml*. Show that **marks** on litre measure each **represent** 100 ml. Pour water into litre measure counting in units of 100 ml as the water reaches each mark. Measure some containers in ml.	Y1 C3.b.4 Estimating how many egg-cups fill containers TA	Y1 86 Finding three containers and ordering them by how many cups they hold	Y2 C3.b.4 Investigating making the largest container possible using A4 card T	Y2 C3.b.4 Investigating making the largest container possible using A4 card T	Show an egg-cup and a litre measure with the half-way marked with a rubber band. Chn predict the number of egg-cupfuls in half a litre. Measure to find out who is closest.	**Y1** • Compare capacities of different containers by measuring in non-standard units **Y2** • Measure capacity in litres and millilitres

Vocabulary
hold
fill
empty
nearly empty
half-full
nearly full
full
more than, most
less than, least
measure
estimate
predict
closest
capacity
level
how many?
compare
order
litre measure
half-litre measure
unit
cup, cupful
litre
half-litre
millilitre
mark
represent
subtraction
addition
multiple
double
clockwise
anticlockwise
turn
right angle

Resources
number fans (one per child)
several transparent containers of differing capacities, including a cylindrical container, a litre bottle and a small beaker
up to four identical cups
lentils, rice, dried peas or sand
red and blue dot stickers
selection of jugs, pots and pans
small 100-squares (one per pair)
counters (one per pair)
place-value cards (T and U)
rubber bands
strips of paper
scissors
sticky tape
individual whiteboards
litre measure
half-litre measure
yoghurt pot
selection of products, e.g. shampoo, juice, squash, milk, bubble bath
digit cards 1–9 (one set per child)
selection of empty containers, e.g. shampoo, bubble bath, shower gel
up to four tablespoons
watering can
funnel
0–20 number lines (one per pair)
egg-cup
sheets of thin A4 card

Year 1 Block C3.a Activities

C3.a.1 A group of up to 8 children working in pairs

Children work in pairs to find out which container holds more, using lentils.

Explain the task. Children first decide which container they think will hold less. They fill this one with lentils. Then they very carefully pour this into the second container. If they were right, then the second container will not be full. But if they were wrong, some will spill. Each pair carries out this task, then they mark their larger container with a red dot sticker and their smaller one with a blue dot sticker. Pairs then exchange their two containers for a different pair's and check each other's results.

Adult support may be useful in running this activity.

two containers of different sizes per pair; lentils, rice or sand; red and blue dot stickers

C3.a.3 A group of up to 8 children

Show the set of containers. Say that we want to decide which is the largest, i.e. holds the most, which is the next largest, and so on. Ask children to discuss which container they believe will hold the least. They must agree this, and then in turn, try filling each other container using this one. If correct, then the smallest container will not fill up any of the others. If incorrect and they find one smaller, they should start again using that one. Select different children to do the pouring. Once you have established which is the smallest, take the next smallest and repeat. Continue until the containers are in order.

Adult support may be useful in running this activity.

five or six containers of different sizes; lentils, rice or sand

Year 1 Block C3.b Activities

C3.b.1 A group of up to 8 children working in pairs

Explain that pairs are going to measure how much their large container holds using lentils, counting the number of pots it takes to fill it. Support pairs, making sure they fill their yoghurt pot level each time, and that they count carefully the number of pots. They may need to make a tally mark for each pot they tip in to help them keep track. Take feedback from each pair and discuss which of all the containers is the largest, i.e. holds the most.

Adult support may be useful in running this activity.

one largish container and a small yoghurt pot; lentils, rice or sand

C3.b.3 A group of up to 8 children

Discuss which container holds most. Which holds least? *We will measure how much each container holds using tablespoons.* Give each child a container, some lentils and a tablespoon. They should measure their container carefully using the lentils and the spoon. They may need to make a tally mark for each spoon they put in to help them keep track. When everyone has measured one container, compare results. Use the measurements to place the containers in order.

Adult support may be useful in running this activity.

selection of empty containers, for example shampoo, bubble bath, shower gel, etc., one per child; tablespoon per child; lentils, rice or sand

C3.b.4 A group of 3 or 4 children

Children estimate which container will need the most egg-cupfuls to fill it, which the least, and place the containers in order of estimated capacity. They measure the capacity of each container by filling the egg-cup with water and pouring it into the container until it is full, counting as they go. Children record results and check their estimated order.

Adult support may be useful in running this activity.

collection of small containers; egg-cup; water

Year 2 Block C3.a Activities

C3.a.1 A group of 4, 6 or 8 children working in pairs

Label a wide selection of jugs, pots and pans: A, B, C etc. Give each pair the same size cup. Ask children to look at each container, estimate how many full cups of lentils (or rice, sand or water) it will hold and record their estimate against each letter. Collect the estimates in a table.

Share out the containers so that each pair measures at least two containers. Ask children to record the actual amount each one holds. Collect the results and write them in the table next to each letter. Discuss the estimates.

Adult support may be helpful in running this activity.

selection of jugs, pots and pans; a matching cup for each pair; lentils, rice, sand, water or similar for measuring

C3.a.2 Pairs of children

Give each pair a container of uniform cross-section (like a cylinder), a felt-tipped pen, scissors and paper. They create a scale to make their container into a measuring cylinder: cut a narrow strip of paper the same length as the container and attach it with Sellotape at the top and the bottom; tip in one cupful of lentils (or rice, sand or water) and mark the level with a line on the strip, labelling it 1; continue to add cupfuls and label the levels one by one. *Does it make any difference if you use rice or sand rather than lentils?*

Adult support may be helpful in running this activity.

cylinder with a uniform cross-section; strip of paper, scissors and a matching cup for each pair; lentils, rice, sand, water or similar for measuring; Sellotape

Year 2 Block C3.b Activities

C3.b.1 Pairs of children

Pairs look at a variety of commercial products bought in liquid form. They see whether each one is more or less than a litre, then consider whether some are less than half a litre. They discuss and make a list of which things we buy in litres.

Adult support may be helpful in running this activity.

selection of shampoos, juices, squashes, milk, bubble bath etc.

C3.b.2 A group of up to 8 children working in pairs

This activity is best done outside. Show a watering can. *We are all going to think of a way to work out how many litres it holds, then measure it to check if we are right.* Encourage children to think of various ways of estimating accurately, for example put in 1 litre and try to make a scale; time how long it takes to tip all the water out of a litre bottle and then how long it takes to tip all the water out of a watering can. Ask each pair to decide on a method, then come up with a sensible, reasoned estimate. Record these, then use a litre container to measure the watering can. Children keep count by recording each litre. Compare the actual capacity with the estimates.

Adult support is needed to run this activity.

watering can; litre bottle; funnel

C3.b.4 A whole class investigation with children working in pairs

Tell pairs that they are going to use a sheet of card to make a container. Give some ideas:

Roll the sheet to make a tall, thin cylinder and stand it on the table.

Discuss how it would need a base. Roll it the other way to make a short, fat cylinder. Create a cone, and so on.

Write: *Who can make the container that holds the most?* Challenge each pair to use only their A4 piece of card. They may fold it, cut it and stick it with Sellotape in any way they like.

Encourage children to think about and give reasons for the shapes they want to try in a systematic way. It may help if they try out how many cups the tall thick cylinder holds, and how many cups the short fat cylinder holds. At the end measure each container in cupfuls to see whose holds the most and/or whose contains nearest to a litre.

Adult support is needed to run this activity.

lentils, rice or sand; measuring cup and a piece of A4 thin card for each pair

Maths Weekly Plan: Year 1 and 2

Block C3.c: Read the time to the hour, half hour or quarter hour
Block C3.d: Y1 Measure time in minutes; Y2 Use hours, minutes, seconds

	Mental oral starter	Objectives	Main teaching	Activities: Group 1 (Y1)	Activities: Group 2 (Y1)	Activities: Group 3 (Y2)	Activities: Group 4 (Y2)	Plenary	Outcomes
Day 1	**Count in 10s from a single-digit number.** Place two 2p coins in a ceramic mug. *How much is in the mug? 4p. Listen carefully as I drop 10p coins into the mug, and* ***count on*** *10 each time you hear a clink.* Drop five 10p coins into the mug; chn count on five 10s. *How much now? 54p.* Count the coins to check. Rpt.	**Y1** • Read the time to the hour and half hour on analogue clocks **Y2** • Read the time to the quarter hour on analogue and 12-hour digital clocks	**All** Set clock to 1 o'clock. *Short hand points at 1, long hand points at 12.* Say time together. Continue showing and saying times up to 12 o'clock. Re-set clock to 1 o'clock. Slowly turn the **minute hand** through a half turn. *This is called half past 1.* Continue like this. **Y2** Set analogue clock to 4 o'clock. Slowly turn hands to 5 o'clock, stopping at half past 4. Repeat, but this time stop after a quarter turn. Use intersecting plates to demonstrate quarter turns. Continue like this for a few 'hours'. **[ITR Y2 D3.d]**	Y1 C3.c.1 Matching clock-faces to given times TA	Y1 1.3 p26 Drawing hands on clocks to match given times	Y2 D3.d.1 TM 14.1 14 Ordering clocks T	Y2 2.3 p38 Writing digital and analogue times	Chant time sequences together with **intervals** of quarter of an hour, eg *6 o'clock,* ***quarter past*** *6, half past 6,* ***quarter to*** *7, 7 o'clock, ….*	**Y1** • Tell time to hour and half hour on analogue clocks • Show time by drawing hands on clocks **Y2** • Tell time: half past, quarter past, quarter to • Count in half hours
Day 2	**Subtract a multiple of 10 from a multiple of 10.** Write 10 **subtractions** on the board using **multiples** of 10, eg 90–50=. Point at one. Chn write their answers on whiteboards. Use 100-square to illustrate the calculation. Rpt for the other subtractions.		**All** Say the o'clock and half-past times together: *half past 12, 1 o'clock, half past 1, … 12 o'clock.* Use the clock to demo, showing how the short hand moves, and its position at half-past times. Repeat, stopping after a quarter turn and asking Y2s to tell time. Use intersecting plates to demonstrate quarter turns. Set the clock to a time. Reveal it. Chn say time. Emphasise where minute hand must point, and that quarter- or half-past times are read by seeing which number the **hour hand** has just left. Choose chn to set random half-past times for the others to read. Choose Y2 chn to set quarter-past times. **[ITR Y1 C3.c]**	Y1 1.3 p25 Joining times to matching clock-faces	Y1 C3.c.4 Playing 'Clock bingo' T	Y2 D3.d.4 Using number cards and setting quarter-past times on analogue clock TA	Y2 100 Writing digital and analogue times quarter of an hour later than given times	Play 'What's my time?' Secretly set an analogue clock to a half-past time. Give clues, eg *It is after 2 o'clock and before 3 o'clock.* Chn say the time. Reveal the clock. Rpt.	**Y1** • Tell time to hour and half hour on analogue clocks • Show time by drawing hands on clocks **Y2** • Tell time: half past, quarter past, quarter to • Say time quarter of an hour later
Day 3	**Recall names and properties of common 3D shapes.** Give one 3D shape to each child. Play *'Stand up'. Give an instruction, eg Stand up if your shape is a* ***cuboid***. Chn holding these shapes stand up. Check them. Rpt, using many different instructions involving names and properties.	**Y1** • Read the time to the hour and half hour on analogue clocks • Begin to use units to measure time: minutes	**All** Set analogue clock to 4 o'clock. Set digital clock to 04:00. *We are going to move each clock on by half an hour.* One child models on each clock. *Remember: there are 60 minutes in 1 hour, so there are 30 minutes in half an hour.* Chn advance clocks by another half hour. **Y2** Advance clocks by quarter hours. Say a quarter-past time. Child sets analogue clock to match. *Where will minute hand point? Hour hand*? Ask chn to write the matching digital time on whiteboards. Set digital clock to correct time and reveal. Repeat.	Y1 C3.d.2 Using a timer to see how many cubes can be joined in 1 minute TA	Y1 1.3 p27 Moving along a dice track for 1 minute	Y2 2.3 p37 Writing digital times to match analogue times	Y2 D3.d.3 TM 14.3 14 Ordering clocks T	Chant digital time sequences together in intervals of quarter of an hour, eg *Three o'clock, three fifteen, three thirty, three forty-five, four o'clock.*	**Y1** • Tell time to hour and half hour on analogue clocks • Show time by drawing hands on clocks **Y2** • Tell time to quarter hour • Know that 30 min = half hour, 15 min = quarter hour

	Mental oral starter	Objectives	Main teaching	Activities: Group 1 (Y1)	Group 2 (Y1)	Group 3 (Y2)	Group 4 (Y2)	Plenary	Outcomes
Day 4	**Recognise the value of digits in numbers greater than 100.** Play 'Number partners'. Give each child a **hundreds**, **tens** or **units** place-value card. Ask chn to get in groups of 3 with one of each type of card. Ask groups to say their 3-digit number. Extend to asking chn to arrange themselves in **order**.	*(Continued)* **Y2** • Read the time to the quarter hour on analogue and 12-hour digital clocks • Use units of time and know the relationship between them: hours, minutes, seconds	**All** Count together from 0 to 10. Then count back to 0. Show a 1-minute sand **timer**. *The sand moves from one part to the other when you turn it. It takes 1* ***minute***. See how many times you can count from 0 to 10 and back in 1 minute. Rpt, counting from 0 to 20 and back. **Y2** Set **analogue clock** to 9 o'clock. What time is it? Time 1 **minute** using a **sand timer**. ***1 minute past*** *9 o'clock*. Advance time on analogue clock by 1 minute. *The* ***long hand*** *has turned*. Rpt for another minute. Continue, showing there are 60 minutes in 1 **hour**. **[ITR Y2 D3.c]**	Y1 1.3 p27 Moving along a dice track for 1 minute	Y1 C3.d.3 Using a timer to see how many numbers can be ordered in 1 minute TA	Y2 D3.c.1 Using a 1-minute timer T	Y2 2.3 p36 Working out how many seconds	Say the letters of the alphabet together from *a* to *z*, then continue from *a* again. Rpt, timing how far you can get in 1 minute.	**Y1** • Begin to measure time in minutes • Use a 1-minute timer **Y2** • Know there are 60 minutes in an hour • Measure time in minutes
Day 5	**Recognise angles which are more/less than a right angle.** Play 'Thumbs up, thumbs down'. Hold up a 2D shape and point at one of its **angles**. *Is this* ***more*** *or* ***less than*** *a* ***right angle***? If they think it is more, they show thumbs up, if less, thumbs down. If equal to a right angle thumbs across. Rpt many times.		**All** Show chn how the timer indicates the passing of 1 minute of time. *Let's see if you can stand on one leg for a minute!* Set the timer. Discuss how many chn succeeded. Reset the timer and try again. Rpt for other physical activities, eg hopping on one leg. **[ITR Y1 C3.d]** **Y2** Set **stop clock** and sand timer going. Show that when the sand runs out, the **second hand** on the stop clock has made 1 complete turn. *Both clocks measured 1 minute, that's 60* ***seconds***. Count 60 seconds together, saying *and* between each number.	Y1 C3.d.4 Using a timer to see how many actions can be performed in 1 minute TA	Y1 1.3 p28 Throwing a dice for 1 minute and recording scores	Y2 2.3 p35 Working out how many minutes	Y2 D3.c.2 Investigating how many minutes it takes to write numbers 1–1000 T	Demonstrate the minutes passing on a **digital** clock. Discuss the number of minutes in half an hour, 1 hour, $1\frac{1}{2}$ hours, 2 hours. Match these to the clock face.	**Y1** • Time activities using a 1-minute timer **Y2** • Know that 60 minutes = hour, 60 seconds = minute • Measure time in seconds

Vocabulary
time
hour
minute
second
long (minute) hand
short (hour) hand
second hand
o'clock
half past
quarter past
quarter to
minutes past
minutes to
interval
analogue clock
digital clock
timer
sand timer
stop clock
count on
multiple
3D shape names
digit
hundreds
tens
units
order
angle
right angle
more than
less than

Resources
2p and 10p coins
mug
analogue clocks with moveable hands
two intersecting paper circles/plates, made by cutting a straight line to the centre of each
11 Post-it notes with analogue clock-faces stamped/drawn on
counting stick
geared analogue clock
individual whiteboards
large 100-square
number cards 1–12
clock-face sheet (Y1 PCM 118)
linking cubes
3D shapes (one per child)
digital clock
large 1-minute sand timer
place-value cards (H, T, U)
up to six sets of number cards 1–20
up to four dice numbered 1–6
2D shapes
stop clock with a second hand
up to four small 1-minute sand timers
up to four calculators

Year 1 Block C3.c Activities

C3.c.1 A group of up to 8 children

Say a time, for example *half past four.* Each child sets their clock to that time. Check each one. Practise this activity two or three times. Then choose one child and say a time, for example *six o'clock.* They set their clock-face to that time. The other children check that they have done this correctly. Then ask the next child to set their clock to the time half an hour later. Discuss this, and support them if necessary. Then ask the next child to set their clock to the time half an hour later than that, etc. Continue like this.
Adult support may be useful in running this activity.

clock with moveable hands per child

C3.c.4 A group of 5 or 6 children

Shuffle the number cards and place them in a pile face down. Play 'Clock Bingo'. All children except one, who is the caller, fill in four different half past times on their clock-face sheet. The caller takes the top card from the pile, reads the number and sets the clock to show half past that hour. For example, if the card is 5, the child sets the clock to show half past five. If a child has drawn in the matching time, they cover it with a cube. The caller continues turning over the cards and setting the clock. The winner is the first player to cover all four of their clock-faces. Repeat the game with a different caller.
Adult support may be useful in running this activity.

1–12 number cards; clock with moveable hands; clock-face sheet (Y1 PCM 118) or sheet of clock stamps per child; cubes

Year 1 Block C3.d Activities

C3.d.2 A group of up to 8 children

Show children the timer and explain that we will try to count for 1 minute. One pair turn over the sand timer and say *Start!* The others count with the teacher: *Elephant one, elephant two, elephant three, …* The aim is to count exactly 60 seconds. When the timing pair shout *Stop!*, everyone stops counting. *How many did we count to?* Discuss how long a minute is. *How many cubes do you think you will be able to join in a tower in 1 minute?* Each child records their estimate. Use the sand timer to test it out. How close were their estimates?
Adult support may be useful in running this activity.

large 1-minute sand timer; linking cubes

C3.d.3 A group of up to 12 children working in pairs

Each pair shuffles their cards. *We are going to see who can put their cards in order to make a 1–20 number line in just one minute.* Start the timer and say Start! When the minute is up, see how far they have got. Award points for every sequence of cards in order, for example if they have got up to 8, they get 8 points. Shuffle the cards and play again. This time encourage children to use a strategy. Encourage discussion and division of labour, for example *You do the numbers up to ten*. Play this several times. How good do they get?
Adult support may be useful in running this activity.

large 1-minute sand timer; 1–20 number cards per pair

C3.d.4 A group of 3 or 4 children

Children use the timer to measure how many actions they can perform in one minute. For example, how many times can they roll a 6 on a dice? How many times can they write the first letter(s) of their name? How many times can they hop up and down on one foot? How many times can they write their ages? How many words in their books can they read?
Adult support may be useful in running this activity.

1-minute sand timer; dice

Year 2 Block C3.c Activities

D3.c.1 A group of 4, 6 or 8 children working in pairs

Explain that you are going to time various activities for one minute. Give each pair a dice. One child rolls and their partner writes a tally mark for every 6 rolled. Say *Ready, steady, go!* to start them off as you invert the 1-minute sand timer. *How many sixes did you roll in one minute? What is the most? What is the least?* Time how many times each child can write their name in one minute, then how many jumps they can do in one minute (one child jumps, one counts). Adult support is needed to run this activity.

large 1-minute sand timer; 1–6 dice per pair

D3.c.2 A group of 6 or 8 children working in pairs

Talk about how to estimate how long children would take to write numbers from 1 to 1000. Explain that they do not actually have to write all these numbers! Agree that pairs should first time how many numbers each child can each write in one minute. They time each other at least twice to get an accurate estimate that they record, for example *Tom: 27, Jane: 34*. They then have to work out how long it might take them to write 1000 numbers. Encourage children to discuss this and decide how they are going to find the most accurate answer. They must be prepared to explain their reasoning. They may need to time each other writing a second set of numbers in one minute to see if they slow down! Adult support may be helpful in running this activity.

calculator and 1-minute sand timer per pair

Year 2 Block C3.d Activities

14.1 14 Ordering clocks

D3.d.1 A group of 6 or more children

Draw 9 o'clock on a Post-it clock-face. Write *9 o'clock* below. Stick it to one end of the counting stick. *Each section of the stick represents half an hour.*
Count along the stick together until you reach half past 12. *What is half an hour later than half past twelve?* If children are unsure, show on the geared clock. Count on to the end of the stick.
Draw 12 o'clock on a Post-it. *Where should it go on the stick? How can we work that out?* Count on from 9 o'clock in half hours and place 12 o'clock. Take another Post-it. *Where should we draw the hands to show half past eleven? Where do we place this time on the stick? Do we need to count from the beginning?*
Do the same for 1 o'clock and other times, with children counting on and back from times already labelled.
Adult support is needed to run this activity.

eleven Post-it notes with analogue clock-faces stamped/drawn on; counting stick; geared analogue clock

14.3 14 Ordering clocks

D3.d.3 A group of 6 or more children

Draw 11 o'clock on a Post-it clock-face. Write *11 o'clock* below. Stick it to one end of the counting stick. Count along the stick together in quarter hours up to half past 12.
What time is quarter of an hour later than half past twelve? If children are unsure, show on the geared clock. Count on to the end of the stick.
Where was 12 o'clock? A child draws 12 o'clock on a Post-it. Stick it to the counting stick. Check the position by counting in quarter hours from 11 o'clock. *What time was at the end of the stick? How can we work this out quickly?* A child draws this time on the last Post-it and sticks it to the end of the counting stick. Point to where half past 11 would be. *What time is here? How do you know? What time goes between eleven and half past eleven?*
A child shows this time on the geared clock. Repeat for other times. Remove the Post-its and stick *12 o'clock* in a new position. *What's the time at the beginning/end of the stick now? How do you know?* Repeat for other times.
Adult support is needed to run this activity.

three Post-it notes with analogue clock-faces stamped/drawn on; counting stick; geared analogue clock

D3.d.4 A group of 8 children working in 4s

Put the shuffled number cards face down in a pile. Pair 1 takes a card, for example 7. Pair 2 sets the clock to show quarter past that hour, for example quarter past seven. Children swap roles and take turns until all the cards have been used. Repeat for 'quarter to' times.

1–12 number cards; clock with moveable hands

Note: Y2 blocks C3.c/d reference activities from original Y2 blocks D3.c/d to allow both year groups to focus on time in C3.c/d.

Maths Weekly Plan: Year 1 and 2

Block D3.a: Add or subtract a 1-digit number to or from a 2-digit number
Block D3.b: Subtract multiples of 10 or 2-digit numbers

	Mental oral starter	Objectives	Main teaching	Activities: Group 1 (Y1)	Activities: Group 2 (Y1)	Activities: Group 3 (Y2)	Activities: Group 4 (Y2)	Plenary	Outcomes
Day 1	**Read the time to the half hour on an analogue clock.** Play 'Clock pointing'. Each child places a clock board (Y1 PCM 117) in front of them. *Show me **half past** 3.* Chn point to the correct clock on their board. Rpt many times for different clock times.	**Y1** • Subtract a 1-digit number from a 2-digit number by counting back, not crossing 10 • Subtract a 1-digit number from a 2-digit number by counting back, crossing 10 **Y2** • Add a 1-digit number to a 2-digit number, bridging a multiple of 10 without crossing 100 • Add two 2-digit numbers using an appropriate strategy • Partition additions into T and U, then recombine	**All** Draw 40–60 number line. Draw fish on **multiples** of 10. Write *48 + 7 =*. Stick shark above 48. *How far does shark need to move to meet a fish?* Point to 8 in 48. *8 + 2 = 10*. Move shark to 50. ***How many more***? **Count on** 5 more. Write *55* to complete **addition**. Rpt for 46 + 8. **[ITR Y2 D3.a]** **Y1** Stick shark on 10 on a 1–20 number track. Stick fish on 17. Chn identify both numbers. Write *17 – 5 =*. *Remember, we **count back**.* Point at 17, then at –5. *Fish is going to swim back 5 spaces.* Hold up 5 fingers. Start at 17 and count back 5. Complete the sentence. Rpt for 19 – 6.	Y1 D3.a.2 Subtracting and looking at units patterns T	Y1 1.3 p30 Subtracting using number lines	Y2 D3.a.1 Adding to make the next 10 TA	Y2 2.3 p31 Adding two 2-digit numbers	Play 'Bingo'. Chn write 3 numbers 2–10 on whiteboards. Write a 1- or 2-digit number on board. *What **adds** to this to **make** 10/the next multiple of 10?* If chn have answer written, they cross it out. Rpt.	**Y1** • Subtract a 1-digit number from a 2-digit number by counting back • Use number lines to count back **Y2** • Add to make the next 10 • Add two 2-digit numbers
Day 2	**Subtract 9, 19 from a 2-digit number.** Play 'Fan-tastic'. Write about 10 **subtractions** on the board, each involving subtracting 9 or 19 from a 2-digit number. Point at one. Chn calculate mentally. On the command *Show me!* they show their answers using number fans.		**All** Show frog. *Frog likes to count back in 1s.* Count back from 25 to 1 on number line with 'wolf numbers' (multiples of 10). Write *14 – 5 =*. Put frog on 14. Point at –5. *We'll count back 5.* Hold up 5 fingers. Start at 14, move frog back 5. Rpt for 13 – 5 and 22 – 4. **[ITR Y1 D3.a]** **Y2** Use 100-square with multiples of 10 highlighted. Show shark. Write *32 + 26 =*. *We add by counting on, tens first.* Count on 2 **tens** from 32. Then count on 6. Write *58* to complete. Rpt for 48 + 36, add **tens** first, then add 6, bridging across 60.	Y1 1.3 p29 Counting back using number lines	Y1 D3.a.4 Using number cards to make TU–U subtractions TA	Y2 2.3 p30 Counting on, bridging 10	Y2 D3.a.2 Adding two 2-digit numbers T	Play 'What is the **take away**?' Give an answer, eg 8 or 19. Chn invent subtractions that have this answer. Record different suggestions on the board. Check them using number cards pegged to a washing line. Rpt.	**Y1** • Count back from a 2-digit number • Subtract by counting back using a number line **Y2** • Add two 2-digit numbers • Use knowledge of bonds to 10 to solve addition
Day 3	**Partition numbers into tens and units.** Children each place their 100-square in front of them. *Show me 3 tens and 2 **units***. Chn point at the correct number. Use a large 100-square to demonstrate. Rpt many times.		**All** Show jar containing 14p. *Frog has saved 14p.* Count the money. Write *14p – 6p =*. ***How much** will he have **left** after spending 6p?* Chn hold up 6 fingers. Take away 4 coins to leave 10p. Change 10p coin for ten 1p coins. *How much left?* Write *8p* to complete. Rpt for 23p – 7p. **Y2** Give one child 56p and another 25p, using 10p and 1p coins. *How much **altogether**?* Write *56p + 25p =*. Point to +25p. *We add the tens first.* Count on in 10s from 56. Point at 5 in 25p. *We now add five 1p coins.* Count on in 1s from 76p. Write *81p* to complete. Rpt for 65p + 28p.	Y1 D3.a.3 Investigating how many times a baker can reduce prices by 2p, 3p, 4p or 5p TA	Y1 D3.a.3 Investigating how many times a baker can reduce prices by 2p, 3p, 4p or 5p TA	Y2 D3.a.4 Looking for patterns in addition T	Y2 p28 Adding two 2-digit numbers	Give child 28p in 10p and 1p coins. They give 7p to another child. *How much does she have left?* Check. Child then gives 4p to another child. *How much does she have now?* Rpt, writing subtractions for each stage.	**Y1** • Subtract 1-digit numbers from 2-digit numbers • Investigate subtraction using coins **Y2** • Add 2-digit numbers • Identify patterns in addition

	Mental oral starter	Objectives	Main teaching	Activities: Group 1 (Y1)	Activities: Group 2 (Y1)	Activities: Group 3 (Y2)	Activities: Group 4 (Y2)	Plenary	Outcomes
Day 4	**Double numbers 1 to 15, and halve corresponding numbers.** Play 'Front and back'. Hold up card 1, facing the chn. *What is* ***double*** *1?* Chn respond. Turn the card around to reveal the answer. Rpt for each card in turn. Shuffle cards and present randomly.	**Y1** • Subtract one multiple of 10 from another **Y2** • Subtract one 2-digit number from another using an appropriate strategy • Understand that subtraction is the inverse of addition, using missing number sentences	**All** *Bisky Bat counts in 10s.* Rehearse counting in 10s from 0–100, moving Bisky along the line. Write *40−20=*. Place Bisky on 40. Point to −20. *We have to count back 20, that's 2 tens.* Hold up 2 fingers. Count back 20. Complete the subtraction. Rpt for 70−30. **[ITR Y1 D3.a]** **Y2** Give a child 58p in 10p and 1p coins. *How much left if he buys a cake for 25p?* Write *58p−25p=*. Point at 2 in 25p. *How many 10s do we need to count back?* Start at 58 and count back 2 tens. *He still needs to pay 5p.* Count back 5. Write *33p* to complete. Rpt for 75p−32p=.	Y1 D3.b.1 Counting back in 10s using coins TA	Y1 1.3 p32 Subtracting multiples of 10	Y2 D3.b.1 Subtracting 2-digit numbers T	Y2 2.3 p34 Completing missing number calculations	Ask chn to say some subtractions that have an answer of 20, using 10s only, eg *50−30=20*. Record suggestions on the board. Extend to answers of 30.	**Y1** • Count on and back in 10s • Subtract multiples of 10 by counting back in 10s **Y2** • Subtract TU−TU by counting back tens then units • Split numbers into T and U
Day 5	**Recall addition pairs of multiples of 10 to 100.** Play 'Ping-pong'. Say a number, eg *20*. Chn say its partner to 100, eg *80*. Start slowly, then gradually increase the pace. Occasionally say *Ping*, to which the response is *Pong*, or vice versa.		**All** Write *36−23=*. Discuss how to subtract. On 100-square, start at 36 and count back 20 to 16, then 3 more to 13. Write *13* to complete. Write *23+_=36. What is the missing number? Let's count on from 23 to find out.* Count on 10 to 33, then 3 more to 36. Write *13*. **[ITR Y2 D3.b]** **Y1** *Bisky Bat has 70p.* Drop seven 10p coins into a mug, counting the clinks as they go. *Bisky gives away 30p.* Write *70p−30p=*. *We will count back 3 tens.* Hold up 3 fingers. Count back from 70 to 40. Choose child to complete the subtraction. Rpt for similar subtractions.	Y1 1.3 p31 Counting back in 10s	Y1 D3.b.2 Subtracting multiples of 10 from amounts over £1 T	Y2 2.3 p32 Subtracting 10s	Y2 D3.b.2 Creating all possible TU−TU subtractions using four number cards TA	Show class 2 towers of bricks, one of 36 and one of 25. Ask pairs to find the **difference between** the numbers. When done, discuss which pairs counted on, and which counted back. Rpt.	**Y1** • Subtract multiples of 10 by counting back in 10s **Y2** • Solve missing number subtractions using addition • Count on in 10s and 1s

Vocabulary
multiple
add, addition
count on
altogether
how many more?
equals
total
sum
make
subtract, subtraction
take away
difference between
count back
how much left?
tens
units
half-past
o'clock
double
half, halve

Resources
clock boards (Y1 PCM 117)
picture of a shark
Blu-tack
1–20 number track
picture of a fish
up to six 1–30 number tracks
up to six counters
individual whiteboards
number fans (one per child)
picture of a frog
1–30 number line
large 100-square with multiples of 10 highlighted
number cards 1–50
up to 100 linking cubes
large 100-square
washing line
30 pegs
small 100-squares (one per child)
jar
up to twenty 1p coins
up to fifteen 10p coins
number cards 1–15, each with its double written on the back in a different colour
picture of Bisky Bat
up to four sets of multiple-of-10 cards 10–100
mug
dice numbered 1–6
up to four £1 coins
about five sets of digit cards 1-9

Blocks D3.a and D3.b

Year 1 Block D3.a Activities

D3.a.2 A group of up to 12 children working in pairs

Write *–3* on the board. Explain that we are going to subtract 3 from different numbers. One child in each pair picks a starting number, for example 14. Their partner writes this on their whiteboard, then places a counter on that number and counts back three steps along the track. The first child writes the rest of the subtraction, for example *14 – 3 = 11*. They show the teacher who records this on the board, listing subtractions with the same units together so children can see a pattern: *4 – 3 = 1, 14 – 3 = 11, 24 – 3 = 21*. Continue. At the end, discuss the unit patterns with the children. Photocopy their whiteboards to record their work.
Adult support may be useful in running this activity.

1–30 number track per pair; counter; individual whiteboard per child

D3.a.3 Whole class investigation, children working in pairs

Discuss how to subtract small amounts from larger amounts by counting back. *A baker reduces his prices through the day to make sure his cakes and biscuits sell before they go stale. If he starts at 20p, how many times can he subtract 4p? or 3p? or 2p?* Pairs have different starting prices (10p, 20p, 50p, £1, depending on the level of attainment) and investigate how many times we can subtract 2p, 3p, 4p or 5p. Can they see a pattern?
Extend by asking more able children to find out what amounts have to be subtracted to leave a reduced price which ends in 9. Try different starting prices, e.g. 25p, 35p, 45p or 55p.
Adult support is needed to run this activity.

D3.a.4 A group of 6 children working in pairs

Shuffle the cards and put them in two piles face down. Pairs select one card from each pile, e.g. 42 and 3, and write a subtraction, e.g. *42 – 3 = 39*. Pairs check each other's answers. If correct, they collect cubes to match the units digit of the answer. Have five rounds each. Which pair collects the most cubes?
Adult support may be useful in running this activity.

20–50 number cards and 1–9 number cards per pair; cubes

Year 1 Block D3.b Activities

D3.b.1 A group of up to 8 children working in pairs

Together count some 10p coins into the mug: *Ten, twenty, thirty, forty, fifty*. Shake the mug and agree how many coins are in the mug. Now visibly remove some coins, for example two 10p coins. Ask each pair to find the card that tells us how much is left. Encourage children to count back the number of coins removed. Remind them of the starting number, i.e. how much we have in the mug. Tip out the coins left in the mug and check against children's cards.
Who was correct? Repeat at least six times. If required, the subtractions may be recorded, for example *50 – 20 = 30*.
To extend, use starting amounts above 100p such as 120p.
Adult support may be useful in running this activity.

10–100 multiple of 10 cards per pair; mug; 10p coins

D3.b.2 A group of up to 8 children working in pairs

Choose a child and give them a £1 coin. *You have a pound and with that you have to buy a bus ticket for 20p. How much change will you have?* Encourage children to suggest that the pound is 100p. Substitute ten 10p coins for the £1. They can then count back in 10s to work out the change. Ask each pair to record the subtraction: *£1 – 20p = 80p*.
Now ask each pair to 'buy' a different bus ticket (30p, 40p, 50p, 10p). Each pair should record their subtraction, using the 10p coins to help them count back if required. Continue like this, giving each pair different subtractions involving £1. Extend either by going above £1 to £1·10 or £1·20, or else by subtracting multiples of 5, for example £1 – 25p.
Adult support may be useful in running this activity.

10p coins and £1 coin per pair

Year 2 Block D3.a Activities

D3.a.1 A group of up to 8 children

Give each child a 2-digit number with a units digit more than 4. Ask them to count on to work out how many to the next 10, using the number track and their fingers for support. They show you how many on their fingers. Check that each child is correct before they write a matching addition, for example a child has 36, they show you four fingers and write *36 + 4 = 40*. Children swap additions to check each other's, giving them a tick if they are correct. Repeat this process five or six times.
Adult support is needed to run this activity.

1–50 number track (or use number cards); 1–100 number cards

D3.a.2 Pairs of children

Remove multiples of 10 and numbers where the units digit is less than 4 from a set of 10–50 number cards. Shuffle the remaining cards and place them face down in a pile. Each child takes a card. Pairs then work out the total of their two cards, adding the smaller to the larger, and use the 100-square to help them count on, first in 10s and then in 1s, for example for cards 45 and 27, start with 45, count on 20 to 65, then add 7 to make 72. Both children record this addition on their whiteboards, then take another card each and start again. Children should do six additions: photocopy their whiteboards at the end.
Adult support may be helpful in running this activity with several pairs of children.

10–50 number cards; large 100-square; individual whiteboards

D3.a.4 A group of up to 8 children

Give each pair a 2-digit number. Ask all children to add 21. Demonstrate how to add 20 by counting on in 10s and then adding 1 more. They each record the completed addition. Ask children to add 32 to the same starting number. Again, they count on in 10s and then in 1s. Repeat for adding 43. Give each pair a new starting number and add the same three numbers in turn. Encourage children to notice the patterns and to start predicting answers. Repeat with new starting numbers.
Adult support is needed to run this activity.

100-square for each pair

Year 2 Block D3.b Activities

D3.b.1 Pairs of children

Child 1 writes a 2-digit number with both tens and units digits more than 5, for example 67. Child 2 rolls a dice twice to generate a 2-digit number to subtract, for example throw a 3 and a 4 and write *34*. Both children perform the subtraction and see if they agree the answer. They record the subtraction. They then reverse the digits of the dice number and subtract it, for example subtract 43 from 67. Repeat the process to continue the activity with new numbers.
Adult support may be helpful in running this activity for several pairs of children.

100-square; 1–6 dice

D3.b.2 Pairs of children

Give each pair four digit cards, for example 9, 8, 3, 2. They arrange the digits to perform all the possible TU – TU subtractions (12). They must show you that they have found them all.
Adult support may be helpful in running this activity with several pairs of children.

four digit cards

Maths Weekly Plan: Year 1 and 2

Block D3.c: Y1 Add two 'teens' numbers; Y2 Add 1-digit numbers to multiples of 10 and 100
Block D3.d: Y1 Add/subtract 9, solve real-life problems; Y2 Create and interpret tables

	Mental oral starter	Objectives	Main teaching	Activities: Group 1 Y1	Group 2 Y1	Group 3 Y2	Group 4 Y2	Plenary	Outcomes
Day 1	**Say a number 10 more/10 less than a 3-digit number.** Write 10 to 15 3-digit numbers on the board. Make two teams: '**10 more**' and '**10 less**'. Point to a 3-digit number at random. Chn in '10 more' team say the number that is 10 more, then the '10 less' team say the number that is 10 less. Rpt.	**Y1** • Begin to add two 'teens' numbers, not crossing a multiple of 10 **Y2** • Add and begin to subtract a 1-digit number to and from multiples of 10 and 100	**All** Draw 2 biscuits. Write *14p* and *15p*. *How much to buy both?* Write *15p+14p=*. *What coins will we use to* ***make*** *this amount? 15p is 10p and five 1ps. 14p is 10p and four 1ps. So we have two 10ps: 20p. And nine 1ps: 9p.* Write 29p to complete. Rpt for 16p+12p. **[ITR Y1 D3.c]** **Y2** Use Turkey to **count back in 100s** from 1000 to 100 along number line. Write 400–3=. Demo how to work out. First: show 100-square. *What is 3* ***less than*** *100?* Second: *What is the 100s number before 400?* Link to counting back in 100s. Write 397. Rpt for 500–2. **[ITR Y2 C3.c]**	Y1 D3.c.1 Adding using coins TA	Y1 1.3 p34 Adding two numbers using place-value cards	Y2 C3.c.1 Creating subtractions from additions T	Y2 2.3 p27 Adding and subtracting 1-digit numbers to/ from multiples of 10	Write *11p + 11p, 12p + 12p, 14p + 14p* and *15p + 15p* in a column down left-hand side of board. Write *30p, 22p, 28p, 24p* down right-hand side. Chn work individually to match each addition to its correct answer.	**Y1** • Add 'teens' numbers using coins • Add by partitioning numbers into T and U **Y2** • Count in 100s • Add and subtract 1-digit numbers to/ from multiples of 100
Day 2	**Add a 1-digit number to a 2-digit number, without crossing a 10.** Play 'Thumbs up, thumbs down'. Write 10 additions of 1-digit and 2-digit numbers on the board, some correct, some incorrect. Point to one: *Thumbs out*. Chn show thumbs up if correct, thumbs down if not. Rpt.		**All** Show a £1 coin. Write *£1* on board. *How many pence are there in one pound? 100.* Demonstrate. Write *£1–4p=*. Re-write as *100p–4p=*. *What is the number 4 less than 100?* Use 100-square to help. Rpt for £1–8p. **Y1** Draw a train ticket. *This costs £13. I want to buy 2 tickets.* Write *£13+£13=*. Point at the 1 in 13. *This is 10.* Use place-value cards to show that 13 is 10+3. Show that we have 10+10 and 3+3. Write £26 to complete the addition. Rpt for £17+£12.	Y1 1.3 p33 Adding two amounts using coins	Y1 D3.c.3 Using number cards to make additions of two 'teens' numbers T	Y2 C3.c.3 Subtracting 1-digit numbers from multiples of 100 and looking at units pattern TA	Y2 C3.c.3 Subtracting 1-digit numbers from multiples of 100 and looking at units pattern TA	Write five pairs of additions, eg *10–3=7 and 200–3=197*, mixing them up so that the additions from each pair are not adjacent. Chn find the matching pairs by identifying the additions that are related.	Y1 • Add two teen numbers, not crossing 10 • Partition numbers into T and U **Y2** • Subtract 1-digit numbers from multiples of 100
Day 3	**Recognise the value of digits in 2-digit numbers.** Play 'Number partners'. Give half the chn a **tens** place-value card each, and the other half a **units** card each. Put chn in pairs, with one T and one U card per pair. Ask pairs to say their 2-digit number. Highlight numbers on a 100-square. Extend by **ordering** numbers.	**Y1** • Add and subtract 9 by adding and subtracting 10 • Solve 'real-life' problems involving money (change)	**All** Show a purse. *This purse has 14p in it. It has 3 coins. Which coins?* Show line of coins and go through which it might be, pointing to each one in turn. Place 10p beside purse. How much more than 10p? How could we make 4p? Encourage them to say two 2ps. **[ITR Y2 D3.d]** **Y2** *Write 10–4* on the board. Chn answer: 96. Write *200–4. Does the answer to the 1st* ***calculation*** *help us do the 2nd?* Write answer: *196*. Encourage chn to see the link. *If we know one fact, we can use it to help us do a harder calculation.* Rpt, using 10–8=2 to find 600–8=592.	Y1 1.3 p35 Using coins to make amounts	Y1 D3.d.1 TM 14.3 14 Word problems TA	Y2 2.3 p27 Adding and subtracting 1-digit numbers to/ from multiples of 100	Y2 C3.c.5 Using dice and place-value cards to create additions and subtractions T	Write *_+9p=36p*. Ask chn to try out various numbers to find out which one is the missing amount.	**Y1** • Solve addition and subtraction using money • Recognise coins **Y2** • Add and subtract 1-digit numbers to/ from multiples of 100

	Mental oral starter	Objectives	Main teaching	Activities Group 1 Y1	Activities Group 2 Y1	Activities Group 3 Y2	Activities Group 4 Y2	Plenary	Outcomes
Day 4	**Recall addition pairs to 10.** Play 'Quick on the draw'. Say a number up to 10, eg *6*. Chn hold up fingers to match its partner to 10 as quickly as possible, eg 4. Rpt for all pairs to 10.	*(Continued)* **Y2** • Organise information in a table • Interpret information from a table	**All** Draw **table**: 9 **rows**, 5 **columns**. Column headings: *Name, Age, Brothers, Sisters, Height. Rows go across, columns go down*. Two chn are height measurers. Each child has their height measured and fills in their details. Ask questions to help **interpret** the data. **[ITR Y2 C3.d]** **Y1** Show small toy **priced** 46p. *Someone offered to* ***pay*** *9p more. How much did they pay?* Write *46p+9p=*. Point at +9. *It would take a while to add nine 1p coins. Let's add 10p instead*. Write *46p+10p=56p*. *We added 1p too much. We need to* ***take away*** *1p*. Complete the addition.	Y1 D3.d.3 14.1 14 Word problems T	Y1 1.3 p36 Using coins to add amounts	Y2 C3.d.1 Creating a table of ages TA	Y2 2.3 p29 Completing a simple table	Draw table with column headings *Name, a, e, i, o, u*. Chn write their names and tick or cross each column to show whether the letter appears in their name. Discuss results.	**Y1** • Add near multiples of 10 • Solve problems involving money **Y2** • Organise information in a table • Interpret information from a table
Day 5	**Find coin totals (3 and 3+ coins).** Stick a 10p, 5p and 2p coin onto the board. Chn show the total number of pence with their number fans. Check answers. Rpt for different sets of 3 coins.		**All** Draw items priced 9p, 19p, 29p and 39p. Point at 9p. *How much is this* ***nearly****?* Show on 100-square that it is nearly 10p. *If I pay 10p, how much* ***change*** *will I get? 1p*. Rpt for other items. *We will have 1p change for all items. How much to buy all four items? 96p*. **Y2** Draw table: 7 rows, 5 columns. Column headings: *Number, Odd, Even, Digit total, Digit difference*. A child selects a number card, eg 32. Write it in Number column. Chn help fill in the rest of the row. Rpt until the table is full. Ask questions to help interpret it.	Y1 95 Solving addition word problems	Y1 D3.d.4 Writing word problems TA	Y2 2.3 p29 Completing a simple table	Y2 C3.d.2 Investigating digit sum patterns and recording them in a table T	Ask each pair of chn to write two numbers ending in '9' which will add up to either 28, 58 or 108. Give them two or three minutes and then take suggestions for each number.	**Y1** • Solve problems involving money **Y2** • Draw a table from information collected • Interpret information from a table

Vocabulary
add, addition
make
subtract, subtraction
calculation
count on
count in 10s
count back
take away
'teens' number
multiple
nearly
how much more?
coin
cost
price
pay
change
table
row
column
interpret
10 more
10 less
tens
units
order

Resources
Turkey from *The Owl and the Pussycat* by Edward Lear
0–1000 number line with multiples of 100 labelled
large 100-square
individual whiteboards
lots of coins of all denominations
up to four dice numbered 1–6
teddy or other small toy
place-value cards (H, T, U)
two sets of number cards 11–19
linking cubes
Post-it notes
purse
cards saying *altogether*, *more*, *left*
five blank cards
height measurer, for example tape measure attached to wall
large cardboard coins 1p–£1
Blu-tack
number fans (one per child)
number cards 10–100
up to four small 100-squares

Year 1 Block D3.c Activities

D3.c.1 A group of up to 8 children working in pairs

Give teddy an amount, for example 34p. *How much does teddy have?* Each pair makes this amount using 10p and 1p coins. Ask each pair to add 11p. They count on 10p, and then 1p, *Forty-four, forty-five*. They write 45p on their whiteboard. Then they check using 10p and 1p coins to add that amount. Were they correct? They show you. When all the pairs have completed this, write a new amount and repeat the activity. Do this at least six times.

Adult support may be useful in running this activity.

individual whiteboard per pair; 10p and 1p coins per pair; dice per pair; teddy or other toy

D3.c.3 A group of 4 children working in pairs

Shuffle the cards and place them in a pile face down. Each pair chooses two cards from the pile, for example 11 and 14, and writes an addition: *14 + 11 = 25*. Pairs check each other's additions. The pair with the largest answer collects 10p and 1p coins to match the answer. Reshuffle the cards and repeat several times. At the end, check which pair has the most cubes.

Adult support may be useful in running this activity.

two sets of 11–19 number cards; 10p and 1p coins; loose cubes

Year 1 Block D3.d Activities

14.3 14 Word problems

D3.d.1 A group of 6 or more children

Ask children to think of an addition fact, for example *6 + 4 = 10*, and write this on a blank card. Repeat for a subtraction fact. Read the vocabulary cards together. *We can use these to make up word problems.* Say that there are a number of people on a bus. Sometimes people get on, and sometimes they get off. *Which words might we use for our addition fact 6 + 4 = 10?*

Together write a word problem such as: *There are 6 people on the bus. 4 more get on at the next stop. There are now 10 people altogether.*

Repeat this for another addition fact.

Then do the same for two subtraction facts.

Ask children to think of three numbers whose total they know. Write this on the fifth blank card, for example *5 + 3 + 2 = 10*. Together write a word problem using this fact.

Adult support is needed to run this activity.

cards saying 'altogether,' 'more,' 'left'; five blank cards

14.1 14 Word problems

D3.d.3 A group of 6 or more children

Ask children to think of an addition fact, for example *3 + 2 = 5*, and write this on a blank card. Repeat for a subtraction fact.

Read the vocabulary cards together. *We are going to use these to make up word problems.* Say that there are a number of people on a bus. Sometimes people will get on, and sometimes they get off. *Which words might we use for our addition fact 3 + 2 = 5?*

Together write a word problem such as: *There are 3 people on the bus. 2 more get on at the next stop. There are now 5 people altogether.*

Repeat this for another addition fact.

Then do the same for two subtraction facts.

Adult support is needed to run this activity.

cards saying 'altogether,' 'more,' 'left'; four blank cards

D3.d.4 A group of up to 8 children working in pairs

Explain that you would like children to write addition word problems for each other involving either the 100-square or the coins. They should write the problem and work out the answer. Give some examples: *A frog starts at 56 on the grid and hops down two rows and three spaces to the right. Where does he end up? Fred has 38p and his mum gives him another 25p. How much does he have now? …* When each pair have written and agreed two problems, put the pairs into fours for each pair to solve the other pair's problems.

Adult support may be useful in running this activity.

100-square per pair; 20p and 1p coins per pair

Year 2 Block D3.c Activities

C3.c.1 A group of up to 8 children

Give each pair a number in the nineties, for example 97, 93, 91, 95. Ask them to work out and show you on their fingers how many more to make 100. Check that they are right before they write the matching addition on their whiteboards, for example *93 + 7 = 100*. Repeat this, giving each pair a different number in the nineties. Record all the additions: *91 + 9 = 100, 92 + 8 = 100…* in order on the board. Point out the number bonds to 10: 9 + 1, 8 + 2… Now write up: *100 – 5 = ?* Discuss with children who has written an addition that helps with the subtraction. Point to 95 + 5 = 100. *We know that we add five to ninety-five to get one hundred. If we take off the five from the hundred, we must get back to ninety-five.* Demonstrate this on the 100-square by starting at 100 and counting back five. Children record the subtraction on their whiteboards: *100 – 5 = 95*. Repeat this for other subtractions, for example 100 – 7, 100 – 4.

Adult support is needed to run this activity.

large 100-square; individual whiteboards

C3.c.3 A group of 8 children working in pairs

Shuffle hundreds and units place-value cards and place face down in two piles. Children take one hundreds card and one units card. They write these in a subtraction, for example *500 – 3 =*. Children each write their answer on a Post-it without discussing it, then compare answers. They agree an answer and write it to complete the subtraction. They study their answer and decide whether they would be able to use either of the cards they have already used to make it. They then replace the cards on the bottom of the shuffled piles and do five more subtractions like this.

Adult support may be helpful in running this activity.

place-value cards (H and U); Post-it notes

C3.c.5 Pairs of children

Each pair spreads out the place-value cards (H only) face down. One child reveals a card, for example 400, and the other rolls the dice, for example 5. Each child writes both an addition and a subtraction, for example *400 + 5 = 405*; *400 – 5 = 395*. They check each other's answers and replace the card. Repeat several times.

Adult support may be helpful in running this activity with several pairs of children.

place-value cards (H only); 1–6 dice

Year 2 Block D3.d Activities

C3.d.1 A group of up to 8 children

Explain to children that you are all going to make a table of the ages of people in everyone's family. Discuss the range of ages: some children may have baby brothers or sisters who are less than one year old; some may have parents or grandparents who care for them who are more than 50 years old. Draw a table with 8 columns headed: 1–4 years old, 5–9 years old, 10–14 years old, 15–19 years old, 20–29 years old, 30–39 years old, 40–49 years old and 50 and over. Children write on the whiteboards the names or initials of at least four but not more than six people in their family, including anyone who cares for them as well as siblings or cousins. They write their ages beside the initials. Take feedback, asking children in turn to tell you the age of their first person. Children cross that person off their list as you record them in the table by ticking the matching column. Continue in the same way and study the table together when it is complete. *Which column has the most/fewest ticks? …*

Adult support is needed to run this activity.

individual whiteboards

C3.d.2 Pairs of children

Tell children that they will draw a table that sorts numbers from 1–60. They must find the sum of the digits in each number to find which column to write it in, for example 34 has a digit sum of 7; 23 has a digit sum of 5… Draw column headings marked from 1 to 9 and ask each child to copy the table and fill in the numbers 1–60 under the correct heading for their digit sum. If the digits add to 10 or more, they add the digits of the total, for example 48: 4 + 8 = 12; 1 + 2 = 3, so the digit sum of 48 is 3. When children have written in all the numbers from 1–60, they talk about the patterns with their partner. *Where are the numbers in the three times-table? Where are the numbers in the nine times-table?*

Note: Y2 blocks D3.c/d reference activities from original Y2 blocks C3.c/d to allow both year groups to focus on time in D3.c/d.

Maths Weekly Plan: Year 1 and 2

Block E3.a: Y1 Count on in 2s or 5s; Y2 Understand multiplication as repeated addition
Block E3.b: Y1 Begin to recognise odd and even numbers; Y2 Know ×2, ×5 and ×10 tables

	Mental oral starter	Objectives	Main teaching	Activities: Group 1 (Y1)	Activities: Group 2 (Y1)	Activities: Group 3 (Y2)	Activities: Group 4 (Y2)	Plenary	Outcomes
Day 1	**Partition numbers into tens and units.** Play 'Number partners'. Give each child a **tens** or **units** place-value card. Each child with a tens card finds a partner with a units card. Choose a pair to hold up their cards and say their 2-digit number. Highlight the number on a 100-square. Rpt.	**Y1** • Count on in 2s or 5s up to 100 • Begin to count on in 3s from zero **Y2** • Begin to understand multiplication as repeated addition or as describing an array • Begin to understand division as the inverse of multiplication	**All** Divide the class into 2 teams. The class counts from 1 to 100, with teams saying 10 numbers each and then swapping. When they say numbers ending in 5, they wave one hand in the air. When they say numbers ending in 0, they wave both hands in the air. Write the **multiples** of 5 and look at the **pattern**. *Bisky Bat **counts in 10s***. Count in 10s from 10–200. Write *5 × 10*. Point at 5. *This tells Bisky **how many** 10s to count*. Hold up 5 fingers. Count five 10s, folding down fingers. Write *50*. Rpt for 7 × 10 = 70. Write *_ × 10 = 90. How many 10s must we count to **make** 90? Write this as 90 ÷ 10 = _. **Division** is how many **sets** make the **total**.*	Y1 E3.a.1 TM 15.1 15 Counting in 2s and 5s T	Y1 98 Counting in 5s by circling numbers on a 6 × 10 grid	Y2 E3.a.1 Using towers of cubes to model division TA	Y2 2.3 p41 Completing multiplications and related divisions	Ask 3 or 4 chn to chant the multiples of 5 together. Invite the rest of the class to help them if they get stuck. Rpt. Ask some chn to **count back** in 5s from 50.	**Y1** • Count in 1s, noting multiples of 5 and 10 • Count in 5s **Y2** • Multiply by 10 by counting in 10s • Begin to see division is inverse of multiplication
Day 2	**Add to make the next multiple of 10.** Play 'Quick on the draw'. Say a 2-digit number, eg *24*. Chn decide what must be added to reach the next multiple of 10, eg *6*. Give chn thinking time, then on the command *Go!* they hold up fingers to match the answer. Rpt.		**All** Show Attery Squash. *She **counts in 5s***. Put Attery Squash on 25 on 100-square. Count on in 5s, moving Attery as you count. Chant the multiples of 5 together. Drop five 5p coins into a mug. Chn count on 5 at each clink. *How much is in the mug? 25p.* Write *5 × 5 = 25*. Rpt. Put 40 pegs on the washing line. Write *40* on board. *We want to pack the pegs in sets of 5*. Write *40 ÷ 5 = _. 40 is how many sets of 5?* **Group** pegs to find out. Show 8 fingers. *There are 8 fives in 40*. Write *8* to complete the division. **[ITR Y2 E3.a]**	Y1 1.3 p38 Counting in 5s along a number track	Y1 E3.a.4 TM 15.3 15 Counting in 2s and 5s T	Y2 22.3 p39 Linking multiplication and division	Y2 E3.a.4 Using towers of cubes to write multiplications and related divisions TA	Choose a child to write on the board a **multiplication** involving multiples of 5, eg *3 × 5 =*. Drop a matching number of 5p coins into a mug. Chn count in 5s as they hear each clink. Rpt.	**Y1** • Count in 5s and 2s • Identify units pattern when counting in 2s and 5s **Y2** • Multiply by 5 by counting in 5s • Understand division is inverse of multiplication
Day 3	**Name and recognise the properties of 2D shapes.** Play 'Shape pointing'. Each child places a shape board (Y2 PCM 123) in front of them. Give an instruction, eg *Show me a shape with 5 **sides***. Chn point to the matching shape. Rpt, including different properties of shapes.		**All** Show Bisky Bat, Attery Squash and Pobble. Child chooses number on 100-square. If multiple of 5, use Attery to count on/back in 5s. If not, use Pobble or Bisky to **count in 1s** or 10s. Put multiple-of-5 cards in order. Count along. Remove a card. Chn say which is missing. **Y2** *I have 35p in my bag. How many 5p coins do you think I have?* Write number sentences: *_ × 5 = 35*, *35 ÷ 5 = _*. Chn shut eyes. Drop seven 5p coins into mug. Chn count in 5s with each. Write *7* to complete sentences. Rpt, starting with 16p in the mug and adding 2p coins.	Y1 E3.a.3 Matching multiples of 5 to 5p coins TA	Y1 1.3 p39 Matching a multiple of 5 to a set of 5p coins	Y2 E3.a.3 Finding a number which divides by 2, 5, and 10 with 1 left over each time T	Y2 E3.a.3 Finding a number which divides by 2, 5, and 10 with 1 left over each time T	Shuffle a set of multiple-of-5 cards 5–50. Lay them in a line. *We need to put the multiples of 5 in **order***. Choose different chn to move one card at a time, aiming to get them all in order. Each child may move only one card.	**Y1** • Count in 5s and 2s using 5p and 2p coins • Begin to count how many 5s in a multiple of 5 **Y2** • Solve divisions using coins • Investigate multiples of 2, 5 and 10

	Mental oral starter	Objectives	Main teaching	Activities: Group 1 (Y1)	Activities: Group 2 (Y1)	Activities: Group 3 (Y2)	Activities: Group 4 (Y2)	Plenary	Outcomes
Day 4	**Count on or back in 10s.** Play 'Birdsong'. Divide class into 3 or 4 groups of birds. Say a start number, eg *7*. Choose a group to start 'singing', ie counting on from 7 in 10s. After 3 or 4 counts, another group takes over the count. Rpt for counting forwards and back in 10s from different numbers.	**Y1** • Begin to recognise odd and even numbers up to at least 20 **Y2** • Know by heart the multiplication facts for 2, 5 and 10 times tables • Begin to recognise 2-digit multiples of 2, 5 and 10	**All** Show Attery Squash. *She counts in 5s.* Write 3 × 5 =. *Attery knows the answer. She doesn't need to work it out! Do you remember how to do it?* Chn hold up 3 fingers and count in 5s. Write out ×5 **table**. Point to answers. Encourage chn to try to memorise them. **[ITR Y2 E3.b]** **Y1** Show Pobble. *He counts in 1s. We will count in 1s, with soft and loud numbers!* Divide class into 2 teams: soft and loud. Count to 20, saying **even** numbers loudly and **odd** numbers softly. Stress the pattern. Rpt, writing 'loud' numbers in red and 'soft' numbers in blue.	Y1 1.3 p40 Writing sequences of odd/even numbers	Y1 E3.b.3 Investigating patterns of digits in odd and even numbers T	Y2 1.3 p42 Completing ×5 multiplication facts	Y2 E3.b.3 TM 15.3 15 Number detective TA	Give chn five multiplications to answer, eg *What are 3 lots of 5?* They write the answers on their whiteboards. Keep it pacy. Ask them to mark their own work. Give lots of praise!	**Y1** • Recognise odd and even numbers to 20 • Sort numbers into odd or even **Y2** • Learn ×5 table by heart • Begin to learn ×2, ×5 and ×10 tables
Day 5	**Round 2-digit numbers to the nearest 10.** Draw unnumbered 0–100 number line with marks for 10s and 5s. Label the ends *0* and *100*. Ask a child to select a number card, eg 57. Chn **round** the number to the **nearest 10** and write the multiple of 10 on whiteboards. Check answers. Rpt.		**All** Make 2 teams: soft (odd), loud (even). *You'll each collect numbers.* A child chooses a number card, and reads it. *Is it loud or soft?* Count, soft and loud, up to the number. Pass card to correct team. When all numbers are collected, order **smallest** to **largest**. **[ITR Y1 E3.b]** **Y2** Show Bisky Bat. *He counts in 10s.* Write *3 × 10 =*. *Do you know answer without working it out? 30.* Write *30 ÷ 10 =*. *How many 10s in 30? Do we have to work this out? If we know the multiplication, then we also know the division!* Rpt to learn ×2 table.	Y1 E3.b.2 Identifying odd and even numbers up to 20 TA	Y1 1.3 p41 Identifying odd and even numbers	Y2 E3.b.2 TM 15.1 15 Number detective T	Y2 p31 Multiplying and dividing	Two chn stand at front of class. On count of 3, each child brings their hand out from behind their back with some fingers standing and some folded down. Chn count total number of fingers standing. *Is it even or odd?* Rpt.	**Y1** • Sort numbers into odd or even • Know even numbers are multiples of 2 **Y2** • Learn ×2, ×5 and ×10 tables by heart • Identify multiples of 2, 5 and 10

Vocabulary
count in 1s, 5s, 10s
count back
how many?
make
multiply, multiplication
multiple
divide, division
sets of
groups of
lots of
total
× table
pattern
even
odd
order
smallest
largest
tens
units
2D shape names
side
corner
angle
round
nearest 10

Resources
place-value cards (T, U)
large 100-square
picture of Bisky Bat
100-bead string
up to 50 interlocking cubes
picture of Attery Squash
up to forty 5p coins
mug
40 pegs
washing line
number cards 1–100
shape boards (Y2 PCM 123)
picture of Pobble
up to four sets of multiple-of-5 cards 5–50
up to twenty 2p coins
up to four sets of number cards 1–9
cards saying *greater than, less than, between, odd, even, multiple of 5, multiple of 10, greater than 10, less than 10, between 5 and 10*
0–20 number line
individual whiteboards
up to eight 1–20 number grids (two rows of 10)
red and blue dot stickers

Year 1 Block E3.a Activities

15.1 15 Counting in 2s and 5s

E3.a.1 A group of 6 or more children

Use the bead string to count in 5s to 100, moving 5 beads along the string at a time. *What do you notice about every other number?* Agree that every other number is a multiple of 10. *What do you notice about the numbers in between?* Agree that these all have 5 at the end.
Now use the bead string to count in 5s to 100, gradually building up speed.
Ask children to help you to write the numbers 5, 10, 15, …, 50 on the board. Draw attention to the multiples of 10 ending in 0 and the other numbers ending in 5. Read the numbers together, forwards and backwards.
Use the bead string to count back from 100 in 5s, moving 5 beads at a time back along the string. Repeat, gradually increasing speed.
Adult support is needed to run this activity.

100-bead string

E3.a.3 A group of up to 8 children working in pairs

Each pair sets out their multiple of 5 cards in order. Choose a multiple, for example 35. Ask children to match this to 5p coins. When each pair has had a go, count in 5s, holding up one finger for each number spoken. *How many fingers? Seven. How many 5p coins? Seven.* Repeat this for other multiples.
Adult support may be useful in running this activity.

set of 5–50 multiple of 5 number cards per pair; ten 5p coins per pair

15.3 15 Counting in 2s and 5s

E3.a.4 A group of 6 or more children

Use the bead string to count in 5s to 100, moving 5 beads along the string at a time. *What do you notice about every other number?* Agree that every other number is a multiple of 10. *What about the numbers in between?* Agree that these all have 5 at the end. *If we carried on counting in 5s, would we get to 70? to 85? to 87? Why not?* Test the answers.
Now count back from 100 in 5s, moving 5 beads at a time back along the string. Repeat, gradually increasing speed.
Use the bead string to count in 2s to at least 30. *If we carried on counting in 2s, would we get to 40? to 41?* Test the answers. *When we count in 2s, the numbers are even.* Pull 12 beads along to the left of the string. Fold this part of the string in half to show two equal parts. *We could share 12 beads evenly between 2 people. What do you think will happen if we share 15 beads?* Do this and show that 1 bead will be left. *We call these odd numbers.*
Adult support is needed to run this activity.

100-bead string

Year 1 Block E3.b Activities

E3.b.2 A group of up to 8 children

Children stick red dot stickers over all the even numbers on their grid.
Now count along the grid, saying the 'missing' even numbers. Count along the grid again, saying the odd numbers.
Now ask each child to cover all the odd numbers with a blue dot sticker. Can they still count along the odd numbers, although they cannot see them?
Adult support may be useful in running this activity.

1–20 number grid (two rows of 10) per child; red and blue dot stickers

E3.b.3 A group of up to 8 children working in pairs

With all the children identify the even numbers up to 100, using a 100-square. Discuss how we know a number is even or odd. Pairs use their 1–9 number cards to create even and odd numbers. They explore making odd numbers with one even and one odd digit, for example 45, 27, etc. They also explore making even numbers with one even and one odd digit. *Which digit tells us if a number is even or odd?*
Adult support may be useful in running this activity.

100-square; 1–9 number cards per pair

Year 2 Block E3.a Activities

E3.a.1 A group of up to 8 children working in pairs

Work with the group to make some towers of 5 cubes. Line up seven towers. Ask each child to count in 5s to write the matching multiplication: $7 \times 5 = 35$. Repeat this with eight towers of two for 8×2 and three towers of ten for 3×10. Show children a pile of 40 cubes. *I have forty cubes here. How many towers of five can I make?* Write: $\_ \times 5 = 40$. Pairs count in 5s to try to work out how many towers of five can be made from 40 cubes. Once they have had a go, take forty cubes and make the towers. Show how to write 8 in the missing number space in the multiplication. Repeat the process, showing 20 cubes and asking how many towers of 2. Then try 70 cubes and ask how many towers of 10. Continue like this.

Adult support is needed to run this activity.

interlocking cubes

E3.a.3 A whole class investigation with children working in pairs

Move on from the whole class teaching: counting in 2s to make 16. *Eight lots of two make sixteen. Do you think we could count in twos to make seventeen?* Discuss why/why not. Use towers of two cubes to demonstrate that the count reaches 16 and then there is one left over. *We cannot count in twos to seventeen. There is one left over!* Repeat for counting in 5s to 22. Discuss why/why not. *How many are left over this time?*

Write up: *Challenge! Find a number where there is always just one left over when you count in twos and fives and tens.* Put children in pairs or threes to investigate this, encouraging them to be systematic in their trials. Extension for those who find this easy: Find a number where there is always one left over if you count in twos and threes and fours and fives and tens!

Adult support is needed to run this activity.

interlocking cubes for support

E3.a.4 A group of 2, 3, 4 or 5 children

Children make ten towers of five cubes. Deal one card from a shuffled set of 1–10 number cards, for example 4. Children collect a matching number of towers, count the number of cubes, for example $5 + 5 + 5 + 5 = 20$ and write a matching multiplication, $4 \times 5 = 20$, and a matching division, $20 \div 5 = 4$. Replace the towers and continue for each card in turn. Repeat the activity with towers of a different height.

Adult support may be useful in running this activity.

interlocking cubes; 1–10 number cards

Year 2 Block E3.b Activities

15.1 15 Number detective

E3.b.2 A group of up to 8 children

Hang 1–20 number cards in order on a washing line. Read the vocabulary Post-its together. Pick up the *greater than 10* Post-it. Point to 7. *Is this number greater than 10?* Agree that it is not and put the Post-it down. Pick up the *less than 10* Post-it. *Is this number less than 10?* Agree that it is and stick it to the bottom of the 7 card. Work through all the Post-its until all the relevant ones are stuck to the 7 card. Read through them explaining that they all describe the number 7. Choose another number and repeat.

Adult support is needed to run this activity.

Post-it notes with: *greater than 10, less than 10, between 5 and 10, odd, even, multiple of 5, multiple of 10*; 1–20 number cards; washing line and pegs

15.3 15 Number detective

E3.b.3 A group of up to 8 children

Give out the cards. Play 'Guess my number': Ask a pair of children to think of a number between 0 and 20 and to keep it secret. Children use the words on the cards to ask the pair questions to which they can only answer *yes* or *no*. Make a note of the questions. When the pair answer the questions, the other children help them to cross out those numbers on the number line that cannot be their number, for example if they ask if the number is odd, and the pair answers *no*, they help them to cross out all the odd numbers. Repeat the game, this time asking a different pair of children to think of a mystery number. Challenge other children to guess the number using fewer of the cards.

Adult support is needed to run this activity.

cards with: *greater than, less than, between, odd, even, multiple of 5, multiple of 10*; 0–20 number line

Maths Weekly Plan: Year 1 and 2

Block E3.c: Y1 Exchange coins for smaller coins; Y2 Double/halve multiples of 5/10
Block E3.d: Y1 Add sets of coins; Y2 Know relationship between halves and quarters

	Mental oral starter	Objectives	Main teaching	Activities: Group 1 Y1	Activities: Group 2 Y1	Activities: Group 3 Y2	Activities: Group 4 Y2	Plenary	Outcomes
Day 1	**Recall multiplication and division facts for ×5 and ×10.** Hold up counting stick. Point to the divisions on it as chn **count in 5s** from 0–50. Start in sequence both forwards and backwards, then point randomly. Repeat for 10s.	**Y1** • Exchange coins up to 10p for equivalent in smaller coins **Y2** • Double multiples of 5 up to 50 • Halve multiples of 10 up to 100 • Add by identifying near doubles for multiples of 5	**All** Read *The Owl and the Pussycat*. Show large moneybox. Show 10p **coin**. Ask chn to whisper to a partner what this coin is called. Choose chn to each say something different about the coin, eg *It is silver*. Rpt for each coin from 1p to £2. Put the coins in **order**. **[ITR Y1 E3.c]** **Y2** Child has 20p. *Your mum has* ***doubled*** *it!* Write *double 20p*. Stick two 10p coins on board. Stick 2 more beside them. **Count in 10s** to show you have 40p. Write *double 35p*. *When we double it we* ***add*** *3 more 10p coins and 1 more 5p coin.* Count in 10s to 70p. Rpt for double 45p.	Y1 E3.c.1 Recognising coins 1p to £2 TA	Y1 1.3 p43 Matching coin sets of equal value	Y2 E3.c.1 Doubling multiples of 5 T	Y2 2.3 p44 Doubling and halving	Place all the coins (1p to £2) in a cloth bag. Choose a child to secretly withdraw a coin. They describe it to the class, eg *It is small and silver with seven sides.* The other chn say the name of the coin. Rpt.	**Y1** • Know value of coins 1p to £2 • Know equivalent values of coins **Y2** • Double multiples of 5 • Halve multiples of 10
Day 2	**Count on and back in 2s.** Play 'Birdsong'. Divide class into 3 or 4 groups of birds. Say a start number, eg *2*. Choose a group to start 'singing', ie counting on in 2s. After 3 or 4 counts, ask a different group to take over the count, and so on. Rpt.		**All** Write *50p*. *I want to* ***share*** *this amount between 2 chn.* Point at 5 in 50. *Five 10p coins*. Divide five 10p coins between 2 piles. *What shall we do with the fifth 10p? What is* ***half*** *of 10p?* Write *5 + 5 = 10*. **Exchange** 10p for two 5p coins. Write *half of 50p = 25p*. Rpt to **halve** 30p. **Y1** Show 1p, 2p, 5p and 10p coins. *Which is* ***worth*** *the* ***most****? Which is worth the* ***least****? Owl and Cat have only got 1p coins. They want to* ***buy*** *a chocolate biscuit. It* ***costs*** *2p.* Show how Owl and Cat can **pay** for this. *Two 1p coins are the* ***same*** *as one 2p coin.* Rpt for 5p and 10p.	Y1 1.3 p42 Sorting and identifying coins	Y1 E3.c.3 Making amounts using the fewest coins possible T	Y2 E3.c.2 Investigating repeated halving TA	Y2 E3.c.2 Investigating repeated halving TA	Give each child a coin (1p, 2p, 5p or 10p) to hold secretly. Ask a child to show on fingers how many 1ps their coin is worth. The other chn say the name of the coin. The child reveals the coin. *Who was correct?* Rpt.	**Y1** • Know value of coins 1p to £2 • Know equivalent values of coins • Make amounts using coins **Y2** • Double multiples of 5 • Halve multiples of 10
Day 3	**Recognise odd and even numbers.** Play 'Stand up'. Give each child a number card 1–100. Give instructions, eg *Stand up if your number is* ***odd***. Check numbers before chn sit down again. Rpt for other instructions, eg *Stand up if your number is* ***even*** *and* ***between*** *ten and twenty.*		**All** Write *15p + 15p =* on the board. Write *double 15p*. In pairs chn work this out using this method: add 10p and 10p to make 20p; add 5p and 5p to make 10p; add 20p and 10p to make 30p. *Double 15p is 30p.* Discuss how 5p + 5p is the same as 10p; 10p + 10p is the same as 20p. Write *15p + 16p =*. *15p + 16p must be* ***1 more than*** *15p + 15p.* Write *31p* to complete the **addition**. Rpt for other additions of **near doubles**. **[ITR Y2 E3.c]**	Y1 E3.c.4 Making coin values using 1p coins TA	Y1 1.3 p44 Exchanging coins for lower denomination coins	Y2 2.3 p44 Doubling and halving	Y2 E3.c.3 Adding near doubles T	Pairs choose two 'next-door' numbers to add together, eg 25 + 26 (Y2s), or 5 + 6 (Y1s). They write them on their whiteboards and calculate answer. Choose pairs to show their addition. Check answers together.	**Y1** • Know value of coins 1p to £2 • Make amounts using coins • Exchange coins for others **Y2** • Add near doubles (near multiples of 5) • Halve multiples of 10